Business
and
Public Policy

Books by Karl Schriftgiesser

Families: From the Adamses through the Roosevelts.

The Amazing Roosevelt Family: 1613–1942.

Oscar of the Waldorf.

The Gentleman from Massachusetts: Henry Cabot Lodge.

This Was Normalcy.

The Lobbyists.

Farmer from Merner: A History of State Farm Mutual.

Business Comes of Age.

Business and the American Government.

Business and Public Policy.

PRENTICE-HALL, INC.
Englewood Cliffs, N. J.

KARL SCHRIFTGIESSER

Business
and
Public Policy

The Role of the Committee
for Economic Development: 1942-1967

© 1967 by Karl Schriftgiesser

Printed in the United States of America

Prentice-Hall International, Inc., *London*
Prentice-Hall of Australia, Pty. Ltd., *Sydney*
Prentice-Hall of Canada, Ltd., *Toronto*
Prentice-Hall of India Private Ltd., *New Delhi*
Prentice-Hall of Japan, Inc., *Tokyo*

FOR RUTH, AGAIN

The basic purpose of CED is to develop, through objective research, findings and recommendations for business and public policy which will contribute to the preservation and strengthening of our free society, and to the maintenance of high employment, increasing productivity and living standards, greater economic stability, and greater opportunity for all the people.

—FROM THE BY-LAWS OF CED

". . . the words of business must be heard and will be sought after; and in a few great issues, the opinion of business can be decisive."

—BEARDSLEY RUML

The purpose of this book is to give a brief history of the major economic trends in the United States during the past 25 years in which the Committee for Economic Development has been suggesting business and public policy through nearly 100 published statements. Earlier, in *Business Comes of Age* (1960), I have told the story of the establishment and early accomplishments of CED. This story is here carried forward, but with less attention to institutional details and more attention to the influence of CED's thinking upon policy making at the federal, state, and local levels of government. In preparing and writing this book I have had the help of persons, within and without the committee, too numerous to mention. I repeat the following from the preface to *Business Comes of Age*: "in the preparation of this book I have had the fullest cooperation of CED—its board of trustees, officers, and staff. However, my arrangement with CED was that I should have the fullest freedom. This is not, then, an 'official' history of CED, but my own independent interpretation. The opinions expressed herein are my own. The errors of judgment (and of fact) that may have crept in are my responsibility." I renew my thanks to the trustees of CED for this freedom—the existence of which has endeared CED to its staff and advisors for a quarter of a century.

K. S.

Preface

Contents

The Committee for Economic Development was organized in 1942. At that time it had three major purposes. The first and most important was to convince the business community that the key to staving off a postwar economic disaster was through high employment. The second was to prove that this could be accomplished by free enterprise if both big and small business, General Motors and the corner dry cleaner alike, would start then to plan for its place in the postwar world. The third was to probe the mysteries of economic policy to find new ways to solve the old problems that would reappear when the wartime boom ended.

The idea for such an organization had a dual origin. The pragmatic planning approach was born at the staff level in the United States Department of Commerce and brought up through channels to the receptive office of Secretary Jesse Jones. The idealistic research approach was born in the fertile minds of Paul G. Hoffman, then president of the Studebaker Corporation, and William Benton, a co-founder of the adver-

I

The Postwar Road

tising firm of Benton and Bowles. In between was Marion B. Folsom, then treasurer of Eastman Kodak Company and a leader in the Business Advisory Council. As the two ideas were becoming one, many other persons became involved, a small elite of business leaders from all parts of the country.

As conceived by these men CED was a simple organization. Its membership was culled entirely from businessmen; its funds derived solely from business coffers. Its membership, a self-perpetuating board of trustees, was small. Paul Hoffman was chairman; Mr. Benton, as vice chairman, was his right-hand man. Mr. Folsom headed its postwar planning efforts and Ralph Flanders, then a Yankee toolmaker, led its research program.

The committee was divided into three divisions. The largest was Mr. Folsom's Field Division, with headquarters in New York, which itself was divided into twelve regional sections. The Field Division was a small but high-powered group whose function was to set up regional committees to carry out its postwar planning schemes. Before the war ended there were more than 2,000 autonomous committees actively at work across the nation. Under this set-up the CED promotion, which included detailed instructions for every imaginable type of industry or service, as well as evangelism, was spread everywhere. It was taken seriously. Plans were laid out on drawing boards and the backs of envelopes. Whole regions and industrial cities, as well as individual concerns, were brought within its fold. That it had a profound effect upon the avoidance of a postwar depression, especially because its drive for full employment was in tune with the times, is unquestionable.

While this exciting experiment in planning was going full steam, Mr. Flanders' more esoteric Research Division was laying the groundwork for CED's quarter of a century labors in the field of national and international economic policy. It concerned itself at first with short-run problems. Its very early statements were directed toward ways and means of discontinuing war contracts with the least disturbance to employment. Its eight businessmen, working with seven economic advisors, headed by the late Professor Sumner Slichter, and its small staff under Theodore O. Yntema, then a professor at the University of Chicago, were, however, more concerned with fiscal and monetary programs for the long run.

The third division was that of Public Information. During the war this was intricately interwoven with the Field and Research Divisions. It was not until later, when postwar organizational changes were effected, that it came into its own as a distributor of economic knowledge and an educator on a large scale.

Through a sort of gentleman's agreement with the National Association of Manufacturers (NAM) and the U.S. Chamber of Commerce, CED was pledged to dissolve itself after the war. But during that period the committee's concern with economic policy had become overwhelming. This was, in great measure, due to the widespread acceptance of, and general tolerance for, certain of its statements on national economic policy. It had, in these papers, rejected much of the classical ideology then espoused by these two national organizations which represented business. It felt there was a vast amount of work to be done and that it probably would *not* be done elsewhere.

Institutionally CED had no desire to compete with either the NAM, a trade organization, which CED emphatically was not, nor with the Chamber. For these reasons it dissolved its Field Division entirely and reorganized itself as a nonprofit, nonpolitical, educational, and research committee. This postwar policy-making organization is the subject of this book. The story of CED's early years and personalities has been told elsewhere in considerable detail.[1] Some of it, however, bears brief retelling as background to the fuller history of CED's deep involvement with most of the major economic problems of the past twenty-five years.

Almost coincident with the war's end, scores of predictions arose to the effect that there would be an army of at least 10 million—perhaps as many as 19 million—unemployed persons walking the streets within thirty days of Japan's surrender. Dire estimates of disaster, most of them from eminently reliable sources and backed with frightening statistics, filled the press. The outstanding economist, Robert Nathan, spoke for most of their authors when he said: "There are a lot of changes we've got to make in our economic thinking to prevent a depression. If nothing is done to stabilize the economy and to get high employment in another two or three years, then we are going to have a depression that will shake the free enterprise system to its very foundation."

With the need for changes in the economic thinking of all Americans, the trustees of CED were in general agreement. In those days economic illiteracy was rampant, and arrogant wrong-headedness

---

[1] Karl Schriftgiesser, *Business Comes of Age* (New York: Harper & Brothers, 1960).

was the usual business posture in public policy matters. But, if Mr. Nathan's prediction of disaster was true, then CED must admit that all its wartime efforts had gone for nought. It was not ready to admit this was true. A report which it issued (prepared by a special field division committee and not by Flanders' research group) vehemently denied it. Based on questionnaires sent to a vast number of marketing experts, manufacturers, and trade associations, the report concluded that, if the level of manufacturing volume that was foreseen by them materialized, the United States should have "substantially full employment" in the first full year after reconversion. It set the top potential of employed persons at 57 million and the minimum at no less than 53 million. From this grew the legend that CED had made a fantastic prediction, within 50,000 of actuality. But, since its median figures had been 53,448,000, its estimate was in reality some 3,602,000 too low. Nevertheless, the optimism of this report, coming as it did from a group of substantial businessmen, received national attention. This was of far greater importance. Even if its assumptions were wrong and its method of projection erroneous (as has often been pointed out) it contributed a breath of fresh air to help clear the climate of economic doom then overhanging the countryside. And it put the Committee for Economic Development on a sound relationship with the public, the press, and the government.

During the negotiations between Secretary Jones and Paul Hoffman that had preceded the founding of CED, the latter had insisted upon including in the committee's charter a provision for a separate research organization, a policy-making group removed from the day-to-day action of the far-flung field division, for postwar planning. Such a provision had not been included in the original concept. Jones, somewhat chary of the idea, asked Hoffman what he proposed to have the group study. Hoffman's reply, which captivated Jones, was succinct: "Taxes."

True to this promise, the first significant "statement on national policy" to emerge from the group headed by Ralph Flanders—in September 1944, nearly a year before the end of the war—was entitled *A Postwar Federal Tax Plan for High Employment*. This statement is of historic importance, both to CED and to any account of economic policy since the war. It brought a significant group of important business leaders within range of the Keynesian revolution and started them on their long and unbroken concern with the uses of fiscal and monetary policy as tools for stabilization of the "full employment economy" that has been the

2

Taxes
and Heretics

dominant objective of government policies, in the postwar era. The seeds of CED's stabilizing budget policy—a policy which has become a part of the conventional wisdom of our time—take root in this document. At the time, and considering its business-based origin, it was little short of revolutionary.

The Flanders group, which included Paul Hoffman, William Benton, Beardsley Ruml, then treasurer of R. H. Macy and Co., Inc., and Harry Scherman, creator of the Book-of-the-Month Club, began its work in March 1943. Aiding them was Harold M. Groves, professor of economics at the University of Wisconsin, Henry C. Simons, from the University of Chicago, and William A. Paton, from the University of Michigan. As they got down to business, the end of the war was not in sight. The Battle of the Bulge had not yet taken place. Victory in the Pacific was far away. As they began their studies, the use of fiscal policy to help control the ups and downs of the economy, and especially its use as an anti-recessionary measure, was not a generally acceptable practice. Taxation, it was almost universally held, was merely a source of revenue, not a tool. It was openly used as a tool only in war time, for instance during World War I when an excess profits tax was imposed. When this tax was again imposed in 1940 it was done not so much to raise money as to restrain business from profiting unduly from the burgeoning defense effort.

During the intensive defense buildup there was little open demand for increasing taxes. Priority went to the mobilization of idle resources. But within the government, which was attracting more and more young economists to its ranks, and especially after John Maynard Keynes had visited Washington in 1941, five years after publication of his *General Theory of Employment, Money, and Interest*, the idea of government intervention through fiscal policy was taking hold. Indeed, plans for the use of restrictive fiscal policy were even then being drawn up for use when, as seemed reasonably certain to happen in the near future, full employment would be reached.

After the United States entered the war, tax policy was openly used for restriction as well as to raise needed revenue. The 50 per cent excess profits tax was imposed not only to prevent profiteering but to make more palatable to the American people the use of the income tax and other measures primarily designed to prevent inflation. Personal income tax exemptions were reduced and individual income tax rates were raised. After the war, Secretary of the Treasury Morgenthau said that this program, abetted by the sale of Treasury bonds to the public, "effectively supported the economic stabilization program [which included wage and price controls and rationing of scarce goods] by removing billions of dollars of excess spending power from the hands of civilians." The program, too, was greatly helped by the adoption in 1943 of the withholding of income taxes on salaries and wages. This was the brain-child of the same Beardsley Ruml who was now a most vocal member of the Flanders group. After the war, tax withholding was retained and it quickly became one of the most effective tools for effectuating the speedy use of fiscal policy as a safeguard against recession and inflation.

A *Postwar Federal Tax Plan's* exciting conclusions were based upon an estimate that total federal expenditures, not including social security and retirement of debt, would amount annually to between $16 and $18 billion. This seemed startlingly large to some observers, especially those who dreamed of returning to a world of laissez-faire and annually balanced budgets. But CED was not alone. Other groups, in and out of government, predicted the need for high government expenditures. All, of course, based their assumptions on a return to a truly peaceful world—they did not foresee the cold war, nor the race to the moon, nor Korea, nor Vietnam. They hoped to walk peacefully toward a Great Society. But at the moment they were all haunted, as were the CED policy makers, by bitter memories of the Great Depression and by President Roosevelt's warning that the federal government must not allow the 10 million men in the armed forces to be "demobilized into an environment of inflation and unemployment to a place on a corner selling apples." [1]

But, as Philip D. Reed of General Electric said several years later, "to put aside any suggestion that we have built national CED economic policy on idealism alone, I think it is only fair to say that where fiscal matters are concerned we have sought earnestly to learn how much of our tax bill is *more* than we have to pay for even a civilized society."

The 1944 policy statement was CED's first step toward learning the answer.

The basis of the statement was that "the tax structure and the budget should be so drawn as to make possible substantial reduction

---

[1] At this period Congress was looking ahead. In 1944 it passed laws that awarded mustering out bonuses and readjustment benefits to servicemen; a liberal war contract settlement act; a surplus property act; a federal highway act for matching grants to the states; and an omnibus flood control act for "useful and worthy" postwar public works.

of the federal debt at a high level of employment. As much debt should then be retired as is consistent with maintaining high levels of employment and production." [2] As we shall see, the approach was couched in familiar conservative terms. Left unsaid was the corollary: at less than high employment, the budget would run a deficit.

The statement then cited Federal Reserve Board and Department of Commerce figures to show that "after reconversion of industry is completed, a net national income of about $140 billion, figured at 1943 prices, would be attained, if we have a satisfactory high level of employment."

High as this "optimistic" estimate was, the committee was convinced that such a national income was not only attainable but would be surpassed within the first postwar decade. "The sole reason for being of the Committee for Economic Development," the report said, "is to help make that happen. . . . Indispensable to this achievement, however, is a drastic and courageous revision of our tax system, removing the many blocks . . . that will prevent the needed growth in the number of jobs."

Many facets of this 1944 statement are of interest twenty-three years later in light of the committee's continuing efforts to achieve, sometime and somehow, a more nearly perfect revenue system. In this statement, for instance, began CED's preference for the income tax as a source of federal income over any form of sales or excise taxes, since both of the latter were generally hidden from the eye of

---

[2] Keith Carlson in an interesting article in the *Federal Reserve Bank of St. Louis Review* (Vol. 49, No. 6, June 1967), on "Estimates of the High Employment Budget: 1947–1967," tries to trace the origin of the concept of the full employment budget. He refers to *Fiscal and Monetary Policy*, National Planning Pamphlet No. 35, published in July 1944, by Beardsley Ruml and H. Christian Sonne. This, he says, "is supposedly the first to discuss budget policy in high-employment terms." The CED policy statement, *A Postwar Federal Tax Plan for High Employment*, was published in August 1944. Beardsley Ruml was a member of the Research Committee of CED at the same time he was collaborating with Mr. Sonne (not then a CED trustee, but one of the guiding lights of the National Planning Association). Since the two pamphlets appeared within a few weeks of each other the evidence points strongly to Beardsley Ruml as the father, or at least the uncle, of the high-employment budget concept. In discussing the 1944 policy statement in his forthcoming book, Herbert Stein, chief economist of CED, says: "Essentially CED elaborated the ideas which Ruml had put forth during the war, stating them and their exceptions more precisely than he had done, spelling out their implications for objectives other than economic stability, and relating them to other economic policies, notably monetary policy and debt management."

the taxpayer. The income tax was the "fairest form of taxation" for many reasons but especially because it is "the only one that can be closely adjusted with ability to pay," and because "where the burden falls and who pays it is clearly evident."

The committee's defense of open taxation was rigorous. "All taxes have to be paid by living persons" and the "mere fact that in many cases the taxpayer may be unaware of the tax does not alter the fact that he is paying it." Its rather violent dislike for excise taxes and sales taxes was not to last forever. A decade later CED grudgingly admitted that, if the then vainly hoped for repeal of all but the historic excises on tobacco, whisky, and gasoline should deprive the federal coffers of needed revenue, a turn to "a more general consumption tax such as a retail sales tax" *might* be the answer. But even then it turned shudderingly away from a tax at the manufacturers' level because such a tax would not be "direct and visible to the ultimate taxpayer."

In 1966, however, CED startled its old friends by coming out strongly if lonesomely for a "value-added tax" at the manufacturers' level—an obviously "hidden tax" that, it had to admit, would undoubtedly be passed onto the ultimate consumer. But in 1944 it wanted no part of excise or sales taxes, or any form of taxation that the taxpayer could not see and feel.

Many other problems that were not to be solved soon, or perhaps ever, were recognized in this historic paper of 1944. On one—the matter of corporation taxes—it took a firm managerial stand. Since all taxes were paid by individuals, it felt, the corporation tax merely conceals the division of the burden as between stockholders, workers, and consumers. Taxes on profits were damaging to employment because they weaken the profit incentive (the key to capitalism) and take earnings that otherwise would be invested in production, and because they limit the capacity of management to increase wages and lower prices. The "inequity" of taxing the same income at two points disturbed CED then, as it did later. Its most controversial stand was its proposal to eliminate all corporate taxes—except for a single flat tax corresponding to the basic normal tax on individual incomes—and to exempt from normal taxes the money received in dividends by individuals.

But perhaps historically the most important aspect of the statement was the committee's implicit acceptance of deficit financing. In words that were then considered heretical it said:

"The Committee does not consider justified the apprehensions sometimes voiced about the size of the federal debt, so long as there is a manifest national resolution to stop its further increase, except under clear conditions of slump in industry and trade. That resolution can be demonstrated in no other way than by taxation adequate to the necessities of the budget."

Thus CED set itself firmly on the side of those who would balance the budget only when the economy is balanced first. This willingness to accept an increase in the federal debt, under clear conditions of slump in industry and trade, while at the same time offering a fiscal program that would make a sizable debt retirement possible at a $140 billion national income, set CED firmly on the side of the Keynesian angels and struck consternation in the classical camp. Businessmen were not expected to talk that way.

In 1944, however, CED's concern was less with theory, Keynesian or otherwise, than with the practical and critical problem of unemployment that even the most sanguine feared would exist after the war. And so it said that "the obvious wise course for the nation is to say in effect to all its most enterprising citizens: 'Go ahead; risk your money and put all the effort and brains you have into increasing the nation's production. By doing this *you will be creating jobs for other people*, while making money for yourself, and this continuous job-multiplication is the main thing we want to see happening in this country. You will have to pay in taxes a good share of what you make, but you will also have left a sufficient share for yourself to make your efforts worthwhile.' "

This statement is historically interesting also because it contains the first of scores of dissenting, critical, or querulous footnotes that have peppered CED statements over the past twenty-five years. Such footnotes have always been an integral part of the so-called "CED process"—indications of the committee's willingness to give both sides of a question and to maintain that intellectual freedom and objectivity that have been characteristic of the organization and won it such friendly welcome in academic circles. The first footnote was contributed by Ernest Kanzler, then chairman of the Universal Credit Corporation, Detroit, Michigan, who questioned whether the CED plan would be "politically acceptable as a whole," and thought it would take taxpayers a long time "to grow up to the plan" and develop that "understanding and sympathetic support upon which the proposed plan . . . depends."

In a special message to Congress in September 1945, President Truman asked for a "transitional bill" that would provide for limited tax reductions to remove "the barriers to speedy reconversion and to the expansion of our peacetime economy." But he warned against excessive cuts, fearing they would further upset the budget. Estimates at that time were for receipts in fiscal 1946 of $36 billion and expenditures of about $66 billion.

Shortly thereafter Secretary of the Treasury Vinson suggested a tax cut of $5.2 billion—to be effected through repeal of the 3 per cent normal tax on individual incomes, repeal of the excess profits tax, and reduction (but not repeal) of certain excise taxes. He also urged postponement of an increase in social security taxes scheduled for January 1946.

The revenue act, as finally passed early in November of 1945, cut the individual surtax rates three percentage points and gave a combined normal-surtax reduction of 5 per cent. It repealed the excess profits tax as of January 1946. It left the excise taxes alone but ordered a reduction of corporate income taxes to a range from 21 per cent to 38 per cent on incomes over $50,000. This provided for an estimated $5.9 billion of tax relief. The postponement in social security taxes for one year amounted to another $1.5 billion.

It cannot be said that the 1945 tax law was greatly influenced by the CED statement. It had called for elimination of the 3 per cent normal tax but not in the way the law provided. It had called for repeal of the excess profits tax, which was granted. That was all.

That "time, understanding, and sympathetic support" are necessary for bringing about any tax reform is now obvious. The late President Kennedy could have vouched for that. The truth of this statement became clear very early to the CED policy makers, who, as we shall see, from time to time were to try to find methods to speed up the process of raising or lowering taxes for countercyclical purposes. The Commission on Money and Credit earnestly urged a major reform in this direction in 1961.[3] President Kennedy endeavored to put it into practice. Nearly a quarter of a century of earnest educational effort was needed to convince Congress and the people that there might be a propitious time to cut taxes, as was achieved finally in 1964, when for the first time in history a reduction was enacted specifically to stimulate the economy. Even more sympathetic support and public understanding are called for, if the efficacy of the other side of the fiscal coin—a tax boost to curb inflation—is ever to be used in timely fashion.

---

[3] For details on the Commission on Money and Credit, see p. 222.

When President Truman stepped into the White House on April 12, 1945, he was faced with many problems besides the decision to drop or not to drop the Bomb. From mid-April to mid-June there was the charter for the new United Nations to be forged in San Francisco. From mid-July until the early days of August there was the fateful Potsdam Conference. There was little time for Truman to devote to the confusing problems of the national economy. It was not until September 6 that he sent his first, lengthy, all-inclusive economic message to the Congress. It was an important message, offering twenty-one suggestions for legislation aimed at full employment and prosperity in the postwar years ahead.

What was about to happen in the factories and on the farms was anybody's guess. That there was to be a great struggle over policy was obvious. Defenders of the old myths would not admit that they had lost their battle first in the days of the New Deal and again when the amazing industrial Arsenal of Democracy was built to win the war, so they stood firm for a return to laissez-faire.

3

Economic Tasks of Peace

The government, they said, must loosen its hold upon on the economy. All war-imposed controls and priorities must be abandoned overnight. On the other hand, President Roosevelt, until his death, and President Truman, whose whole political life had been spent in the atmosphere of the New Deal, wanted none of this. They had devoted their political careers to directing the power of the federal government to strengthen, indeed to save, the private enterprise system. All their thoughts in this direction were gathered together in the phrase that now was heard everywhere—full employment.

"We must help develop the human standards and material resources of the nation," Roosevelt had said in his final budget message, "which in turn will tend to increase our productivity and most effectively support business expansion, and employment." Now in his September message to the 79th Congress, President Truman added, "We must look first and foremost to private enterprise" to provide the jobs needed in a full employment economy. "Every government policy and program will be pointed to promote maximum production and employment." But he noted that it was "the ultimate duty of government to use its own resources if all other methods should fail to prevent prolonged unemployment."

The year 1945 was also to be a crucial year in the history of CED. Its membership was determined to have its voice heard on those problems which it considered most vital. It had already proved that it would be listened to. Its small research committee, still under the leadership of Ralph Flanders, rolled up its sleeves for its busiest and most exacting year.

"If the heretics on the other side of the gulf are to demolish the forces of 19th Century orthodoxy," John Maynard Keynes had said in 1925, "they must attack them in their citadel. I was brought up in the citadel and I recognize its power and might." The committee members were willing enough, then, to consider themselves heretics (up to a point), and they, too, had been brought up in the citadel. They were not afraid of the power of government but were determined to use it, on their own terms, to make the private enterprise system work in the way they knew it could.

In a paper issued at this time by the research group, William Benton had said:

"In a democracy there is a place for private enterprise and there is a place for public enterprise and it is necessary to clarify basic lines of division between them. The area for private enterprise should extend to the limit of the ability of private individuals to better serve the common good. Beyond this limit, government enterprise can better serve that good."

In this credo for business policy Mr. Benton also had said: "Prolonged and severe depressions . . . cannot be accepted as natural and irremediable phenomena. The people's elected representatives and the agencies of government are responsible for establishing fiscal, monetary, and other policies that help prevent the fever of inflation and the paralysis of deflation and depression. Constructive policies respecting taxation and public expenditures (including expenditures for public works), intelligent handling of the national debt, and enlightened control over money and credit can greatly retard or prevent excessive swings of the business cycle."

Upon looking back at this period a decade later, economist John Kenneth Galbraith discussed the still prevalent myth of automaticity which held that the economy works best if left to itself. He had this to say:

"While the defense of the assumption of automaticity foundered on the rock of practical experience the opposing view required steady enforcement. Two events might be singled out. There was, of course, the publication of Keynes's *General Theory* in 1936 and its immediate widespread influence on professional economic thought. There was also the formation in 1942 of the Committee for Economic Development. The primary motivation of CED was the fear of what another depression might do to the reputation of American capitalism. At least initially, many of the business members of the organization hoped that by encouraging individual firms to plan for enlarged investment after the war it might be possible to forestall government planning. This looked like a plausible formula for escaping the seemingly untenable assumption of automaticity without accepting the unpalatable corollary of government responsibility. However, CED soon came to accept a conservative measure of government intervention as a requisite for good performance. And the rejection of automaticity was explicit. The defection of the CED businessmen was a serious blow to all who argued for the automatic economy."

In an interesting aside, Galbraith pointed out that the fact that CED was a business organization was especially important. "In our tradition of economic debate, a proposition can often be more economically destroyed by association than by evidence. . . . The charge that an idea is radical, impractical, or long-haired is met by showing that a prominent businessman has favored it. Businessmen—

successful ones at least—are by definition never radical, impractical, or long-haired. It is obvious, in this context, that the rejection of the doctrine of automaticity by a group of influential businessmen was important. The position of CED was henceforth regularly cited in the argument over automaticity and government intervention."

To this Galbraith might have added that there is another side to the picture. CED's acceptance of some government intervention, its rejection of the ever-balanced budget, its stand on tariffs, on East-West trade, on the farm problem, have always won it its share of opponents, both within and without its membership. For CED merely to espouse a new policy—or even to apply an old policy to a new situation—for many years almost invariably won it rejection by the editors of *The Wall Street Journal*. "And so CED's main concern," Herbert Stein,[1] who participated in the discussions of this exciting year, wrote in 1958, "has been with the functions of government and the manner in which they are executed. . . . The critical question is not how much government should do but what kind of things it should do and how it can do them effectively. . . ." CED began to exhort this main concern in 1945 with a series of five statements on national policy.

In the closing days of the war the economic atmosphere was disturbed by a dark ideological cloud. "How is one to tell which kind of law applies in a given case?" John Maurice Clark, then professor of economics at Columbia University, asked in a series of lectures delivered in 1946. "Laws from the orthodox front side or the Keynesian back side of the looking glass? The simplest formula is that Keynesian laws apply until we get full employment, and orthodox laws after that." But there seemed then to be no "machine-made way of deciding which kind of law holds." Re-examination of each problem in the light of the possibilities suggested by both kinds of theory—that of Keynes and that of Friederich von Hayek, whose now forgotten *Road to Serfdom* was then the Bible of the old guard— was necessary. Keynes was "the antithesis to orthodoxy" and it was necessary to use him to "break through the crust of outworn ideas," and to "fashion a synthesis in both theory and in policy."

To the policy makers of CED the great question was, "Will this synthesis be possible?" The committee was determined to try

---

[1] Herbert Stein joined CED in 1945 and succeeded the late Howard Myers as director of research in 1956. In 1966, he became vice president and chief economist.

and find out. It set out to do so at a time, again to quote Clark, when the world was "in the grip of a mighty struggle. On one side are forces driving toward chaos and anarchy, political, social, economic and moral. On the other side are forces of centralized control. Between them stand the forces and men who are trying desperately to salvage a workable basis for a humane and ordered community, in which some effective degree of freedom and democracy may be kept alive, without wrecking society by their undisciplined exercise and disruptive excesses."

Although the CED statements issued in 1945 dealt with immediately pressing problems they contain much that is of lasting value to the understanding of CED's close relationship with economic policy making during the next twenty-five years. These papers dealt with the problem of postwar employment, the removal of wartime controls, international trade, and (of greatest historical significance) with the full employment bill then pending before Congress.

As CED took up these "economic tasks of peace," two shadows fell over its shoulders. One was the shadow of 1919–20, the end of the first World War. Then prices surged upward—by as much as 25 per cent in a single year. In almost every daily newspaper the initials "HCL"—for high cost of living—were a headline commonplace. But at the same time jobs were plentiful and profits were high, if not excessive. The United States was in the throes of inflation. As was inevitable, this led to collapse. In mid-1920 industrial production dropped with a bang—down 35 per cent. Farm prices fell—down 50 per cent. Non-farm prices fell—down 40 per cent. Unemployment soared.

The other shadow in 1945 was that of 1939—the end of twenty years of peace—which saw, in spite of all the efforts of the New Deal, 9 million still unemployed, one-half of the nation's corporations operating in the red, and one-fifth of farm income coming from the federal government. Which was to happen now—depression or inflation? Or could wise policies be devised to avoid them both?

In 1945 certain figures reflected the state of economic affairs. Unemployment was low. People were hungry to spend their money on long-denied goods and services. Business was anxious to put its expanded productive facilities to profitable peacetime use. The individual income tax had risen, in five years, to the highest effective rates in United States history—ranging from 11.5 per cent on net incomes of $1,000 to 88.9 per cent on those of $500,000. Corporate income and excess profits taxes had gone up—the latter to 95 per cent. From these and other sources, notably excise taxes, net annual budget receipts had risen from $7.1 billion in 1941 to $44.5 billion in 1945. The total receipts for the five years had totaled $130 billion. But in those same five years the federal government had spent almost $320 billion, of which the greater part had gone to fight the war. The difference—$190 billion—had been borrowed from the public. In 1945, too, wages, prices, and resources were under rigid governmental controls. Yet over the nation hung a cloud of fear that something would happen and all would end in disaster. This was perhaps best expressed in the debate that began that year in Congress after Senator Murray introduced his famous bill designed to assure, by governmental effort, employment for all those willing and able to work.

To the CED policy makers, their academic advisors, and their staff this hovering cloud was not impenetrable. But the uncertainties of the situation caused them to ask questions. Could business undertake to provide adequate assurance that if price controls were immediately removed and if government policy did not curb effective demand, prices would not rise rapidly? Or, could business undertake to maintain satisfactory levels of employment, even if the government were indifferent to the inadequacy of demand? Business, of course, could do its share—even more than it had done before the war—but it could not do it alone. Government must play its part— a greater part than most conservatives could countenance.

On the home front the dangers were clear. But, at the same time, no return to isolationism could be risked. America must show the way to restoring international economic equilibrium. Should inflation or depression come to the United States, the international repercussions would be disastrous. Either would force foreign nations to insulate themselves from us and our markets. Either might reduce the possibility of establishing those nonrestrictive international economic arrangements that were so necessary for world prosperity and peace.

Although there were many immediate problems (such as months of acute shortages, industrial tension, surplus disposal, production controls, labor relocation, etc.) to worry the business community, the CED "heretics" turned their attention to a larger issue— the implementation of sound economic policy that would smooth the transition period and put the nation on the road to a workable full-employment economy. It would seek ways to reduce the armed forces and military production to a peacetime basis, to transfer resources to peacetime production, to restore peacetime markets free of price and production controls, and to bring *aggregate demand and supply into balance at high employment and without substantial price increases*.[2]

How to do this? The CED program, as variously expressed in four of the five statements on national policy which the Research Committee produced between April and October 1945, was detailed, well-documented, and determined. In essence it called for the adoption of unpopular precautionary measures even if their execution was not immediately apparent or necessary, and might never have to be called for. Such measures should be so designed that drastic action could be taken *promptly* when the event making them mandatory occurred. Price controls should be streamlined and liberalized, but they should not be abandoned for at least another year, in spite of the universal clamor from people in all walks of life urging their immediate disposal. Income tax reductions should also be postponed. And strong, if unfamiliar, fiscal and monetary powers should be exercised—by presidential direction, if necessary—in such a way as to prevent an excess, or a deficiency, of aggregate demand.

---

[2] Among some of its many recommendations of a short-run nature were: Increased and lengthened unemployment compensation; a shelf of needed federal public works "in case expected private demand does not materialize"; additional federal appropriations to "further encourage advance planning for needed public construction"; expansion and adoption by large and small businesses of in-plant training activities; the use of "traditional federal aid for education"; support of the GI-Act of 1944, especially its provision for educational opportunities; and federal aid to the states to assist unemployed workers during the transition period.

By the fall of 1945 nearly 5 million persons had been discharged from the armed services. Other millions had left their wartime jobs. Nevertheless, unemployment—once so dreadfully feared—stood at about 2 million persons. Outside the military some 52 million men and women were at work. Here and there arose complaints about critical labor shortages. Everywhere it was all but impossible for producers to meet the clamorous demands for goods and services. With all this, prices were pressing hard against the ceilings. Inflation became a threat to national economic stability.

A postwar depression was out of the question by the end of the year and even a recession seemed improbable. With a potential runaway of prices the growing threat, the attention of the committee turned naturally in this direction. Suddenly monetary policy became important. The pertinent question was: Are the monetary policies of the past adequate to the current situation? The committee did not have an immediate or easy answer. Certain actions of the Federal Reserve, however, made it wonder. Were the money authorities pursuing proper

4

The Employment Act

means for adopting the quantity of money and credit to the needs of the economy?

In view of the accumulation in private hands of government securities directly convertible into cash, and in view of the volume of currency outstanding, would the policies of the Federal Reserve be sufficient to damp inflationary pressures, or conversely, to promote expansion? What changes in existing controls over the volume and terms of credit were required if this powerful instrument were to serve the purpose of high productive employment? In 1946 (September) when inflation had, as CED put it, "mounted to grave proportions," it issued a statement on this subject.

But, in the midst of these worrisome circumstances, it was the full employment bill that occupied most of Congress' attention. CED quickly became involved in this debate. Although the committee engaged in no active lobbying on the Washington scene, the principles involved in the bill were such that it could not stay out of the fight. Its participation, however, was on a lofty and aloof plane.

In his book, *Congress Makes a Law*, the classic study of the history of the Employment Act of 1946, Stephen Kemp Bailey has this to say about CED's role: "The CED is not included as a 'pressure' group because it made no attempt to initiate direct or indirect pressures on legislatures. It testified when called upon, and, at [Rep.] Will Whittington's [D. Miss.] suggestion submitted a bill draft which was important in the history of S. 380. But it has intentionally stayed as far away as possible from conventional pressure activities." [1]

While the National Association of Manufacturers and hundreds of local units of the United States Chamber of Commerce vociferously and expensively fought the full employment bill, CED spoke softly in favor of it. But, as it turned out, it carried the big stick.

---

[1] As a nonprofit research and educational organization CED has made it its inflexible rule to testify on legislation only when specifically invited to do so by a committee of Congress. This has sometimes brought criticism because CED has seemingly not tried to carry through its policy recommendations by political action. Its reasons for this rule are only partially to be found in the code of the Internal Revenue Service. It was never intended to be an "action" organization. When congressional committees do invite CED to testify on legislation within its competence it restricts its comments to recommendations made in statements already published or approved for publication. When trustees of CED wish to go beyond a CED recommendation they make it clear that they are departing from the CED text and speaking as individuals. Under these conditions CED has testified some 99 times before congressional committees since 1945.

To the CED committee[2] the bill had several weaknesses. One lay in its working title—"full employment." To the Flanders group this was delusionary because, under any workable system, there would always be some people who were unemployed, if only temporarily. CED preferred "high employment"—an attainable and desirable state of affairs. The final act omitted both adjectives.

But even more unfortunate from CED's point of view were the original provisions which declared it to be the policy of the United States government "to assure the existence at all times of sufficient employment opportunities to provide jobs for all persons able and willing to work." And, to the "extent that continuing full employment cannot otherwise be achieved, it is the further responsibility of the federal government to provide such volume of federal investment and expenditure as may be needed to assure full employment." The bill provided machinery to carry this out through what it called a "national production and employment budget" to be submitted annually by the President and reviewed by a joint congressional committee.

The CED thought this was carrying government intervention too far. Conservative groups lobbied vigorously against it but none offered any alternative to satisfy the widespread hunger for some kind of a law which would enlist the federal government reasonably on the side of economic stability through high employment. The CED group did have one.

In August 1945, Paul Hoffman, in his capacity as chairman of CED, was invited to appear before the Senate Banking and Currency Committee. There he proposed two ideas that were not in the bill under discussion. After much debate the CED committee hammered them into shape. Early in October they were made public in a state-

---

[2] Under the by-laws of the Committee for Economic Development, statements on national policy may be issued *only* by vote of the Research and Policy Committee of the CED. Therefore, it is technically incorrect to say that CED issued a statement. However, for the sake of simplicity throughout, the terms "committee" or "CED" or "the CED committee" will be used rather than "the Research and Policy Committee of the Committee for Economic Development." When CED publications other than statements on national policy are referred to (such as statements by the Program Committee, which may issue statements based on previously published policy statements of the Research and Policy Committee of the CED, or supplementary papers, or research studies), the difference will be apparent in the text.

ment on national policy entitled: *Toward More Production, More Jobs, and More Freedom.*

The statement was forthright. "The most vital function," it said, "is to establish conditions under which a free enterprise system can operate most effectively and to counteract the tendencies in that system toward booms and depressions."

Unfortunately, it added, no clear-cut, consistent policy pointing in this direction had yet been put forward by the government. But the magnitude of the public debt and the anticipated volume of regular public expenditures made public policy such a dominant factor in the economy that "clarity, consistency, and coordination became imperative."

From only two sources could clarity, consistency, and coordination emerge—the President of the United States and the Congress. To them should go a mandate—"one specific assignment, and one only," the statement proclaimed—the development of a "coordinated and progressive program of measures designed to meet the responsibilities of the federal government for a more stable and prosperous society."

The committee declared it was the continuing duty of the President and the Congress to affirm that "the attainment and maintenance of high level production and employment within the framework of a free enterprise economy is a major objective of policy."

Unlike the Murray bill,[3] the CED fiat did not call for "maximum purchasing power." Nor was it prescient enough to foresee, or proclaim, that possible inflation might some day call for a national policy on prices. The Murray bill, also, neglected to mention price stability as a national purpose, although "maximum purchasing power" has long been interpreted to mean this. Several years later this omission was to open up a national debate over whether "price stability" should be added to the Employment Act's purposes. This grew especially clamorous after the Council of Economic Advisers presented its "Wage-Price Guidelines" in 1963.

Having made the bold declaration on national economic policy, the committee then offered two clearly stated proposals for effectuating its demands:

1. A PRESIDENT'S COMMISSION ON FULL EMPLOYMENT. *This commission should be headed by a representative of the President. It should be a*

---

[3] Senator James E. Murray (D. Mont.) introduced S. 380, the so-called full employment bill, in January 1945.

small working body composed of the ablest men to be found. Its members should be chosen as representatives of the general public interest (particular economic groups or viewpoints can be represented through advisory groups). The commission should be serviced by a staff of the most competent authorities in the various fields. It should make policy recommendations to the President periodically, beginning as promptly as possible. It should lay the groundwork for the development of a continuing and coordinated program of government action.

2. A JOINT CONGRESSIONAL COMMITTEE ON FULL EMPLOYMENT. This committee should be composed of the ranking members of Senate and House committees which now deal with major problems affecting the economy. It too should be adequately staffed. It should receive reports from the President with regard to such matters and should work toward the development of a coordinated congressional policy.

Even before the CED statement was published, advance copies had quietly been circulated on Capitol Hill. One fell into the hands of Will Whittington, a moderate conservative from Mississippi, who was one of the congressmen entrusted with redrafting the bill for the House. As Dr. Bailey puts it, he was "striving for a bill that would exclude the last remnants of what he considered to be dangerous federal commitments and assurances (including the wording of the title), but would provide for an *economic planning mechanism* . . . in the executive and legislative branches, and for a moderate program of public works."

This was essentially the goal of CED as was set forth in the two proposals. Spurred by the CED statement and with the help of others in and out of Congress, Mr. Whittington wrote into the revised draft the sections calling for the present Council of Economic Advisers and the Joint Committee on the Economic Report (now the Joint Economic Committee). These then startling but now commonplace provisions were in the version passed by the House. They survived the deliberations of the conference committee and became the law of the land. At the same time the use of the phrase "full employment" went by the boards.

The version that became law did not have a universal appeal. Representative Celler of New York called it "something written by the best minds of the eighteenth century." Populists of Representative Wright Patman's school damned it as a "sell-out." Men of Senator Taft's stripe thought it went too far to the left. For those on the right, the *New York Herald Tribune* spoke. The Employment

Act of 1946 was, the paper said, "perhaps the most serious threat to free enterprise and democracy with which this country has been confronted in its 170 years of existence."

Despite these words of disappointment and disparagement, the Employment Act has stayed unsullied on the books for twenty-one years. Four Presidents have not only used the power it has given them but have leaned upon it in times of both prosperity and economic stress.

The year 1947 opened auspiciously. On the last day of 1946 President Truman had officially proclaimed the war to be at an end. When he went before Congress to deliver his State of the Union message he was able to announce that the nation was enjoying "virtually full employment." But he was not in an entirely optimistic mood. Prices, he warned, were threatening to rise so high that people might not be able to afford to buy all the goods and services that were expected to pour forth in the coming year. Most of the wartime controls had been removed. Unfettered by government, it was up to private industry to hold prices in line and it was up to labor not to demand "unjustified" wage increases. The about-to-be-familiar postwar pattern had begun.

Two days later Mr. Truman sent to Congress another message, the first annual *Economic Report of the President* to be issued under the mandate of the Employment Act of 1946. The Report was a mixture of review and forecast. It was based on his interpretation of "expert and lay opinion" which, he said, is in agreement on the rules of "sound public finance that call for a surplus in government revenues over expendi-

5

Stability
and Flexibility

tures while employment is high and the total income is large." The President indicated that he had been doing his best to obey the rules. As far back as August he had ordered stringent cutbacks in federal expenditures and, looking ahead, he had practiced what he called "stringent economy" in preparing the budget for fiscal 1948, which he was about to submit to Congress.

When the budget appeared it projected federal expenditures for basic national requirements of $37.5 billion, for which there would be receipts of $37.7 billion. The President hoped that, if business activity were to be slightly higher in 1947 than in the year just past, the precariously slim surplus might be enlarged. However, under these circumstances, Congress should take no chances. It should not reduce taxes. Instead, it should increase postal rates and postpone the scheduled reduction of excise taxes. By doing these things, he reasoned, the surplus could be raised to $1.8 billion.

These words fell chillingly on the ears of the Republicans who dominated the new 80th Congress—that Congress which, not without some provocation and justification, President Truman was to call the "worst Congress in history," as he trudged across the country on his amazing road to victory in 1948.

At this juncture in history when, unrecognized by most people, an era of new approaches to economic policy making was taking place, the Committee for Economic Development was itself undergoing some disturbing moments. The time had come for it to make its most important inner decision. Its frank, unorthodox, and seemingly Keynesian utterances on federal wartime controls, on taxes, on tariffs and trade, on the Marshall plan, and on agriculture and small business, had by now won it a share of enemies. CED had already been accused in one Wall Street publication and before at least one large organization of businessmen of displaying socialistic tendencies. This, of course, worried some of its wartime supporters and its treasury sank to a precarious level. Its only financial support then came from the voluntary contributions of business corporations. With all this in mind, Paul Hoffman spoke to his fellow trustees:

"I think it is very important that we as a group think of ourselves not as right, left, conservative, or radical, but as *responsible*. What we are trying to do is to get at the facts about the way this economy functions, and then go down the roads indicated."

The somewhat harried group of businessmen took this abjuration to heart. They adopted the shortened phrase—"Neither right nor left but responsible"—as CED's motto. Shortly after this declaration Paul Hoffman resigned to become the head of the Economic Cooperation Administration. He was succeeded by W. Walter Williams, then president of Continental, Inc., who brought from the West Coast considerable organizational ability. Under his chairmanship, CED was reorganized pretty much in the form under which it operates today. Many original trustees—Beardsley Ruml; Raymond Rubicam, a co-founder of Young and Rubicam, Inc.; Marion B. Folsom; Wayne C. Taylor, former Under Secretary of Commerce—stuck with the revised organization and were joined by many newer men—including James Brownlee, partner of J. H. Whitney and Co.; Philip D. Reed, then chairman of General Electric Company; and J. Cameron Thomson, then president of Northwest Bancorporation—all of whom helped revitalize CED. Mr. Reed took over the chairmanship of the newly devised Research and Policy Committee, which became the committee's only official mouthpiece. Important administrative staff changes were made. An expanded information committee was assigned to spread the CED story on a much wider and more popular scale than heretofore. But most important was the adoption of the following resolution as the key statement of CED's purpose:

> To develop, through objective research and discussion, findings and recommendations for business and public policy which will contribute to the preservation and strengthening of our free society, and to the maintenance of high employment, increasing productivity and living standards, greater economic stability, and greater opportunity for all the people. To bring about increasing public understanding of the importance of these objectives and the ways in which they can be achieved.

This reorganization of CED was completed by the spring of 1948. In the meantime and despite this inner turmoil, the small research group kept doggedly at its task of "finding the facts and going down the road indicated." In November 1947, the CED issued a 75-page document that turned out to be of far greater significance in the economic history of the United States than any of its many authors then dreamed. Because of its wide influence on the economic thinking of the past twenty-five years it is worth examining in some detail.

Taxes and the Budget was what its subtitle said it was—"a program for prosperity in a free economy." It sought to disabuse the belief in the inevitability of economic instability. It offered a simple and flexible formula to meet almost any economic contingency that might occur. It would replace the orthodox belief in the sanctity of the annually balanced budget, and make a virtue of deficit financing under certain adverse conditions. It was built on the concept of high employment and production and did not preclude the use of government spending as an economic instrument. It did not guarantee prosperity, nor did it pretend to obviate the need for a sound monetary policy and a constructive debt management policy. It depended upon certain well spelled-out automatic reactions that could be expected to respond without political promptings, to the conditions of the market as they occurred from time to time. In brief, it was a policy prescription intended to enable government and private enterprise to carry out the mandates of the Employment Act. As such, it went counter to the two major prevailing policies—the annual budget-balancing policy of long tradition and the newer "managed-compensatory" budget policy then striving for dominance on the economic scene.

The committee gave it a name—the Stabilizing Budget Policy. It was not, of course, entirely new. Its virtue was that in it CED found a new way to express a hitherto unsynthesized prescription in simple form. It was to sink into the consciousness of the American government and of business during the next two decades. It was then, as the *Washington Post* said of it in 1966, a "sophisticated concept" that, in the words of Leon Henderson, would "tax your credulity."

The search for such an approach to economic stability had been going on in academic circles for some time. Lord Keynes's American disciples, particularly Alvin Hansen and Abba P. Lerner, had led the way. But it had made little impression on Presidents or Congressmen or even the public, nor was CED's document to win universal acceptance overnight. The belief that nations, like families, should keep their budget always balanced still prevailed.

President Truman believed this. He did not readily countenance new trends in economic thinking. Although he was not, as sometimes accused, an "economic illiterate," it is true that he trusted old-fashioned virtues as exemplified by such men as Secretaries of the Treasury Fred Vinson and John Snyder, more than he did the thinking of the economists he appointed to the first Council of Economic Advisers, Edwin Nourse, Leon Keyserling, and John Clark. He himself has said in his *Memoirs* that "the federal budget was one of my more serious hobbies." He regarded its preparation as "one of the most serious responsibilities of the President." But for what has been called "the generalities of policy," he had little use.

Walter W. Heller, Chairman of the Council of Economic Advisers from 1961–64, and others have shown that the economic philosophy of CED can be traced to such diverse writers as Swedish economist Gunnar Myrdal and Beardsley Ruml. Its more immediate sources are less esoteric. They lay in the simple fact that a small but an intelligent group of businessmen were unable to accept as infallible the old-fashioned belief that federal outgo should never exceed federal income in a given year.

"Insofar as this principle was rationalized at all," Herbert Stein has written, "it was rationalized along the following lines. The economic system, if let alone, or perhaps if assisted by wise monetary policy, would do all that could be done to maintain high employment. If there is any employment-creating effect from unbalanced budgets it is likely to be temporary and will prevent the natural forces of the market from producing recovery. If the annual-balanced-budget rule is given up, no principle at all can be substituted for it. Budgetary management would have no guide or limit but political expenditures and debt."

This view did not meet any of the four tests which CED said must be met if budget policy were to contribute to, rather than impair, healthy economic growth. First, the CED policy said, budget policy must help to make the economy more stable by acting to restrain the demand for goods and services when inflation prevails, and to stimulate demand when depression exists. Second, it must foster economy in government. Third, it must provide for reduction of the federal debt. And, finally, it must avoid frequent changes in the tax rates because of their unsettling effects upon business and personal planning.

The traditional system failed the first test because it actually contributed to instability. A budget that was balanced in a recession, CED said, accentuated recession while a budget that was balanced in prosperous times stimulated inflation by failing to reduce the spending power of the public. It only partially met the second test because the requirements of the balanced budget tend to forestall only new expenditure that would cause a deficit unless tax rates are raised; expenditure of the growth in tax revenue could be unrestrained. As to debt retirement, it also failed because it tended in good times to draw off, into expenditure increases and tax cuts, money which ought to go to retiring debt. In bad times its efforts to prevent deficits are "usually in vain." And, finally, it failed because it calls for frequent and disturbing changes in tax rates in order to maintain balance.

Having dismissed as irrational and unworkable this standard policy of the past, the committee looked at another policy that was growing in acceptance in government, academic, and public sectors —that of "compensatory public finance." One major premise of this newer theory was that the so-called *natural forces* of the economy could *not* maintain high employment. Nor could monetary policy make good the deficiency. Therefore the rate of government expenditure was the key to high employment and stability.

Simple and direct in its thrust, this policy tended to put all the burden on government. It said that when employment is judged (by the government) to fall below a specified (by the government) high level, then a combination of tax cuts and continued or increased government spending should be made in the amount necessary to keep the predicted (by the government) decline from eventuating. If, on the other hand, prices were expected (by the government) to rise above a certain "proper" level, then taxes should be increased and government spending cut in order to draw off excess purchasing power.

The greatest danger in this formula, as CED pointed out, was its dependence upon the art of forecasting. Not yet forgotten by the committee were the series of erroneous forecasts of a severe depression that had appeared toward the end of the war. They had done little to enhance prognostication (although even at this early date efforts, in which CED was to join, were being made to improve the collection and use of statistics for this purpose). The CED was not about to support any system that depended on what Walter Heller has called "human frailties and institutional imperfections." This, perhaps more than anything, moved them toward automatic and away from discretionary fiscal rules. Another important factor was skepticism over the willingness, or ability, of the Executive or Congress to move quickly enough in times of economic peril. This doubt was, of course, one reason why CED was to lay such heavy stress on monetary policy, whose inbuilt flexibility was supposedly more responsive to situations that had to be met, or reversed, quickly.

Another consideration helped move CED toward its stabilizing policy. "Once conservatives give up rigid adherence to the annually-balanced-budget principle," Herbert Stein wrote in a CED staff paper, "they become free to participate in discussion of the particular form that a flexible budget policy should take." Having arrived at this state, CED was able to suggest budget policies that would give weight to such conservative values as economy, limitations of government intervention in the market, and stability of tax rates. CED concluded that "the really frightening possibility" was that national policy would "oscillate between adherence to the annual balance principle in prosperity and belief in compensatory spending in depression." This could only mean endless ascent to higher and higher government spending, in both prosperity and depression.

Out of this welding of conservative value judgments with the new economic thinking came the stabilizing budget policy in November 1947.

Taxes and the Budget set forth four aims of budgetary policy to be reached through a rounded program of government and private action. The first should be to ease fluctuations in total demand, thus stabilizing employment and prices. Second, it should restrain "unnecessary" expenditures and stimulate efficiency in government. Third, it should provide for reduction of the public debt under conditions of "reasonable" high employment and production. And, finally, it should avoid reliance on the ability to forecast economic fluctuations.

With these dicta in mind the CED policy makers set forth this key to their new over-all policy for the promotion of stability, government economy, and debt reduction:

> *Set tax rates to balance the budget and provide a surplus for debt retirement at an agreed upon level of high employment and national income. Having set these rates, leave them alone unless there is some major change in national policy or condition of national life.*

The key phrase of this key statement was, of course, *tax rates*. As the statement pointed out, collections by the government under any system of unchanging tax rates would be larger as the national income rises, and smaller as it falls. It would also be true that some kinds of federal expenditures, notably unemployment compensation payments, would automatically go up or down with changing economic conditions. Some other expenditures, such as public works, while not responding automatically, might also be advanced or held back as the economic situation warranted.

With tax rates set to yield a "moderate" surplus at high-employment national income, larger surpluses would result when the national income went above that level, and smaller surpluses would result when it dropped. If national income went below "some point" it would bring a deficit. Surpluses which would come when national income exceeded the standard high employment level should not be used to increase government expenditures. "A direct consequence of the stabilizing budget principle is that fluctuations in the national income do not call for fluctuations in the tax rate, or in expenditures except for the automatic response of some expenditure items."

But there are exceptions to every rule. Tax rate and expenditure changes are appropriate under certain circumstances. Even back in 1947 the prime example given by the CED was that if defense expenditures could only be cut, then it would be proper to lower the tax rate. But this did not mean that Congress should then go on a spending spree. If it did, people ought to pay for their excesses through increased tax rates.

The edict to set tax rates and then leave them alone did not mean that tax rates should never change from what they were in 1947. Indeed, the report said, they should be adjusted periodically, perhaps every five years, to keep them in line with the growing population of the United States and with the growing national income that a healthy economic society could expect. There would of course be times when the nation would be faced with extraordinary expenditures of a temporary nature. Such needs should not be met by raising tax rates sharply and then cutting taxes as soon as the situation eased. Such a situation called for a smaller tax increase extended over a longer period. Much of the money for this purpose should be obtained by prudent borrowing.

In the case of a national economic crisis—a severe depression or a major inflation—the situation should be met by deliberate and drastic action by Congress, which should order as much of a tax cut or increase as might be necessary. This would be the "most effective and least dangerous" of all available courses. CED did not, in this respect, subscribe to the then emerging belief that in such circumstances the Congress should give the President restricted power to raise or lower taxes. This possible remedy was to be given wide currency by the Commission on Money and Credit in 1961. This plausible prescription was to trouble CED policy makers for many years.

The committee did not insist that its stabilizing budget policy could, by itself, divert the nation from economic trouble at all times. It recognized the need for the "interdependence of all aspects of economic policy." Wise action in the field of money and banking was also necessary. With this went sound management of the public debt, both by the Treasury and the Federal Reserve System. A reasonable price-level policy was called for. The individual income tax should remain the primary source of federal revenue. Many reforms, especially in the corporate field, should be made in the tax system. Finally, business and labor should adopt "far-sighted" policies affecting the over-all economy, as well as their own interests. Technical progress should be used to increase productivity, and improve the flow of savings into constructive investment.

The committee then turned to the then current economic scene. It deftly inserted some significant figures into its stabilizing formula. Tax rates, it said, should be set sufficiently high to yield a surplus of about $3 billion at a national income corresponding to about 96 per cent of the labor force. At the 1947 size it estimated this to mean a $3 billion surplus when unemployment was 2.5 million.

CED did not claim the formula or figures were infallible. "The policy recommended here cannot be adopted and left to run without common sense and vigilance." All CED claimed to do was present principles that were essential to making the decisions that must be made. "The policy will not yield the results of which it is capable unless the principles are consistently followed and reasonably interpreted."

Election year, 1948, witnessed much confusion on the economic front. Neither political party did anything meritorious to stop it. Congress passed the Taft-Hartley labor act over President Truman's angry veto. Twice it enacted measures calling for 20 per cent tax cuts, only later to sustain the President's rejection of them. Fearful that inflation would get entirely out of hand, President Truman vainly sought acceptance of his 10-point anti-inflation program that would have reimposed drastic restraints upon the economy. He did not ask for the tax increase that the stabilizing budget policy of CED seemed to call for under the inflationary conditions. In Washington hot debate raged as to the relative priority of tax reduction over debt retirement, with neither being accomplished. Vainly the President pressed for his long-deferred public housing bill, for increased welfare funds, for a civil rights law. Harried on all fronts, economic and political, he went to the country and surprised the world by his amazing re-election to the Presidency.

While all this was taking place, and the Federal Reserve was trying to quiet the inflationary trend by raising the discount

6

The First
Postwar Recession

rate, deflationary gnomes were invading the economy. New housing starts, always an important early indicator, dropped sharply. Manufacturing investment slumped. Net foreign exports were down. In the third quarter of 1948 retail sales leveled off. There was a sharp rise in personal savings. In brief, the first postwar recession was setting in.

At first nobody wanted to admit it. In a divided Council of Economic Advisers, Chairman Edwin L. Nourse and Leon Keyserling were sending conflicting advice to the White House. Even different advice came from Secretary of the Treasury Snyder. Everywhere there was reluctance to admit the change in economic climate. Since then, several historians have pointed out that the signs were obviously pointing downward. (Criticism today of the failure of the Truman Administration to read them then as quickly as it should have is not ex post facto.) In January 1949, both the President and his Council were still warning that "our prosperity is threatened by inflationary pressures at a number of critical points." The President therefore called for a balanced budget, and a substantial surplus "to reduce inflationary pressures" and permit "a sizable reduction in the national debt," which was then at the high point of $252 billion. But his budget submitted a few days later projected a $900 million deficit.

Faced with this, Mr. Truman asked for a $4 billion increase in revenues, to come from additional corporation taxes, revised estate and gift taxes, and higher rates in the middle- and upper-income brackets. Congress refused his requests. Instead, the 81st Congress launched an "economy drive." Before the Korean War interrupted, it had cut $1 billion from the Administration's defense requests that had been necessitated by the signing of the North Atlantic Treaty. Congress also reduced appropriations for highway, aviation, and water resource projects. It failed to liberalize social security. It had kept excise taxes unchanged. And it had failed to raise postal rates.

The recession did not cause widespread public discomfort or concern. In mid-year the President withdrew his request for a $4 billion tax increase.

Between June 1949 and January 1950, however, a change in the economic thinking of the Administration took place. During that time the principles of the stabilizing budget policy, as propounded by CED in 1947, were given explicit endorsement.

When Mr. Truman sent his budget message to Congress on

January 9, 1950, he broke with tradition. He projected, and defended, a deficit of $5.1 billion for the coming fiscal year. He announced that for fiscal 1951 receipts would amount to $37.3 billion to cover expenditures estimated at $42.2 billion.

"Our general objective," he said, "should be a tax system which will yield sufficient revenue in times of high employment, production, and national income to meet the necessary expenditures of government and leave some surplus for debt retirement."

This was a far cry from what Secretary Snyder had said two months earlier. Then he had warned there were no hard and fast rules applicable to over-all spending and taxing policy except that receipts and expenditures must be examined each fiscal year and that a deficit was wrong.

The special tax message that Mr. Truman sent to Capitol Hill on January 30 was what has been called a "tax rearrangement," which was designed to bring in $1 billion additional revenue in fiscal 1951. Excise taxes, especially those on freight transportation, were to be cut, loopholes were plugged, estate and gift taxes were to be revised, and the corporate income tax was to be raised from 38 to 42 per cent on large corporations to bring in another $1 billion.

This proposal set off the longest, if not the most lucid, debate over taxation the nation had endured for many years. It lasted for nearly six months. The House version of this tax bill was not passed until four days after the Korean War started. The Senate took it up on July 5, but under an agreement that, if war conditions warranted, action on the bill would stop and new measures would be considered. That is what happened.

On July 19, Mr. Truman sent Congress a new message asking for a revenue act that would raise federal receipts by $5 billion per year, by eliminating excise reductions, raising the corporate income tax to 45 per cent, and increasing personal income tax rates. Within the surprisingly short time of three months Congress gave him what he had asked for, effective as of October 1, 1950.

When Mr. Truman reluctantly and perhaps more out of necessity than deep conviction, submitted his unbalanced budget in January, he had said that "nothing could be more foolhardy than to bring about a balanced budget in 1951 by measures that would make it impossible to maintain a balanced budget in the following years." He went even farther along the lines espoused by the CED stabilizing budget policy. In his final budget message (that for fiscal 1954) he said: "The financial program of the federal budget cannot be planned in the terms of a single year. It must be planned in the light of security, economic, and budgetary goals—not just for the ensuing year, but for three and even four years ahead."

An annual budget, he added, may be necessary for pragmatic reasons but the "major functions and programs of government" are continuous. "Budget and fiscal policies are the tools of national policy. As such," he said with the voice of experience, "they are the subjects of controversy and evolution."

The policy makers of CED seem always to have been aware of one indisputable fact: when it comes to economic problems the questions still outnumber the answers. They knew that all the answers to the economic perplexities of the 1940's did not lie in the stabilizing budget policy. Necessary as it was, by itself it could not insure continuing equilibrium. Perhaps this could never be attained in a market-dominated economy with its inevitable ups and downs. But they were certain that better approaches to stability were possible if proper tools were used.

In order to find them, the committee explored many areas. Wages and price policies were important. The structure of markets for labor and goods had to be examined. Agricultural policy, foreign trade and international finance, the volatile construction industry, and savings and investment institutions were other dark areas awaiting new light. The committee would come to them in due time. But first things first.

For this reason the committee turned next to that most perplexing of all problems, monetary policy, realizing that, as the economist Henry Wallich has put it, "a good monetary system is part of our social fabric,

7

A Monetary Impasse

like our system of laws. Lack of trust in stable money means lack of trust in all economic relationships. It has been well said that an inflationary economy is like a country where nobody speaks the truth."

Late in 1948 the committee published a statement on national policy, *Monetary and Fiscal Policy for Greater Economic Stability*. In it CED presented a policy which it considered to be of equal importance to the stabilizing budget policy when properly applied at the right time. This was called a Flexible Monetary Policy.

This policy was based on the simple assumption that the market is the key economic institution in a free society. The freer it is to make its own decisions the more effective it will be. In a free society there is a strong presumption against government intervention by such devices as wage, price, or distribution controls. These are acceptable only in times of war or of economic disaster.

This does not mean that the government does not have certain indispensable economic functions. It does. But these should be limited in scale and character, and should be enforced when necessary without "arbitrary discrimination and coercion of individuals."

Monetary policy, in short, should be used to affect the "general behavior" of the economy and to "promote economic stability" as mandated by the Employment Act. This means that responsibility must be shared—by business, labor, the banks, and other private and public institutions.

The outstanding virtue of monetary policy is that its impact upon the economic life of the nation is "indirect and impersonal," a condition that was quite the reverse of CED's interpretation of the direct and personal virtues of the individual income tax. Of almost equal importance is its virtue of flexibility. Available on an almost day-by-day basis, it can assert itself quickly, or reverse itself with equal speed. Under most circumstances, either can be done without asking permission of the Congress. Furthermore, monetary policy involves no "enlargement of the sphere of government action." By its very constitutional nature, government has all the powers and responsibilities it needs in order to move in the field of money. As every schoolboy knows, the government alone can issue money; by orderly extension of the rule, it can control the rest of the money supply—bank notes and deposits.

The key to this control, developed over the years, is that imperfect but necessary institution, the central bank—in the United

States, the Federal Reserve System. This mechanism is geared to control the money supply deliberately through its power to control the volume and cost of vital reserves of the banks. Through this great power—in the opinion of some observers a power too great to be vested in a quasi-governmental institution—the Federal Reserve System can encourage credit expansion when the economy needs it or restraint when expansion is undesirable. Furthermore, from time to time in the wisdom of Congress, the System can be given additional temporary powers further to control the economy through selective instruments such as control over margin requirements or installment loans. Since it is independent of Congress for operating funds, and is independent of the Executive, its power is great. In the late 1940's CED favored giving the System even further power by removing it from the domination of the United States Treasury.

Monetary policy, it has often been said, *is* the Federal Reserve System. Through its influence over the supply, cost, and availability of bank reserves, it has great influence on the cost and availability of loans to business and to the public. It is therefore a major force in fighting inflation. Almost all the great inflations have been preceded or accompanied by large expansions of the money supply.

Because CED felt that inflation ranked as high as, if not higher than, unemployment as a public enemy, the committee lent great weight to monetary policy as a weapon. It was, however, candid enough to admit that monetary policy was not likely to be a very effective curb against depression. But, if monetary policy alone cannot combat depression, it can help by providing liquidity up to that point beyond which it can do harm.

Having thus asserted its confidence in monetary policy, the committee laid down monetary rules for both inflationary and recessionary situations:

> *First, hold tax rates stable, so that revenues will rise as the national income rises and government surplus will increase. Then tighten the reserve position of the banks, by Federal Reserve sales of government securities in the open market, by increase of rediscount rates and/or by increase of reserve requirements. Use the government surplus to retire the debt held by the commercial banking system, including the Federal Reserve Banks. Refund maturing government debt in a way that will reduce the holdings of the banking system. Re-*

duce the volume of government loans and guarantees of loans.

So much for *inflation.* For *recession* CED offered these rules:

> *Hold tax rates stable, so that tax revenues will fall as the national income falls and government surplus will decline or fall into a deficit. In extreme conditions a temporary reduction of tax rates may be desirable to stimulate private expenditure. Expand the money supply and increase bank reserves by open market purchase of government securities; further ease the reserve position of the banks by reduction of rediscount rates and/or by reduction of reserve requirements. Finance a deficit, if there is one, by borrowing in a way that will induce the banking system to acquire government securities, with such Federal Reserve action in providing additional bank reserves as may be necessary for this purpose. Refinance maturing federal debt in part by borrowing from the commercial banking system, including the Federal Reserve Banks. Expand the volume of federal loans and guarantees of loans within the scope of the federal loan program accepted as appropriate in the long run.*

Early in its role as policy maker CED had been seriously warned by one trustee that it should not consider itself an "economic fire engine," rushing off to every fire that might break out. Heeding this advice, it had restrained its impulses and dedicated its efforts to policies for the long run. But now a situation had developed which CED thought had got out of hand. It was no longer a small fire; it had reached the stage of a conflagration. CED therefore went to the scene.

The monetary policy statement had asserted firmly that "in its decisions as to the purchase and sale of government bonds, the Federal Reserve should act on the basis of *its* judgment from time to time as to the effect of such action *on the economy as a whole.*" When deciding on the character of its continuous refinancing, the Treasury should give "great weight to the effects of different kinds of borrowing on the general inflationary or deflationary situation." In 1948 neither was the case.

These CED "directives" were, of course, primarily aimed at a situation that had existed since the start of World War II—the "pegging" at par of the market for government bonds. In CED's opinion (and in the opinion of Thomas B. McCabe, a former

CED trustee who was then chairman of the Federal Reserve Board), this custom, while perhaps necessary during World War II, now opened the way to coercion of the Federal Reserve by the Treasury, forcing the central bank to "act too narrowly in the meeting of specific difficulties and in the solution of specific problems." In other words, CED would restore to the Federal Reserve that degree of "independence" it had so deeply cherished and which its adherents deemed necessary if it were to live up to its commitments as defender of the value of the dollar. Thus CED stepped into the middle of the great monetary debate of the 1950's.

The document's flat recommendation was:

> *In its decisions as to purchase and sale of government bonds, the Federal Reserve should act on the basis of its judgment from time to time as to the effect of such action on the economy as a whole. This assumes accepting continuing responsibility for maintenance of an orderly market for government bonds. It also assumes that due consideration will be given to requirements arising out of unsettled international relations. The Federal Reserve should feel free to reduce the support level unless it finds a superior alternative way of bringing about a monetary restriction if and when that is required by the objective of economic stability. It should regain the initiative in its open market operations, rather than let the initative remain with the market. Passive open market policy is not consistent with the effective regulation of the money supply.*

This view attracted wide attention at the time. It came at a moment when the subject of monetary and debt management policy was disturbing the peace of both financial and government circles. Less than a year after the statement appeared the Treasury-central bank issue became a matter of serious concern in Washington. Senator Joseph O'Mahoney, chairman of the Joint Committee on the Economic Report, had been casting a critical eye on the situation. Events that had disturbed CED were disturbing him and other leaders. Testimony from a wide number of political, academic, and business witnesses, pointed up the gravity of the situation. Marriner Eccles, former chairman of the Federal Reserve Board, had already warned that under the policy of supporting the prices of Treasury obligations the Federal Reserve had become "an engine of inflation." As a result of this unnerving testimony, the Joint Economic Committee ordered a subcommittee, specially created for the purpose, to conduct a full study and investigation into the "effectiveness and coordination of monetary, credit, and fiscal policies in dealing with general economic policy."

The chairman of this subcommittee was Senator Paul Douglas, Illinois Democrat. The scholarly senator had come to the political arena from a long professorship of economics at the University of Chicago, where so many of CED's advisors had made their reputations. Under the erudite but politically aware guidance of Senator Douglas there began a continuing public postgraduate course in political economy. Over the years this process has made the Joint Committee one of the most educationally productive committees in congressional history. Ralph Flanders, now a senator from Vermont, was one of its most articulate members. He, of course, not only had been trained in but was a prime originator of CED's own process of open discussion and objective research, on which the Joint Committee modeled itself.

The Douglas subcommittee called a wide variety of witnesses before it. One of them was J. Cameron Thomson, chairman of the CED committee which had issued *Monetary and Fiscal Policy*. In the ensuing years he was to make frequent visits to Capitol Hill to explain CED policies to many committees. On this occasion he appeared with a 23-page essay which set forth the essence of that statement. It was a persuasive document, as the Douglas committee later acknowledged in its *Report*.

The voice of CED might be heard in the words of Federal Reserve Chairman Thomas B. McCabe: "I cannot emphasize too strongly the difficulties we are placed under when many of the most vociferous supporters of free enterprise, businessmen and bankers and their organizations, criticize the possession and use by the Federal Reserve System of necessary authority over the cost and availability of credit as if the delegation of this authority were characteristic of a 'managed economy' or an 'administered state.'" Education is not always an easy process.

The subsequent *Report* of the Douglas committee reflected CED philosophy in many ways. It rejected the annually balanced budget ideology *in toto*, looked also with skepticism upon the imperfections of forecasting, and warned against its use as a reliable economic tool. It went into more details than did CED in listing several institutional reforms it considered necessary for better conduct of fiscal policy. But it followed CED suggestions that the salaries of Federal Reserve Board members be raised to Cabinet level and that, in the name of efficiency, the membership be cut from seven to five. These proposals have today only partly borne fruit.

In one important matter the Douglas committee and the CED both agreed and disagreed. This was on the necessity for the creation of a National Monetary Commission. The CED group had suggested empowering a temporary commission to make a "comprehensive study of the possibilities of improving the structure and policies of monetary, budgetary, and related institutions." This commission was to be established by act of Congress but CED urged strongly that it should be composed of private as well as public members. The Douglas committee had a different concept. It urged creation of a permanent national monetary council without private citizens as members, but consisting of the Secretary of the Treasury, Chairman of the Board of Governors of the Federal Reserve, Comptroller of the Currency, Chairman of the Federal Deposit Insurance Corporation, Chairman of the Council of Economic Advisers, and the heads of all federal lending or guaranteeing agencies.

The primary purpose of this powerful junta would be to coordinate all economic programs within the government, thus assuring that their individual policies coincided with the over-all economic policy of the administration. In the domestic field it would thus have the same functions that the National Advisory Council then had in the international lending field. It would keep all the various agencies informed as to problems and policies of the others. This, of course, was in keeping with CED thinking when it had said:

> Federal credit agencies in such fields as housing should not pursue policies of a promotional, easy-money kind at a time when monetary authorities are endeavoring to combat inflation.

Under the leadership of the Chairman of the Council of Economic Advisers, this commission would provide a forum for discussion of common economic problems, solve disagreements by negotiation, bring others to the attention of the President, and call to the attention of Congress types of legislation needed "to secure more appropriate and better coordinated policies."

The set-up offered in the CED report had suggested a federal loan council to coordinate the activities of the federal government's various lending and loan guarantee agencies. Neither CED's nor Douglas's suggestions made headway at the time. Years later, however, similar reforms became matters of deep concern to the Commission on Money and Credit. They were to be the subject of painful inquiry by CED itself when inflation again became a major problem in 1966.

The most nourishing sustenance the Douglas committee drew from the CED statement lay in its animadversions on the "independence" of the Federal Reserve System. The Douglas report concluded that "the advantages of avoiding inflation are so great and a restrictive monetary policy can contribute so much to this end, that the freedom of the Federal Reserve to restrict credit and raise interest rates for general stabilization purposes should be restored, even if the cost should prove to be a significant increase in service charges on the federal debt and a greater inconvenience to the Treasury in the sale of securities."

This, of course, was what CED had said, one year before.

The underlying thesis of the CED statement was upheld even further when the Douglas committee said:

> The primary power and responsibility for regulating the supply, availability, and cost of credit in general (should) be vested in the duly constituted authorities of the Federal Reserve System, and that Treasury actions relative to money, credit, and transactions in the federal debt (should) be made consistent with policies of the Federal Reserve.

No action in this direction was quickly taken. Congress ignored the Douglas proposal for a joint resolution by Congress which would issue "general instructions" to the Treasury and the Federal Reserve making clear the division of authority between them, and telling them that the "power and responsibility" for regulating the supply of credit was indeed vested in the duly constituted authorities of the central bank.

Fourteen months later, however, a crisis occurred and the two suggestions bore fruit. As relations between the two authorities deteriorated, the Treasury argued for the maintenance of the pegs on government securities. In its opinion they held down the public debt, maintained confidence in the public credit, and kept the cost of borrowing low. The Treasury also felt that monetary policy was ineffective against inflation and saw no compensatory benefits inherent in the suggested removal of Federal Reserve support.

The crisis of January 18, 1951 came when Secretary Snyder told a New York audience that, after consultation with President Truman and Chairman McCabe, it had been decided to freeze the 2.5 per cent long-term interest rate for the duration of the Korean emergency. This decision, apparently news to some Federal Reserve officials, caused a national stir of excitement.

President Truman called the Open Market Committee of the Federal Reserve to the White House, the first time a President had ever so openly attempted to influence the presumably independent central bank. But no open commitments were asked or made. The next day the Treasury announced that agreement to keep the peg had been given. This was denied by the Federal Reserve. The fight was now front page matter. Something had to give. The result was the famous "accord" announced on March 3, 1951.

By virtue of this agreement the Federal Reserve was freed at last from its long subjection to the Treasury. At last a flexible monetary policy was possible—and on exactly the same lines proposed three years earlier by CED.

The stabilizing budget policy and the flexible monetary policy had been worked out through an adaptation of academic theory to business pragmatism in many heated and hard-fought sessions of CED's research group. In 1949, it had other effects upon the national economic thinking than those just mentioned. For one thing, it inspired a group of 16 outstanding economists to meet under the auspices of the National Planning Association for a full discussion of the questions raised.

Such disparate academic thinkers as Howard Bowen, John Kenneth Galbraith, Paul Samuelson, Sumner Slichter, Arthur Smithies, and Jacob Viner gathered solemnly at Princeton. Their findings, known as the "Princeton Manifesto," were widely read, eventually seeping into the textbooks. This group of rugged individuals, of course, differed in their conclusions from the CED statement in many ways.

It left considerable room for discretion in the light of "recent events and the outlook for the near future." For example, it provided that under conditions of unemployment and deflation, tax increases to match new expenditure programs should be suspended until they could be put into effect without impeding recovery. In addition, it urged that the possibilities of "formula flexibility" be explored since auto-

*matic flexibility was no more than a "first line of defense."
The statement also called for "more strenuous fiscal measures
. . . when there is a definite expectation, justified by events,
of serious recession or inflation" . . . a prescription which
left considerable latitude for differences of interpretation among
the signers.* Thus although the Princeton statement represents
the high-water mark of the doctrine of fiscal automaticity
(among economists at least), it did not go as far as CED's
original stabilizing budget formula in relying on automatic
stabilizers.

The Princeton Manifesto and other plans—among them the
noted *Monetary and Fiscal Framework for Economic Stability* by
Milton Friedman, professor of economics at the University of Chicago—had some similarity to CED policy. All had what has been
called "a family resemblance." They agreed, for example, that the
level of business activity should be the determinant of the size of
budget surpluses and deficits, and that this was the fundamental
of fiscal policy. All looked with some suspicion on the unreliability
of forecasting and the difficulty of making rapid changes in tax
rates and spending programs through the usual congressional and
administrative procedure. All depended on fluctuations in tax collections rather than on changes in expenditures to provide desired
fluctuations in the position of the budget. But the Princeton group's
plans on monetary policy were generally less precise than on fiscal
policy. "They seem to fall," Herbert Stein has said, "between the
great confidence in monetary policy that prevailed in the 1920's
and the extreme skepticism about monetary policy that prevailed
in the 1930's." But it was from these beginnings that the CED's
fiscal and monetary policies began to exert their quiet but effective
influence on American economic thought.

Discussing the work of the Research and Policy Committee
a few years later, Theodore O. Yntema, at that time its chairman
and chairman of the Finance Committee of the Ford Motor Company, had this to say about the spreading influence of CED in the
realm of policy making:

*We are often asked how we know that trying to adhere
to these standards pays off. This is a legitimate question. However, it is sometimes asked in a way that seems to call for an
illegitimate answer. We are expected to show that what we
recommended in January is done in June. There are some cases*

like this, but they are not usually significant. Almost always if what we recommended in January is done in June, there is a strong possibility that it would have been done anyway. . . . The more significant test is whether there has been a gradual shift in the climate of public opinion in which policy is made, as a result of national discussion and debate in which CED has actively participated.

The Korean War came quickly at a time when the nation had recovered from its first postwar recession and when most signs pointed toward a period of domestic well-being. Mr. Truman was still in the White House and there was no telling how far he intended to carry out his Fair Deal policies, or at what cost. Now, it seemed that most if not all of his plans would have to be delayed. The nation, faced with the necessity of new military expenditures, would be forced into a rigorous wartime schedule. Imposition of wage and price controls, higher taxes, and all the other dreaded managements of the economy that go with war, were to be expected. Born in the war and matured in the brief but hectic adjustment period that followed, CED was resigned to this. In the policy statements that quickly followed the invasion from the North, it accepted this as a basic fact of life but at the same time it was ready to offer rational policies to keep the economic situation from getting out of hand.

A part of CED's internal postwar reorganization has been the establishment of a small "program committee," as it was called, whose primary duty was to issue

8

Korean Interlude

brief policy statements at times of economic stress. This committee was restricted to patterning established CED policy to the crisis of the moment. At the time the Korean crisis broke this committee was made up of Meyer Kestnbaum, then president of Hart Schaffner & Marx (who had succeeded Walter Williams as chairman of CED); Marion B. Folsom; J. Cameron Thomson; John D. Biggers, then president of Libbey-Owens-Ford Glass Company; Gardner Cowles, then president and publisher of *Des Moines Register and Tribune*; Fred Lazarus, Jr., then president of Federated Department Stores, Inc.; Philip D. Reed; and Beardsley Ruml—a strong and experienced group. Within two months of the Korean outbreak this group issued a special statement, *Economic Policy for Rearmament*.

This statement supported the President's call for a tax increase, accepted a deficit, and predicted that a second tax increase would be needed in 1951. It made the fairly accurate guess that military expenditures, then about $15 billion, would increase to $35 billion within a year. If this $20 billion worth of extra military demand was added to non-military demand, it could produce a dangerous excess of demand. Unless adequate steps were taken to curb non-military demands this would result in a round of general price increases. Inflation would impede the military effort and cause immediate and future hardships to the American people beyond the real requirements of the program. The inflationary potential must be restrained at its source.

The committee offered a five-point program which, it said, would keep the economy stable without recourse to price or wage controls, or rationing. First, cut government non-military expenditures; second, raise taxes to draw off income from private hands; third, increase the sale of defense bonds to the public; fourth, reduce the supply of money by selling more government bonds outside the banking system; and, finally, curtail credit for consumers' durable goods, housing, plants and equipment, and inventories. The program also called for selective excises at a high rate on products needed for military production.

Application of this sound but moderate fiscal-monetary policy might have sufficed the economy had not the war situation worsened. But it did, and the Administration quickly concluded that a more rigorous program was needed. With this, CED agreed. Among Mr. Truman's proposals was the reimposition of an excess profits tax, which was greeted with howls of anguish by most of the business community. In a new policy statement, *Paying for Defense*, CED offered a constructive alternative to the inequitable and inflationary excess profits tax. This was to impose a tax of 15 or more per cent *on top* of the 38 per cent basic corporate tax rate. At the same time it urged general increases in excises as a quick way to bring in large amounts of revenue. It recommended a 5 per cent increase in the income tax rate. The business-minded press of the nation hailed the CED proposal as the only reasonable alternative to the business-dreaded excess profits tax. But Congress would not go for it.

In December the Chinese communists threw themselves into the war and stunning setbacks were sustained by the United Nations forces. *Business Week* spoke to the business community: "The confident days of the ten per cent war are gone. The nation faces its greatest crisis. Nothing less than the fate of our country is at stake." This was, of course, no understatement. It meant that heroic measures were called for to meet the huge budget necessary to prosecute a war that had long since ceased to be a police action.

In March 1951, CED policy makers put the situation explicitly on the line: "Taxes are already high. Now we need still higher taxes: higher than we have ever had, even at the wartime peak."

Estimates for the fiscal 1952 budget were scary—a predicted deficit of $16.5 billion. Finding ways to meet this situation was not easy. Many a turbulent meeting of CED committeemen took place that winter. In March 1951, however, it managed to reach consensus. An "emergency tax program" which it issued that month called for increases in taxes to yield $10 billion more revenue than the already hiked-up rates were bringing in. It asked for a new 5 per cent rise in personal income taxes, a new defense profits tax on top of the excess profits tax, excise taxes of 20 per cent on automobiles, 25 per cent on refrigerators and television sets, and a national 5 per cent sales tax on other items, including clothing and household goods. When one newspaper editor read this austere proposal, he yelped: "An evil scheme by evil men."

President Truman also sought to raise $10 billion more in taxes. He asked Congress to get the additional revenue from the personal income tax to the tune of $4 billion; from the corporate income tax, $3 billion; and from excises, $3 billion. A long and stormy battle over the 1951 revenue bill raged in Congress from early in February to late October. And then Congress gave only $5.7 billion in additional revenue—barely more than half of what both the President and CED had asked. It was certainly no victory for either.[1]

The tax increases, however, did what they were supposed to do. Federal receipts rose rapidly in response to them and to the growth of income that came from the war effort. Of course, recovery from the 1949 recession, begun just before the Korean War erupted, also helped. Revenues continued to rise until the middle of 1953. By that time a new President was in the White House and the second postwar recession had begun.

Looking back on the Korean period most economic historians are agreed that fiscal policy performed reasonably well during the period of hostilities. Indeed, there are some who claim that this was the high-water mark of postwar fiscal policy. Compensatory fiscal action was reasonably prompt and more nearly accurate than at any time since the end of World War I. Furthermore, the tax changes enacted during the first half of the conflict increased automaticity and compensated for the decline in military demands when that came briefly about.

---

[1] About $2.3 billion was to come from the personal income tax, primarily through rate increase of about 12 per cent; $2.2 billion from corporate income taxes through an additional five percentage points on the income tax that raised it to 52 per cent on incomes over $25,000; $1.2 billion from excises that included automobiles, trucks, and sporting goods.

The Committee for Economic Development had just passed its tenth birthday when General Dwight D. Eisenhower became the 34th President of the United States. During that changing decade CED had issued 27 statements on national policy. These had ranged far from its early concern with laying the spectre of a possible postwar depression, and had reflected most of the economic problems facing the nation in that transitional era. In 1944 CED had offered a viable postwar tax plan.

If many of the reforms advanced by the CED program were yet to be accepted, they had already been a challenge to the leadership of the business community and the government. CED had discussed and offered solutions—both long-run and short-run—to such problems as international trade, European economic cooperation, national security and defense, the special problems resulting from Korea, small business, agriculture, collective bargaining, wage and price controls.

9

Conservatism Moves In

All of these had fitted into the economic, political, and ideological debate that marked these years. But of equal, if not greater, importance, had been the committee's deep concern with fiscal, monetary, and debt management policies. In this field it made itself clearly heard, and it pushed forward, although slowly, its philosophical concept of a free society and a mixed economy that was vastly different from what had been acceptable when it entered the national picture.

The many words uttered by CED stood out as perhaps the most generally persuasive echoes of the Keynesian revolution that had quietly taken place in this decade. Although CED's influence may have been intangible, as influence in the policy-making sphere so often is, it had penetrated the higher reaches of Washington, Wall Street, and (not least important) the universities. And it had not gone entirely unnoticed on Main Street. It was listened to, if not always followed. CED's dedication to objectivity, as well as its determination to be neither right nor left, but responsible, had won it a wide and growing readership in professional circles. There its generous employment of well-known economists and other social scientists as advisors and collaborators had made it unique among business organizations.

If some observers, especially in the business establishment, felt that it showed too willing a slant toward accepting government intervention in order to make its policies work, there were others who already detected signs of slippage toward an undefinable right. Both views seemed to show up within the committee as well as without, as evidenced by an increasing number of dissenting footnotes that spotted the pages of its statements. This, of course, reflected a growing conservatism among the American people, as revealed most noticeably in the 1952 election, and in the observable drift toward McCarthyism then arising in certain segments of the population. But a careful reading of these statements reveals few signs of backsliding toward complacency, although certain shifts in emphasis were taking place.

The eight years of Republican rulership now just beginning were to make clear the continuing need for such an organization as the Committee for Economic Development. They were years marked by the international disturbances of the cold war, by periods of recession and unemployment at home, by a creeping fear of inflation, by other strains and stresses within the economic system that called for, but did not always get, sound analysis and pertinent prescription. During these eight years CED was to speak out nearly 25 times. It was to become engaged in several controversies, make new enemies, and widen the horizons of its competency measurably. More uncomfortable under the ambivalent leadership of President Eisenhower than it ever cared to admit, the committee struggled to maintain its reputation for advanced thinking at a time when it would have been easy enough to drop back to the old laissez-faire ways of life.

During this time CED deviated but little from its major concern—fiscal and monetary policy; but even in this field it managed to explore new ground. It turned to the underdeveloped countries and their needs; it explored with harsh eyes the vast agricultural complex of the nation; it made a new accounting of the costs of public education; it penetrated the growing urban areas crying for renewal; it kept its eye on foreign investment and international trade; it worried about the balance of payments and the soundness of the dollar; and it took a hard look at the new European scene, exemplified by the Common Market. In doing all this it helped set the scene for what has been called the age of the New Economics that arrived with such seeming suddenness in the Kennedy-Johnson era.

In circles where CED was best known, it was widely predicted that the Committee for Economic Development would have much to say about the economic policies to be followed by the Eisenhower Administration. As *Business Week* observed, there was "a marked similarity between the CED and the new Administration. Both represent the views of forward-looking businessmen, a sort of progressive conservatism." Furthermore, while acting as President of Columbia University, General Eisenhower had been a trustee of the committee, although he had taken little if any part in its deliberations. Nor, for that matter, had another CED trustee, George M. Humphrey, whom the new President chose as his Secretary of the Treasury, ostensibly the highest economic post in the federal government, or Charles E. Wilson, who was now named Secretary of Defense.

During his presidency Eisenhower was to reach into the ranks of CED more than once. From them he chose Marion B. Folsom, first as Under Secretary of the Treasury and later as Secretary of Health, Education, and Welfare. For Under Secretary of Commerce he chose Walter Williams. Both had been chairman of CED. Meyer Kestnbaum, then CED chairman, became a Presidential Assistant, and James D. Zellerbach, Kestnbaum's CED successor, was named Ambassador to Italy.[1]

Shortly before the inauguration, a small group of CED trustees brought before the President-elect a nine-page statement of its views on the areas of economic policy most in need of attention. These, broadly, were national security, promotion of economic stability, and stimulation of economic growth.

In the first category, the paper repeated the proposals CED had made in 1949, in its statement on *National Security and Our Individual Freedom*, calling for development of the National Security Council as the principal executive agency for formulating and reviewing comprehensive and balanced security policies. It wanted three civilians added to full-time membership on the Council and suggested the setting up of a Committee on National Security in both Houses of Congress.

Next the CED group stressed to the President its belief in the need for a fundamental revision of United States commercial policy and for more effective efforts to strengthen the economies of other free nations.

But of far greater importance at the time, the CED warned Mr. Eisenhower of the "critical requirement" for a strong anti-inflationary policy. This could be accomplished by keeping the cash budget in balance at high employment (as was then being enjoyed) and by continuing the accord between the Treasury and the Federal Reserve to insure that monetary and credit control would be flexibly manipulated to meet the intensity of inflationary pressure. The committee warned of the real possibility that a depression might occur within the next four years and urged the President-elect to start immediately to make economic preparations to avert it. In this respect

---

[1] Government service was not a new experience for CED trustees. Ralph Flanders and William Benton became United States Senators and Mr. Benton held other appointive posts. Prior to the Eisenhower regime high positions in the executive branch were held by Will Clayton, William C. Foster, Paul G. Hoffman, Thomas B. McCabe, Howard Petersen, and Wayne C. Taylor. More recently John T. Connor has served as Secretary of Commerce; John A. McCone as Director of the Central Intelligence Agency; Robert B. Anderson as Secretary of the Treasury; and Erle Cocke as Chairman of the Federal Deposit Insurance Corporation. George C. McGhee is serving as United States Ambassador to the Federal Republic of Germany; William M. Roth as Special Representative for Trade Negotiations; James E. Webb as Administrator of the National Aeronautics and Space Administration; and George Romney as Governor of Michigan.

the committee was not wrong. The first "Eisenhower recession" was already in the making.

The committee then took up the immediate matter of tax reduction and tax reform. When economies in government spending, which should be a priority of the new Administration, were achieved; when the cash budget was balanced; and when tax reduction was thus made possible—but not until all this had been achieved—then priority should be given to elimination of the excess profits tax.

Although it is by now pretty well forgotten, these suggestions had a profound influence on the new Administration. As a result it became the first Administration to give, as the historian, E. Carey Brown, has pointed out, "heavy emphasis to future budgetary considerations rather than to the economic situation as it then appeared. . . ."

When *The New York Times* revealed that CED was advising the President-elect not to eliminate the excess profits tax until the economic situation made such action acceptable, there was consternation in a wide sector of the business community. This was accentuated when CED elaborated upon this theme in *Tax and Expenditure Policy for 1953*, a brief and pungent statement issued in April. Annoyed indeed were the National Association of Manufacturers and many top officials of the U.S. Chamber of Commerce, then vocal in their demand for the immediate death of what the *Chicago Tribune* called "that evil tax."

In an interesting and revealing editorial, *The New York Times* summed up the situation:

> *For many years leaders of the National Association of Manufacturers and the U.S. Chamber of Commerce have omitted no opportunity to proclaim their undying faith in the balanced Federal budget as the cornerstone of a strong and sound economy. Are we to believe that this article of faith contains a proviso, in fine print, that the budget must be balanced by particular kinds of taxes that they happen to like? No one familiar with the views of CED doubts that it detests the excess profits tax quite as thoroughly as do the NAM and the Chamber of Commerce. But the CED has not permitted either its detestation or its zeal for tax relief to blind it to the central issue involved. Because it regards a balanced cash budget to be "an essential safeguard against inflation" it sees no logical alternative to backing the President.*

Thus the battle was joined. At the same time the issue was confused by Representative Dan Reed, an arch-conservative budget-balancer from upstate New York, who was doing his best to force a drastic tax-reduction measure through Congress. This, of course, was in response to the Republican platform, which had put tax reduction at the head of new business for the new Congress. When the Republican President—the first in twenty years—now told them, in effect, that they could not cut taxes, cut expenditures, and balance the budget all at once, they did not like it. Nor did they like CED, which had put the idea in his head in the first place.

The President had good reason for following his course. The budget which he had inherited had a projected income of $68.7 billion to satisfy outgo of about $78.6 billion—which meant a deficit of about $10 billion. This took into consideration a Treasury loss of about $2 billion that would occur when the excess profits tax expired. It also counted revenue losses that would come in April with the scheduled expiration of the 1950 income tax increases, as well as the expiration of part of the corporate tax and excise taxes. All told, if allowed to take place, these changes would amount to a drop in federal revenues of about $8 billion in fiscal 1955.

In January, only a few weeks after his meeting with the CED group, the newly inaugurated President warned the nation that "until we can determine the extent to which expenditures can be reduced it would not be wise to reduce our revenues." In midwinter, despite his ability to get some of his predecessor's appropriations cut down, he was forced to take to the radio to ask for a six-months' extension of the excess profits tax, for postponement of the 5 per cent reduction of the corporate tax due in April, and the postponement of repeal of the excise taxes, also due at that time.

The President's will prevailed, but only at a price. The excess profits tax was kept on the books until January 1954. The Reed tax cut proposals were put aside for promised action the following year. Looking back on this period one cannot escape the conclusion that these events combined were a substantial victory for the CED philosophy as expressed up to that time. While the committee itself did not take an active part in the congressional struggle, testimony by such former CED members as Secretaries Humphrey and Folsom were persuasive. Both of them were later to acknowledge that this enforcement of the stabilizing budget policy in 1953 was one of the brighter chapters of the Eisenhower Administration. In the next few years CED was not always to be as fortunate in seeing its policy carried out.

When President Eisenhower went to the White House he did not take with him any great knowledge of economic affairs. Nor is it clear that he had acquired any deep convictions. Many of the men he chose for his cabinet—George Humphrey, Charles E. Wilson, Sinclair Weeks—were not noted for their mental resiliency. In too many respects their thinking stemmed back to nineteenth century concepts. But he did bring with him, specifically as his Administrative Assistant for Economic Affairs, a younger man who had been one of his chief economic advisers during the election campaign. He was Gabriel Hauge, an ex-journalist who is now president of Manufacturers Hanover Trust in New York.

In a remarkably naive passage in his book, *First Hand Report*, Sherman Adams, that intransigent Yankee who was Eisenhower's Assistant, has said: "Having the President's office budget in mind I was inclined at first toward cutting the Council of Economic Advisers down to one man, whereupon I listened to a stern lecture from Gabriel Hauge on the reasons why he felt Eisenhower's decisions in the field of economics might well spell the success or failure of his Administration."

There was evidence, also, early in 1953, that Congress might starve the Employment Act of 1946 off the statute books. It had already cut the Council's appropriations and it looked as if it might be even more ruthless. Mr. Hauge (who incidentally had arranged the pre-inauguration meeting of Eisenhower with the CED group) persuaded Sherman Adams and Congress to be more liberal.

Later President Eisenhower, also at Mr. Hauge's suggestion, brought Arthur F. Burns, a brilliant, self-confessed non-Keynesian economist, to Washington from Columbia University and the National Bureau of Economic Research, to head and revive the Council. By executive order, President Eisenhower made the chairman of the Council of Economic Advisers the sole boss of that agency, and otherwise strengthened it.

Under Arthur Burns's sojourn as chairman the Council became a strong, consistently well-organized, and productive branch of the executive department. That no President at all concerned about economic stability could do without it has become increasingly obvious in the passing years. What had started out disastrously became a bright chapter in the history of the Eisenhower regime.

Once the reactivated Council got under way it played an important part in directing economic policy toward eliminating the confusion that resulted from the recession that had set in at mid-1953. A wave of real fright spread across official Washington, although it was kept well hidden from the public.

Mr. Eisenhower had come to office on a platform promising Republican prosperity served on a business-like basis. There were moments now of great fear that all would go tumbling down the drain if a depression or serious recession should occur. The first businessman's Administration in twenty years would be discredited; the businessman's Republican party would be destroyed or, at least, set back, perhaps for another twenty years.

Harried, indeed, were the Cabinet meetings of those days, as Robert Donovan has revealed in *Eisenhower: The Inside Story* and as Edward D. Flash, Jr., has elaborated in his study of the Council of Economic Advisers in *Economic Advice and Presidential Leadership*. Seldom was economic advice more greatly needed. The Administration sought it, and took it, and stood firm.

Senator Paul Douglas accused the Administration of pussyfooting, and labor leader Walter P. Reuther accurately pointed out that, early in 1954, the Administration had done little for the growing army of unemployed, which then totaled 3.09 million persons or 5.8 per cent of the labor force; or for industrial production, then down 10 per cent; or for the steel industry, then operating at 74 per cent of capacity. But the Administration was not to be goaded into precipitate action. And so the political climate, as Edward Flash recalls, "was warmed by epithets of 'fear deal,' 'prophets of gloom and doom,' 'trickle down theory' and 'what's good for business.'"

In January 1954, President Eisenhower issued his first *Economic Report*. If nothing else it should have scotched, for the time, the accusation that the Administration did not know what it was doing.

"The government," the President said, "will not hesitate to make greater use of monetary policy, debt management, and credit policy, including liberalized use of federal insurance of private obligations, or to modify the tax structure, or to reduce taxes, or to expand on a large scale the construction of useful public works, or to take any other steps that may be necessary."

It all depended upon choosing the right time to do any or

all of these things. According to President Eisenhower the need for "constant vigilance and preparedness by government does not . . . justify constant stirring or meddling." And so, he said, the "arsenal of stabilizing weapons will be drawn upon boldly by the government, but not more frequently than is required to maintain reasonable stability."

One needs only to read those words to see how far conservative American thinking in the postwar years had moved toward accepting government intervention in the affairs of private enterprise.

At the time the Eisenhower Administration was testing the virtues of the "automatic workings of the fiscal system" and "deliberately pursuing monetary, tax, and expenditure policies that inspired widespread confidence"—as the President modestly described the 1954 situation—CED was completing work on what has long been considered one of its more important educational documents. It was started in the spring of 1952 by a subcommittee on the maintenance of high employment, then headed by Fred Lazarus, Jr., one of the nation's leading retail merchants.

Defense Against Recession, published in March 1954, was a well-researched document. A mass of study material had been contributed to the committee by several outstanding specialists in such fields as business policy, public works, housing policy, state and local finance, federal budget policy, wage and price policy, and the increasingly important problem of distressed areas.

The document was not offered as a "blueprint for action" for the current situation, but as a long-range contribution to greater economic stability. Nevertheless, it did fit the pattern of the day in many respects. The Administration's acceptance of several of its precepts is one reason why Murray Rossant, in an article in *The Reporter* magazine, said that the Administration's economic policies confounded those who had assumed that "Eisenhower Republicanism was merely Hooverism in a soft collar."

In this policy statement the committee made it clear that, in the event of a serious business recession, the federal government should accept *"quite a large deficit"* as one of the most effective of stabilizers. An effort to narrow this deficit through higher taxation or decreased spending would only "deepen the depression." Robert Donovan has said that this was the hardest theory for the President to understand. It was easier for him to grasp the idea that big tax cuts and broad public works programs should be resorted to only when recession resulted from cutbacks in construction and equipment spending rather than from inventory movements—which his advisors said had brought on the 1953–54 recession.

The CED report also called for "easy money" early in a recession, which the Federal Reserve had already mandated by the time the statement appeared. It urged the speed-up of tax refunds, a policy already espoused by President Eisenhower. It called for a two-year carry-back of business losses, a proviso just passed by the House a week before publication. It urged extension of unemployment insurance, which Congress was soon to reject in spite of Administration support. It called for a change in the terms and maturities of federal loans and loan guarantees, especially for housing, a proposal also recommended by the President. It suggested a federal standby system to lend money to state and local governments to plan needed public works, also an Eisenhower proposal. But the Administration skitted away from a further CED suggestion of direct federal loans to states and municipalities to carry out these plans.

The CED statement also recommended some mild reforms for state and local governments, but it did not delve deeply into the problems of economic federalism. (This was to come later when, in 1963, CED set up its wide-ranging Committee for the Improvement of Management in Government under Marion B. Folsom.) It presented some bland recommendations to business, such as the need for development of new products, improved marketing processes, a more stable inventory policy, and the reduction of short-term debt. It also told the bankers not to be "too tightfisted when the economic weather gets cloudy."

The report also touched upon a subject that was to become of perennial interest to CED, of major interest to the Commission on Money and Credit, and, as late as 1967, of continuing interest to the editors of *The New York Times*—namely, finding some constitutionally reasonable method for speeding up the process of lowering or raising taxes for stabilization purposes.

The problem was a sticky one. It caused the committee much trouble. As the members saw it there were four ways in which this vital component of the stabilizing budget policy might be implemented. The simplest, of course, was merely that when the President was convinced of the economic need for tax reduction he would ask Congress for it, and Congress, presumably, would comply with his request. Or, the President might act under authority, previously granted him by Congress, to cut tax rates by limited amounts and for a limited period. Or, the President might act under previously granted authority to cut rates when some objective situation appeared—such as 5 million unemployed. Or, legislation might be passed providing in advance that when such an objective signal flashed, a legislatively specified tax reduction would *automatically* go into effect. Many of the subcommittee's professional advisors argued for the fourth system—automatic action upon an agreed signal. The CED trustees rejected this as not being "practical," then or in the near future. In the end the committee said:

> *If reduction of tax rates is to be an important anti-recession instrument, preparation should be made in advance for its flexible use. The time that is administratively and mechanically necessary between a government decision to change tax rates and the first effects of that decision on taxpayers is short. With a small amount of advance preparation, for example, a decision to cut income tax rates could be felt in withholding and therefore in take-home pay within two months.*
>
> *The main problem is the length of time needed to make the decision. This process would involve an Administration decision to recommend a tax reduction of a particular kind and a congressional decision to approve, modify or reject the Administration's recommendation. In principle it might be possible to short-cut this process by legislation providing for a tax cut to go into effect automatically under certain conditions, or by giving the President authority to reduce certain taxes under specified conditions. There are, however, difficulties, in the way of either procedure. To make the present procedure more flexible, it would be helpful for the Administration to decide: (a) whether in the event of a recession (actual or forecast) it would recommend tax reduction; (b) in what kinds of situations, on the basis of what facts, it would take such action; and (c) what kind of tax reduction it would recommend. The Administration should discuss these plans with congressional leaders and attempt to reach general agreement, by mutual adjustment. These, it should be noted, would be plans, not binding commitments. The plans could be changed. But laying this kind of groundwork in advance will save much valuable time.*

There, for the time being, the matter was allowed to rest.

The year 1954 was a busy one for the policy makers of CED. In addition to *Defense Against Recession*, CED published three other valuable statements on national economic policy. Each had been long months in preparation. None was of an ad hoc nature. One, *Taxes, National Security, and Economic Growth*, published in January, is of historic value because it touches upon issues relating to stabilizing fiscal policy that have been of continuing concern to observers of the economic scene. Another, *Managing the Federal Debt*, filled out CED's developing fiscal policy series. The third, *United States Tariff Policy*, set the stage for the Trade Expansion Act of President Kennedy's Thousand Days.

In the next two years, the period of the Eisenhower boom that ended with the recession of 1957–58, CED published other policy statements on the budget, government expenditures, tax reduction and tax reform. Each in its way had something to contribute to the history of economic thinking and helped disperse those "myths" which were to have their rudest challenge during the Kennedy-Johnson era.

10

Looking for Tax Reform

Taxes, National Security, and Economic Growth indicated a subtle veering toward a new and rocky coast. Hitherto CED (and, indeed, the economics profession as a whole) had devoted but little attention to economic growth as an important national objective. Now a flood of statistical information about the high growth rate boasted by the Soviet Union began to infiltrate the country. This came about two years before Khrushchev's ominous but futile warning: "We will bury you." The CED statement paid passing attention to the implications:

"We should not underestimate the ability of a totalitarian government controlling vast resources and populations to expand its economic potential for making war if it determined to do so. Our economic lead could be dangerously reduced if our economic growth stopped or were retarded."

But there were other reasons closer to home why economic growth was important. One of these was of constant concern to CED:

"The growth of our economy is also an important source from which we can hope to achieve tax reduction in the near future. . . . A proper tax structure, one that does not unduly absorb savings or repress incentives to work or invest, is itself an essential condition for rapid economic growth."

The statement stressed another of the committee's more lasting beliefs. Although it implied that this was based more on empirical judgment than on scientific appraisal, it was an honest conclusion coming, as it did, from a group of management elite. This was that high income tax rates in the upper brackets were undesirable. For one thing they hindered personal effort on the part of corporate managers. More important, they stifled investment, especially risk investment.

Although elimination of these obstructions was paramount, there were other conditions necessary for satisfactory economic growth. Particularly necessary were "adequate markets for the products of an expanding economy." Because of the importance of adequate markets, however, the committee said it is sometimes suggested that tax policy can make its greatest contribution to economic growth by concentrating on tax reductions in the lower and middle income groups. A corresponding insistence upon little or no reduction of the tax burden on the upper income groups is "a mistaken view. It is clear that we need *both* adequate markets *and* strong incentives." This was to be a CED theme song for many years.

When it came to making a choice between tax reforms to stimulate growth and tax reforms to relieve the burdens on the lower and middle income groups, the CED policy makers opted for growth. They rationalized their choice in two ways. First, the cold war international situation made rapid growth of American productivity "essential as a reserve for possible mobilization." Second, most people "had more to gain, in improved living standard, from rapid growth of productivity, than from any feasible shifting of tax burdens."

In the ensuing years CED was to consider the problem of growth in many ways at many times. It was never willing to set a figure for a proper annual rate of growth, nor did it become a member of the "growthmanship" school, whose arguments enlivened economic debate in the late 1950's.

Nevertheless there were certain specific tax reforms of a general nature which CED felt should be given consideration. Most of them centered around the committee's patiently reiterated basic belief that the personal income tax should remain the major source of federal revenue. But, as it was then administered, the personal income tax was a far from perfect instrument. Especially inhibiting were the high rates imposed in every bracket. Taxes should be cut across the board. This should be done by reducing the rate of taxation and not by the special gesture of increasing exemptions. A system for averaging incomes should be devised. All excises except the historic ones on liquor and tobacco should be abandoned.

At this point the CED policy makers paused. They realized that the uncertainties of the market might at any time make it necessary to retain needed federal revenues that would be lost if excises were abandoned. In this event they argued that a more general consumption tax such as a retail sales tax would be desirable.

CED had first proposed such a tax in 1952 when it was expected that the budget for fiscal 1953 would be $10.4 billion in deficit. It had then argued that this budget could be balanced by reduction of federal expenditures "that are, at least during this emergency period, less important to the nation than avoiding either a deficit or a tax increase." But since it felt that Congress might come to a different conclusion, it urged balancing the budget by a "temporary tax on retail sales except sales of food, housing, and items already subject to direct federal excises." This way of financing the excess of expenditures would be less inflationary and less injurious to production than any alternative. What other method was there?

Not corporate taxes: federal taxes were already taking 60 per cent of net income. Not the income tax: that could "not be exploited further." Not more selective excises: there was no "reasonable basis for selecting the objects of such taxes." Because of the defects in the alternatives nothing remained except a "fairly general retail sales tax."

The retail sales tax, which CED now proposed, would be more desirable than one collected, as some economists suggested, at the manufacturers' level. A retail tax would be direct and visible. A manufacturers' tax, on the other hand, might well pyramid retail prices to heights above the tax charged to manufacturers. Not only would this affect the consumer but it would place a serious burden on small business. Furthermore, the sound tax objective of "generality of coverage" would be difficult to achieve, since it would probably be impossible to bring many services within its scope.

This argument met with some sharply footnoted opposition within the CED ranks, where the main objection was that a retail sales tax would be politically unpalatable. An advantage of a tax at the manufacturers' level was that it would be simpler and less expensive to administer and it would not interfere with local and state sales taxes that had already become major sources of revenue in those entities.

In the ensuing years CED was often to flirt with the retail sales tax idea. In 1957, for example, when it called for reduction to 60 per cent of all income tax rates then above that figure, and for elimination of all selective excise, it said that revenue loss could be recouped by "a general consumption tax at quite a low rate." It said, "when progressive tax rates are carried to extremes, when heavy reliance is placed on a corporation income tax that may be capricious in its effects on different businesses, and when consumption taxes [selective excises] are arbitrary and discriminatory [which a general sales tax would not be], the tax system fails to conform either with equity or economic requirements."

This roused the hackles of William Benton, among others, who said he saw "no reason to believe that . . . a general consumption tax will yield a solution to federal tax problems. To install a general federal consumption tax in place of any part of the individual income tax would be unjustified . . . on grounds of equity or economics." When tax reduction is possible, he said, corporate income tax reduction should have priority. "The corporation tax today is largely passed along to the consumer, and is thus a form of general consumption tax, its reduction should bring prices down." This view, that the corporate income tax is passed on to the consumer, had much to do with CED's later advocacy of a value-added tax.

Ten years later, after long and acrimonious debate, the committee completed its full-circle turn around. In 1966 it strongly endorsed a so-called value-added tax at the manufacturers' level. It no longer seemed to be embarrassed by the fact that the value-added tax is a *hidden* tax and one which the taxpayer—the ultimate consumer—might well not know he was paying. It, like the corporate tax, would be passed on.

In 1954 there were other tax reforms on the CED agenda. Reduction of the corporate tax, of course, was a requisite. Others included broadening depreciation allowances and removing "double taxation" of dividends. On the former, the committee urged using a rate twice as high as the so-called straight-line depreciation then in use. Congress adopted it in the Revenue Act passed that year. Widely debated in Congress was the CED theory of discrimination in the payment of taxes on income from dividends. (CED had not yet adopted the view that the corporate tax was passed on.) The committee contended that the distributed income of corporations is taxed both as a part of the corporation's income and as part of the stockholder's income. CED called for allowing deduction of dividend income from gross income and for claiming a credit against taxes otherwise due equal to a percentage of remaining dividends. Congress voted for a token mitigation of this discrimination—a $50 deduction and a 4 per cent credit allowance—in the 1954 Revenue Act. But the relief granted was small, and by no means eliminated the problem of equity.

Along with these proposed reforms CED in 1954 also felt it necessary to modify an important element of its stabilizing budget policy. This was necessary to meet the conditions that had changed since the policy was first enunciated in 1947. At that time it had said "we believe that the useful and feasible meaning of the budget-balancing principle is that the cash-consolidated budget should be balanced—*or yield a moderate surplus*—under conditions of high employment."

But tax requirements had increased in the ensuing years. The additional taxes required to yield a *surplus* at normal high employment were growing so high that they would probably exceed the gains from debt reduction.

Therefore, CED suggested that tax rates be set to *balance the cash budget—not* to produce a surplus—at employment of 96 per cent of the labor force. (Later CED reverted to its original formula; the change was apparently based on expediency.) The 4 per cent unemployment became the CED normal unemployment rate. Many observers thought this was too high a figure. But experience since 1954 has shown it to be a difficult level to maintain.

The recession that had begun in 1953 lasted for only nine months. It was followed by a "boom." During this happy interim the automatic stabilizers of the economy were left pretty much to themselves. Planned stabilization to meet current or future needs was noticeable by its absence. There was some noticeable and effective cutting of federal expenditures. The existing structure of personal and corporate income taxes brought in relatively large increases in revenues. No new tax legislation beyond continuance of the excise taxes was offered by the Administration or by Congress.

President Eisenhower did not think the times propitious for cutting income taxes, although he spoke optimistically of his plans for eventual tax reduction. He constantly warned against incurring inflationary deficits. On all economic fronts there was general expansion. Both the President and CED worried about inflation and so great was the latter's fear that it would get out of hand that, in December 1955, its program committee issued a brief New Year's warning against the potential danger.

I I

Recession in 1958

As the 1956 election year opened, President Eisenhower shied away from any mention in his messages of a tax cut. Instead, he promised debt reduction. CED was soon to follow with a policy statement in which it called for both debt reduction and a tax cut. Since the country was undergoing what Mr. Eisenhower called "conditions of high prosperity," CED felt that the "substantial cash surplus," which it then saw in sight, would justify aiming for tax reduction to begin in January 1957.

Shortly after his re-election President Eisenhower sounded a sharp note of alarm. Prosperity had brought inflation; wages and prices were getting out of hand; the soundness of the dollar was being threatened. In his January series of messages he said:

"Business in its pricing policies should avoid unnecessary price increases, especially at a time like the present when demand in so many areas presses hard on short supply. . . . Increases in wage and other labor benefits negotiated by labor and management must be reasonably related to improvements in productivity. . . . Except where necessary to correct obvious injustices wage increases that outrun productivity are an inflationary factor." Federal taxes, he said, must be kept where they then were. The public debt must be further reduced. Many expenditure programs, even "meritorious proposals," must be postponed.

The winter of 1957 was a rough one for the Administration. When President Eisenhower submitted his budget in January his Secretary of the Treasury, George Humphrey, was unhappy, and said so in words that are still remembered. "There are a lot of places in this budget that can be cut," he told the newspaper reporters. Although he did not name them in detail he challenged Congress to find and do something about them. Otherwise, he said, "You will have a depression that will curl your hair."

Instead of being angry at having his own budget attacked by his own Secretary of the Treasury, the President agreed. He had much support—Senator Byrd of Virginia, the National Association of Manufacturers, the U.S. Chamber of Commerce came vigorously to his side. In the end, Congress did manage to cut the budget, slashing nearly $3 billion, much of it in defense. This was a Pyrrhic victory, for, as the Budget Bureau warned, much of what was cut would have to be restored by supplemental appropriations later. The slowups that followed caused considerable hardship on several business fronts, and accelerated the rate of unemployment.

Early in October the first Sputnik shocked the nation and

was followed by a demand that something be done. At first this resulted mainly in talk about "revving up" the defense program. The President's reaction was to call for cutting back of non-defense expenditures. By New Year, as he was sending his 1958 messages to the Hill, everyone knew that the economic situation had deteriorated greatly. Most economic indexes had gone down in recent months. The nation was in an economic decline. Although it was now a matter for open debate President Eisenhower did not allow this fact to affect his eternal optimism.

The budget for the current fiscal year was only $400 million in deficit and his projected fiscal 1959 budget promised a surplus of $500 million. Many observers were critical and said these figures were far too high. But he did not ask for any precautionary fiscal action beyond a minor tax reduction aimed at helping small business and the perennial request for an increase in postal rates. Instead, he relied on his ingrained belief that "confidence was the major ingredient for an economic recovery."

The Committee for Economic Development's policy makers watched the situation with wary eyes. They apparently did not have as much confidence in "confidence" as did their former colleague. During the winter of 1958–59 several emergency meetings of CED's research and policy committee were held. There were several consultations with government officials. The economic indicators were watched closely. Many members were for immediate action. Preferably this should take the form of an immediate tax cut. At one meeting Arthur Burns, who had left the Council of Economic Advisers to return to his teaching post at Columbia University, took a vigorous position in behalf of reduction. By the end of February or early in March, the committee was moving in that direction.

Even as early as the start of 1958 most economists believed, and rushed into print with their opinions, that the country was facing the severest recession of the postwar years. They based this observation on the evidence of drastic reductions in inventories, sharp cuts in business plans for capital spending on new plant and equipment, and a determined consumers' movement to refrain from buying most durable goods, especially the new and unpopular 1958 model automobiles. There was, of course, a minority of economists who believed that the economy was not too badly off or that, at least, it would quickly reverse itself. They felt that the recession would be no more bothersome than its two postwar predecessors. The January 1958 *Economic Report* insisted that there had already been a considerable adjustment in inventories. It spoke proudly of the "confidence of business concerns in the economic future," evidenced by their "long-range plans for expansion."

The facts, of course, were somewhat different. Almost at the time these remarks were being published, businessmen, as *Business Week's* economist Leonard Silk later recalled, "really began to slash inventories with a passion unprecedented during the postwar period, at an annual rate of nearly $10 billion." And capital spending was running 20 per cent below the 1957 level. Unemployment was then up to 7.5 per cent.

The CED group was disturbed by the seemingly complacent attitude of the Eisenhower Administration, with which, during this period, it remained in close touch. The question they asked was, "What should be done to keep the recession from feeding on itself?"

Many influential persons felt that a "massive tax reduction" was the only answer. Others foresaw an erosion of vital programs such as defense, foreign aid, or urban renewal. They feared that any contraction of the tax base would be more harmful than an immediate boost in public spending on a wide domestic front. But most economists (at least those not connected with the Administration) insisted that a temporary income tax cut, of significant but not too generous proportions, was the best answer.

Presidential advisor Gabriel Hauge received a letter during that period from "a distinguished and conscientious" fiscal expert stating that if the Administration did not endorse a temporary tax cut, such a failure "would be thought of a generation hence in the same category as President Hoover's failure to take the advice of a thousand economists to veto the Smoot-Hawley tariff legislation in 1930."

The Administration hesitated to move because it might be politically impossible to get a satisfactory kind of tax cut. Even then such a countercyclical measure, for all of CED's preaching, was "too novel" to be accepted by Congress. Furthermore, the already unavoidable increases in spending by the government for a housing program, farm support, national security, the challenge of Sputnik, etc., would furnish the very anti-recessionary impact that was needed.

By late winter 1958, CED had made up its mind to speak out. The great question that had deterred the committee was "*When* to act?" After all, this powerful tool—a deliberate tax cut—had never yet been deliberately used for this purpose in United States history.

During their deliberations (and again in a sharp footnote in

Anti-Recession Policy) former President of the New York Federal Reserve Bank, Allan Sproul and Howard Petersen, a leading Philadelphia banker, expressed the opinion that the nation was "closer to the time of decision" than their colleagues were willing to admit. Had their views been followed, CED would have come out for an immediate tax cut in March. The majority, however, insisted upon a more prudent attack.

In its program statement, *Anti-Recession Policy for 1958*, CED said that no tax cut should be made unless the economic situation became clearly worse than it had been in the recessions of 1949 and 1954, from both of which there had been reasonably rapid recovery. If seasonally adjusted production and employment continued for the next two months to drop at the same rate at which they had dropped in the preceding autumn and winter, then there should be a tax cut.

"For the conditions in which a tax reduction would be necessary, we would recommend a cut of one-fifth in personal income tax rates, effective until March 31, 1959. This would mean a tax reduction, computed at high employment income levels, at a yearly rate of $7.5 billion. At the end of the period, the cut would end unless the economic situation at that time demands its extension in whole or in part."

The statement did not call for corporate or excise tax reductions, as CED had previously done under such conditions, for it wanted to concentrate on "the simplest step, on which quick agreement would be most readily forthcoming." Thus CED emphasized the seriousness of the situation. It wanted the slight delay because it did not "wish to fire our heaviest anti-depression artillery each time the business activity slackens, simply because we fear future economic collapse."

The CED suggestions received wide and generally favorable attention in the press, although they were criticized on some fronts as being too cautious. But they failed to bring President Eisenhower, Secretary of the Treasury Robert Anderson, or their advisors out into the open. The Administration, it is now clear, had made up its mind to rely on the automatic stabilizers—and on a relaxed monetary policy—to bring stability back. There is evidence that the Administration did have some vague plans to follow the CED program with both a tax reduction and greater spending for public works if there were no definite signs of recovery by the end of June. But it never told this to the public.

CED acted with perhaps more wisdom and foresight than it realized when it insisted upon the two-month lag in its program for the recession of 1958. Even as it was making its stabilizing policy position clear the economic indexes were shifting their direction and the recession was petering out.

While CED was at work applying its stabilizing budget policy to the realities of the 1958 recession, a problem of more lasting importance was also getting earnest attention. When the Committee commissioned fifty internationally known scholars to prepare papers on the most important economic problems likely to face the United States in the forthcoming decade, a majority agreed that it would be inflation. With their conclusions most CED trustees agreed. They had, indeed, started intensive work on this subject in 1955. The Committee's main objective was to produce a companion piece to its highly successful statement of 1954, *Defense Against Recession*, which it hoped would have an equally effective influence on the mind of America.

When CED first began issuing its statements on national policy, the attainment of high employment and the use of economic measures to sustain it was, of course, the dominant issue. Economic policy had been devised for this purpose. Toward the end of the 1950's it had been used, and its use had become generally acceptable to, and in great measure understood by, the public. But even while this process was de-

12

Defense
Against Inflation

veloping, it became apparent that high employment alone was not the solution to economic growth. With it went a need for price stability.

Fear of inflation disturbed the peace of mind of businessmen, bankers, statesmen, and economists, and gave them sleepless nights. The fact that the average annual price rise from 1948 to 1958 was about 2 per cent, or well below the 3 per cent advance during the golden years from 1895 to 1910, did not assuage their dread. Nor were they comforted by Sumner Slichter's oft-quoted remark, "The problems of creeping inflation are a small price to pay for avoiding the much greater problems of unemployment and a rate of growth that falls far short of our potential." A creep, they kept telling each other, may turn into a gallop. But even if it did not, inflation as a "permanent way of life," which they feared it had already become, was a disease for which a cure must be found.

Inflation during war perhaps cannot be avoided but, as the CED policy makers observed, the three most recent inflationary surges had occurred when there was no war, when productive capacity was high, when there was high employment, when the budget generally was in balance, and when the money supply was increasing at a moderate rate.

The appearance of inflation under these conditions raised questions in their minds. Was this inflation caused by "new forces" that hitherto did not operate or that were hidden by "more powerful influences"? If inflation could happen under these amenable conditions—conditions which they hoped would "be characteristic of America for a long time to come"—a searching inquiry was called for in order to get at the root of this evil.

The resulting statement, *Defense Against Inflation*, rejects the idea that creeping inflation is desirable, or even acceptable, because even at a "creeping" rate, inflation "erodes the value of long-run fixed money obligations, which are important in our economy, and crucifies the weaker groups in our society." Pensioners, holders of annuities and life insurance policies, investors in bonds, government employees, and employees of institutions such as private schools, hospitals, and other endowed institutions, are multitudinous victims of inflation. Against these, inflation imposes "the cruelest tax."

Real growth and sustained productive employment are not stimulated by a rising price level. By distorting normal incentives for efficiency in business and increased productivity of labor, inflation "may well endanger the sustainability of growth." CED's earlier statement published in February 1958, *Economic Growth in the United States*, had made a great point of this. As far back as 1947 the committee had said that high productivity "can make the major contribution to moderating inflation." In 1950 it had argued that any "substantial rise in real wages can be achieved only through an increase in productivity." It was now to make productivity the key to its anti-inflationary policy.

The statement said that, if the people were willing to adopt the right policies, the United States could have both stable prices and high employment simultaneously. But first it must do one thing—"give up the illusion that we can get more out of the economy than we put into it, that we can consume more than we can produce." This truism was followed by exhortation for a joint sharing of responsibilities by government, business, labor, and agriculture.

As usual, CED took a firm stand against the use of specific government controls to combat inflation. Reliance should be placed on the proper use of fiscal and monetary policies to keep demand from rising faster than the nation's ability to produce. There was always a chance, of course, that monetary restraint and tax policy might fail, for a variety of reasons, to keep demand within bounds, thus forcing prices to get out of hand. Should the federal government then impose rigid controls over the causes—wages and prices?

Here CED took its familiar stance, rejecting selective intervention except in times of gravest emergency such as war. "We must rely on the forces of competition and on the voluntary exercise of restraint in prices and wage policies by business and labor to prevent this from happening. . . . Such controls would seriously impair freedom and efficiency of the economy and, in any case, they could not restrain inflation for very long."

CED felt, as it always had, that if the federal government had to intervene it should do it more effectively than was often the case. Among other things the federal government "has the responsibility to enact and enforce legislation to preserve competition in business and labor markets." The committee was to enlarge upon this theme of market power, but before it got to this controversial subject, it offered an imaginatively constructive, but incomplete, suggestion by which it hoped to bring the whole matter of wage-price policy within the province of highest administrative concern—the Presidency.

Since that memorable day when President Truman signed

the Employment Act of 1946, Congress had been unwilling to revise the mandate for maximum employment, production, and purchasing power in any substantive respect. Now, with growing national concern over inflationary possibilities, a doubt arose in Congress as to whether the Act should not be amended to add price stability to its goals. This suggestion was both good and bad.

It was good, for it proved the high status which the Employment Act now came to enjoy as an almost constitutional directive that made national economic responsibility the continuing concern of the chief executive. It was bad, for, by opening the Act to amendment even in so laudable a direction, it opened the gate for other changes its many enemies might invent in order to weaken or even destroy it. It was bad, also, because, as CED admitted, the idea of price stability was inherent in the phrase *purchasing power.* Without price stability maximum purchasing power would, of course, be impossible.

In his first of many exhortations to business and labor to keep wages and prices within the productivity trend, President Eisenhower had not asked for legislative power to implement the policy. After long debate CED came to the conclusion that the omission of price stability from its framework was a mistake. Realizing that the Act had originated out of a desire to stave off depression, it now rationalized that, since "the risk of recession is not reduced, but is increased, by failure to take restrictive action in a boom," cognizance of this should be written into the Act.

Although the committee admitted that a mere statement of the objective would not itself produce stable prices, it believed that it would be helpful for three reasons: First, it would help counteract the view that the commitment to high employment takes precedence over the commitment to stable prices. This may seem a strange thing for CED to be saying, but it is consistent with its own philosophy, as stated in its by-laws, where its "basic objectives" give *equal status* to the maintenance of "high employment, increasing productivity and living standards, greater economic stability, and greater opportunity for all our people." Much as it believed in high employment, CED had never assumed that this alone should have priority over the other economic necessities of a free society.

Second, it felt that such an amendment would "strengthen the determination of public officials to adopt anti-inflation measures when they are needed." In this the committee spoke correctly, for by 1958 the official sanctity of the Act had penetrated the consciousness of most federal policy makers, including the chairman of the Federal Reserve Board.

Its third reason, however, seemed to transcend the others.

> . . . it would require both the President, in his annual Economic Report, and the Joint Economic Committee of the Congress, in its report on the President's report, to place greater emphasis on recent and prospective price trends and to discuss in a more systematic manner methods of achieving price stability.

In many ways this was the bold suggestion written out by CED. It called upon the President (and, of course, his advisers, presumably in the Council of Economic Advisers) to keep a sharp watch on the actions of private enterprise and organized labor, and to examine their motives regarding price or wage increases. It called upon the President to create ways and means (by exhortation or otherwise) to induce business and labor to toe the line of his own suggestion as to the proper level of wages and prices. It suggested giving him no coercive powers, nor did it suggest that he use measures to punish, say, a recalcitrant U.S. Steel Corporation or Walter Reuther's automobile workers. But it did make it his duty, and the duty of Congress, to create wage-price guidelines and to plead publicly for their acceptance.

In calling for "systematic methods of achieving price stability" the CED suggestion opened the way, via the Joint Economic Committee, for public hearings on "recent and prospective price trends," thus making it possible for Congress to dig deeply into both industry's and labor's affairs. If "recent" prices were deemed to be too high, and if "prospective price trends" threatened to go even higher, the proposed amendment would make it mandatory for the President to say so, as loudly or as softly as he wished, and for the Joint Committee to examine the causes and prospects and to suggest proper action, legislative or otherwise. So, too, might the President intervene—with words, if not a big stick—when he felt that evidence revealed the undue use of "administered prices" by certain firms or industries.

There was nothing in the original Employment Act to bar the President or Congress from following this course. As President Johnson later said, when the wage-price debate was again waxing hot in 1965, "I regard the goal of over-all price stability as fully implied in the Employment Act of 1946." So did CED, but in 1958 it wanted to make this explicit. It admitted that its proposal might "precipitate a long and acrimonious debate" which might "result in a rejection of the stable price objective." But it had faith in the public's abhorrence of "inflation as a way of life" and it believed that Congress would not reject this "overwhelming view" if given a chance. CED therefore suggested that Congress go even farther and write into the Act the mandate that *steady economic growth and productivity* was a permanent national objective.

"Business and labor should not force excessive increases in wages," CED said in *Defense Against Inflation*.

> *By excessive, we mean: (a) Average wage rates (including fringe benefits as well as cash wages) should rise as fast—but not faster—than the rise of output per man-hour for the economy as a whole, which has averaged just over 2 per cent a year since 1900 and close to 3 per cent a year since World War II. Larger increases of wage rates would be justified if productivity for the economy as a whole could be raised more rapidly. We emphasize that wages should not rise in line with productivity in particular industries and firms. Moreover, labor and capital should both share the benefits of increased productivity, that is, wages should rise in proportion to the average gain in productivity, but should not absorb the whole gain. (b) Average profits per unit of output would be roughly constant if wages behaved in this way and if prices were stable on the average. The main justification for departure from this average behavior in particular cases is a surplus or shortage of particular categories of labor or product.*
>
> *If the existing degree of competition in product and labor markets should prove to be inadequate*, the CED report continued, *and the exercise of business and labor power insufficiently responsible to preserve general price stability, we shall have to seek measures to strengthen competition. The laws to maintain competition in business need to be more vigorously enforced and constantly reviewed to assure their effectiveness. But the main problem is in the field of labor, where there is no law and not even a public philosophy or policy for the limitation of economic power. There is urgent need for objective consideration of the proper extent, character, and uses of union power in our society. Existing laws*

should be reviewed to see whether they give or leave a degree
of power to labor organizations that is not in the public in-
terest.

In these words the CED added to its formula for wage and price stability. The fundamental lines of defense were the stabilizing budget policy and flexible monetary policy. The mobile forces to deal with breakthroughs were what have come to be called guidelines, backed up by the laws needed to preserve competition. The prescription did not meet with immediate approval, it is true, but its effect in the long run was to be substantial. It raised as many questions as it gave answers, perhaps more. They were, of course, hedged with many explanations, not all of which stood up to future tests. When, for example, a distinguished "task force" was created by CED in 1960, with the then president of the University of California, Clark Kerr as chairman, to make an independent study of national labor policy, it found fault with these explanations, as did William Benton, Elliot Bell of McGraw-Hill, and Allan Sproul, at the time of publication. But the basic principles of the study—that price stability should be a national goal and that wage increases should be based on the national average level of productivity—were quickly swept into the main flood of national debate.

It would be a mistake to suggest that CED presented its wage-price policy as a wholly new concept to an unwary public, as something new under the sun. It, of course, was not. As we have noticed, CED had been aware of the key role of productivity for more than a decade; but this was the first time it had amplified the subject and pulled together all the strands of the argument in its behalf. It was, furthermore, the first time that so comprehensive a plan had been offered by a group of influential business leaders. But its greatest virtue was the timing of its release to the public.

Already a wave of uneasiness over price stability had begun to stir in the Congress. Within a year of publication Congress was flooded with a series of bills designed to amend the Employment Act to include price stability in its list of national goals. Elsewhere various schemes were advanced to implement such an amendment, to give the President power to "enforce" wage-price stability through a variety of ways. Articles and books on the "new inflation" appeared in great numbers. The American Assembly, that earnest discussion group founded by Mr. Eisenhower when he was president of Columbia University, met at Arden House to discuss it at book-length. The Commission on Money and Credit, just beginning its long deliberations on the national economy, made "reasonable price stability" one of its three national goals.

There were many schools of thought on this subject. One might be called the moderate exhortatory school, whose ideas were clearly outlined in the CED document. The most ardent protagonist of this group was President Eisenhower, who succinctly summed up its views in his 1959 *Economic Report*:

> *The Congress will be requested to amend the Employment Act of 1946 to make reasonable price stability an explicit goal of federal economic policy, coordinate with the goals of maximum production, employment, and purchasing power now specified in that Act. Steps will be taken within the Executive Branch to assure that governmental programs and activities are administered in line with the objective of reasonable price stability, and programs for the enlargement and improvement of public information on prices, wages, and related costs, and productivity, will be accelerated.*

The next year he repeated this, adding, "Such an amendment would help accomplish the desired purpose without causing changes in our economic institutions that might be inimical to the freedoms we now enjoy."

The philosophy of the second school of thought was best summed up in a paper read to the National Planning Association in 1959 by Clinton S. Golden, a former vice president of the Steelworkers Union. This plan called for more direct action by the Administration but it stopped short of any direct form of controls over prices and wages. It wanted the annual Economic Report of the President to include a statement on "the kind of wage-price developments that in the ensuing year would obstruct growth and stability."

This would be derived from data obtained by the Council of Economic Advisers at a series of labor-management-consumer conferences which would form the basis for "general guidelines for specific industries." Then a new agency that was to be called the Price-Wage Analysis Board was to be set up within the executive branch. This board would prepare reports on prices and wages in individual industries and apply the general presidential guidelines. Such reports might include past measurable contributions to the gross national product of such basic industries as steel, automobile, chemicals, rubber, transportation, etc., and might project "probable increases in productivity."

With such data available a framework would be created within which the bargaining process could take place. The reports would be made public on request of the President when action was taken in an industry that he felt would make for deficient markets—a price rise in an "administered price" industry, or for inflation—a wage increase substantially in excess of productivity gains. Thus the facts of the issue would be brought before the bar of public opinion. As Mr. Golden said: "The power struggle between big business and powerful labor organizations may force government intervention, unless a 'third party'—other than business or labor— is given a seat at the bargaining table. The third party is the general economic interest, represented by public opinion. However, public opinion can exert a desirable influence only if it is an *informed* public opinion."

This was an extreme example of what Edward S. Mason, George F. Baker Professor of Economics at Harvard University, had described to the CED some four years before as "the 'sawdust trail' brand of economics" which, he had predicted, would work no better than "coercion," which was, of course, anathema to both business and labor.

Representative Henry S. Reuss, a Wisconsin Democrat who, among other things, had served in the Office of Price Administration and been a deputy general counsel for the Marshall Plan, and who was in 1958 a member of the House Banking and Currency, Government Operations, and Joint Economic Committees, represented another school of thought. He entered the lists firmly convinced that the spirit if not the letter of the Employment Act had been violated by the Republican Administration. He was especially disturbed at the failure to obtain any meaningful Administration program for price stability, despite President Eisenhower's lip service to the wage-price-productivity formula. He therefore proposed his own plan for stability through amending the Employment Act.

Mr. Reuss's bill, introduced in 1958, would require the President to include in his *Economic Report* recommendations concerning money and credit policies. He described it as a mandatory "policy directive" to the Federal Reserve and other federal credit agencies. But of more immediate concern was a requirement for the Council of Economic Advisers to collect information concerning price and wage increases that might adversely affect maximum employment, production, and purchasing power. The Council would report its findings to the President who would then be able to make "an informed, appropriate request for voluntary restraint" to the industries and unions involved. The Administration did not support this bill. The Federal Reserve did not like it. Chairman Martin said: "The goal of price stability is now implicit in the Act." He added that, in his opinion, requests for voluntary restraint were neither desirable nor workable.

The Reuss bill, having failed to get anywhere in 1958, was completely revised by its author after hearings had revealed its weaknesses. The new bill, introduced in 1959 at the same time as nine other similar bills were placed in the hopper, added this stronger feature:

> *The President, directly or through any federal agency he may designate, shall hold public hearings concerning price increases, prospective or actual, which in his judgment appear to threaten national economic stability, and wage increases, prospective or actual, and the relationship of the price increases thereto, which the firm involved declares to be a cause of the price increases specified. . . . He shall issue factual summaries of such hearings, and, where he deems it advisable, issue advisory statements.*

When hearings on the Reuss and other bills were held in April 1958, T. V. Houser, then chairman of Sears, Roebuck and Co., and chief author of *Defense Against Inflation*, was invited to testify.

"The people are entitled to know," he said, "what the government policies and intentions are with respect to the price level in the discharge of those government functions that inevitably affect the price level. And the government has an obligation to tell them, as a simple matter of honesty. To allow the public to think the policy is something other than it is, or simply to keep the policy dark, amounts to fooling the people. This is no way to run a democratic society."

Thus Mr. Houser made a firm declaration for an explicit statement in the *Economic Report* of what the national policy objective for the price level is. He was vigorous, however, in his condemnation of the Reuss procedure. He said that it was nothing but "price and wage control without due process." He saw no basic difference between it and controls imposed during wartime—except that the latter had the force of law. It was, as he put it, merely substitution of a "loose process relying upon the pressure of public opinion" for "legal sanctions with legal safeguards," and he wanted no part of it.

As far as the record shows, at no future date did CED go to bat for amendment of the Employment Act to include price stability as a national economic goal. Nor did the Commission on Money and Credit, which placed "reasonable price stability" alongside of adequate economic growth and low levels of unemployment as the three compatible goals of economic policy, suggest its inclusion in the Act. CED did, however, continue to battle in several succeeding statements [1] for adoption of its productivity level formula as the true guide to a noninflationary national policy. In many ways this wage-price policy was to stand on a par with the stabilizing budget and flexible monetary policies as an integral part of CED's over-all economic philosophy that evolved over the years. Nor was CED's concern to abate. In 1967, it again had a subcommittee at work reviewing wage-price policy, along with its other stabilizing policies.

From the beginning education had been an important word in the lexicon of the Committee for Economic Development. Not only had CED educated its own membership, but it had educated countless other businessmen among whom its words of wisdom had been widely circulated. Its statements were a source of knowledge to hundreds of editorial writers and other opinion formers, who never ceased to be surprised, pleasantly or otherwise, by the comparatively forward-looking tenor of its beliefs. Its reputation for reasonable objectivity endeared its manifestos to teachers and librarians long resentful of the laissez-faire propaganda being pushed their way by other organizations. Its quiet persuasion had affected thinking in high administrative and legislative places of government.

Since 1953 CED's statements had come, by request, to the desk of one young United States Senator. He was to continue his subscription even after he became President of the United States. By his own admission, CED played a not inconsequential part in the educational process that made John F. Kennedy the first occupant of the White House to whom economic theory was not an entirely dismal science to be left to the experts.

This is not the place to discuss in detail the economic educa-

---

[1] See *Fiscal and Monetary Policy for High Employment*, 1962; *The International Position of the Dollar*, 1961; *National Objectives and the Balance of Payments Problem*, 1960; as well as relevant CED testimony.

tion of President Kennedy. Walter Heller has done this well in *New Dimensions of Political Economy*, and there are additional details in the memoirs of the 1,000 Kennedy days by Theodore Sorensen and Arthur Schlesinger. But a few words are in order. In reading about the early days of the Kennedy Administration one is sometimes given the impression that John F. Kennedy entered the White House as a dyed-in-the-wool fiscal and monetary conservative. Walter Heller quotes Seymour Harris, the Harvard economist, as saying that he "at first seemed allergic to modern economics." Franklin D. Roosevelt, whose New Deal brought about more economic changes than any previous administration, never learned to understand the language of the theorists. President Kennedy did, although as Heller says, "economic reason and political reality pulled Kennedy in opposite directions." His campaign speeches reveal this. They also lend weight to the assumption that Kennedy needed only a little prodding to lead him to the road of righteousness. And, this, of course, is what happened.

How much direct influence *Defense Against Inflation* had on this evolutionary and educational process is difficult to determine. There were many other economically progressive influences at large at this time. The Joint Economic Committee, for example, was publishing its comprehensive and challenging Staff Report on *Employment, Growth and Price Levels* under the direction of Dr. Otto Eckstein, an outstanding Harvard economist and one time counsellor to CED. The Staff Report and its accompanying research papers tackled the wage-price question from many more angles than CED attempted. Several contributors to it, notably Charles Schultze, later Director of the Bureau of the Budget, had labored in the CED vineyard. And, of course, Walter Heller, now chairman of the Council of Economic Advisers, had been close to the committee, especially at the time when the stabilizing budget policy was being forged. If he did not always agree with CED's findings—as his brilliant 1957 critique of the stabilizing budget policy revealed—he had high respect for the CED process and its output in general.

It is not unexpected that in this climate the Kennedy Administration, pledged as it was to getting the country moving again, would come up with economic ideas and try to apply them to the current economic situation. From Walter Heller's Council came the controversial wage-price guidelines in 1962. President Kennedy paid only passing attention to them in his own *Economic Report*, and then in a paragraph that might have been lifted directly from CED

—or from President Eisenhower. At this time he apparently was willing to "economize by admonition," and to rely as had his predecessor on appeals to "conscience, responsibility, and economic statemanship to stem inflationary price increases." For all he said was this:

> *The nation must rely on the good sense and public spirit of our business and labor leaders to hold the line on the price level in 1962. . . . If labor leaders in our major industries will accept the productivity benchmark as a guide to wage increases, and if management in these industries will practice equivalent restraint in their price decisions, the year ahead will be a brilliant chapter in the record of the responsible exercise of freedom.*

The Kennedy-Heller guideposts were so simply presented that they hid the potential power for controversy that was soon to be revealed:

> *The general guidepost for noninflationary wage behavior is that the rate of increases in wage rates (including fringe benefits) in each industry be equal to the trend-rate of over-all productivity increase. General acceptance of this guide would maintain stability of labor cost per unit of output for the economy as a whole—though not of course for individual industries.*
>
> *The general guidepost for noninflationary price behavior calls for price reduction if the industry's rate of productivity exceeds the over-all rate—for this would mean declining unit labor costs; it calls for an appropriate increase in prices if the opposite relation prevails; and it calls for stable prices if the two rates on productivity increase are equal.*

These general rules were, however, subject to modifications, designed to reconcile them with objectives of equity and efficiency and to adopt them to the circumstances of particular industries.

> *Wage rate increases would exceed the general guide rate in an industry which would otherwise be unable to attract sufficient labor; or in which wage rates are exceptionally low compared with the range of wages earned elsewhere by similar labor, because the bargaining position of workers has been weak in particular local labor markets.*

Wage rate increases would fall short of the general guide rate in an industry which could not provide jobs for its entire labor force even in times of generally full employment; or in which wage rates are exceptionally high compared with the range of wages earned elsewhere by similar labor, because the bargaining position of workers has been especially strong.

Prices would rise more rapidly, or fall more slowly, than indicated by the general guide rate in an industry in which the level of profits was insufficient to attract the capital required to finance a needed expansion in capacity; or in which costs other than labor costs had risen.

Prices would rise more slowly, or fall more rapidly, than indicated by the general guide in an industry in which the relation of productive capacity to full employment demand shows the desirability of an outflow of capital from the industry; or in which costs other than labor costs have fallen; or in which excessive market power has resulted in rates of profit substantially higher than those earned elsewhere on investments of comparable risk.

The key to the Council's guidepost for noninflationary *wage* behavior was out of the CED book almost word for word. But the second guidepost for noninflationary *price* behavior went beyond anything CED had proposed. The major sin of omission in *Defense Against Inflation* had seemed to many to be its lack of a direct guide for price behavior. The CED statement apparently assumed that if labor conformed with the productivity benchmark, prices automatically would respond in the way described in the Council guidepost. But it did not say so and it protested too much.

Even while the guidelines were being issued, the Administration was busily engaged with an attempt to avoid an inflationary wage settlement between the United Steel Workers Union and the powerful, pace-setting steel industry. It was the Administration's hope quickly to reach an agreement that would be in the interest of sustained economic growth as well as general price stability. It wanted no repetition of the 160-day steel strike that had helped cripple the economy during the Eisenhower regime. On the last day of March 1962, a contract was signed. It called for no wage increase for one year but it did provide for fringe benefits estimated to cost 10 cents an hour. It was apparently agreed—although, of course, not written into the contract—that industry would refrain from raising the price of steel. At least, the Administration believed this to be the case. President Kennedy publicly hailed the obviously noninflationary agreement as "industrial statesmanship of the highest order." The statesman-like act, however, was soon subverted. The U.S. Steel Corporation ten days later announced a $6-a-ton increase in the price of steel.

The eruption of bad temper and bad manners which followed this "wholly unjustifiable and irresponsible defiance of the public interest," as President Kennedy called it, did little to endear the Kennedy Administration to the business community. If the methods employed by the Administration to force price cuts by the steel companies which had followed Big Steel's suit exceeded the bounds of proper exhortation, it seemed to many observers that economic justification was on the government's side. Especially if one subscribed to the CED formula, or to the guidelines partially derived from it. Chairman Roger Blough's visit to the White House, where he announced the price increase as a *fait accompli,* and the Administration's threats of intervention by the Department of Justice, were equally ill advised. In many circles Joseph Block's leadership of Inland Steel in rescinding, temporarily, the price rise on the grounds that the economic situation justified the shift, was hailed as good sense and good business. Paradoxically, both Mr. Blough and Mr. Block were trustees of CED.

The guidelines were not destroyed by the unfortunate steel price embroglio. They continued to be the policy of the Administration. And most historians of this period agree that they served the purpose for which they were created. There were, of course, episodes when they seemed to be breached, price-wise, by some aluminum, copper, oil, and other industries, and wage-wise by some powerful unions in the building trades, transportation, electrical, and other sectors. In our free society this undoubtedly was to be expected.

The guidelines were carried over into the Johnson Administration, where they were to assume an importance beyond that originally envisaged. When first set forth in 1962 they were generally considered as a *guide* rather than as a *rule,* providing a clear indication of orders of magnitude that were subject to certain modifications. They were, originally at least, designed to deal with only one phase of incipient inflation—to fill the gap between the action and the application of fiscal and monetary brakes. Indicative of this was the absence of any specific productivity-level figure. This also had been the case in *Defense Against Inflation,* although the latter intimated that the historic annual rise in productivity of 2 or 3 per cent was probably the magnitude that should be followed.

In 1964 the Council of Economic Advisers set an "official" standard for noninflationary wage increases at 3.2 per cent, based on the productivity trend rate of the past five years. By adopting this arbitrary figure the possibly temporary guide somehow seemed to become an established rule. And rules are made to be broken. Spokesmen for labor were disturbed not only by its seeming arbitrariness, but by the amount which they felt was too low and therefore too restrictive for bargaining-table purposes. Dissatisfaction with the guidelines grew. In response, the Council, in 1966, changed the formula because it then found that the figure for the preceding five years, 3.6 per cent, was too steep as a measure of long-term productivity gain. They said this 3.6 reflected a period (1961–1965) of unusually high and uninterrupted business expansion. The true rate of productivity, the Council said, was slightly over 3 per cent— which, of course, was the maximum figure used in 1958 by CED.

As the economy "heated up" in late 1965 scare words about the "threat of inflation" were again heard in the land. There was widespread renewal of demands to create machinery within the government to assure a continuing national wage-price policy. As the Joint Economic Committee had put it earlier, there was "a need, at least on a standby basis, for a fact-finding procedure in key price, and associated wage, increases which seriously threaten economic stability, to be invoked at the discretion of the President, and to result in the issuance of a report and recommendations regarding the justification of such proposed increases."

Once again Representative Reuss sought to create this machinery through amendment of the Employment Act. His 1966 bill called for the Joint Economic Committee to pass each year on the guideposts recommended to it by the Council of Economic Advisers. The Committee would hold hearings at which both industry and labor would have an opportunity to make their views known. If the Joint Economic Committee disapproved of the Council's guideposts, Congress would make the final decision on them. Once the guideposts became effective, the Joint Committee would be advised by the Council of possible breaches which threatened national economic stability. The Joint Committee would then hold public hearings to determine whether the guideposts had been breached, and whether such breach did indeed threaten economic stability. If it did, the committee could make recommendations to the President, or to the parties involved, concerning possible actions that would be in the public interest. These recommendations would be advisory, and—a gesture to private enterprise as well as to labor—would not be binding. But, as Mr. Reuss said, "they would certainly be influential in restraining harmful action."

Again, nothing came of Mr. Reuss's proposal.

A permanent policy for defense against inflation by the use of productivity guidelines may sometime be worked out, with procedures acceptable to business, labor, and the government. As CED proposed in 1958, some such equitable arrangement, preferably without imposing federal restraints, should be a part of the permanent economic machinery. CED itself may devise the blueprint in statements yet to come.

There was no quiet, personal meeting between trustees of CED and the new young President, as there had been with General Eisenhower in the days just preceding his first inaugural. But there was more affinity between the CED and the Kennedy Administration than one at first might suppose. The President's economic understanding was close to fundamental CED policies. His willingness and capacity to learn were similar to that spirit which had made the CED process of give and take between businessman and professional so successful. Because of this there were to be exciting years ahead, marked by ascendancy of the "new economists" in the hierarchy of government under the leadership of a President who was capable of, and willing to make, difficult choices in this most difficult and, as he said, myth-ridden arena.

A few weeks after Mr. Kennedy entered the White House, CED came forward with a statement, *Growth and Taxes: Steps for 1961*. Designed as a prelude to more fundamental tax reforms the committee promised to deliver at a later date, it was a sort of memorandum to the new Administration. It pointed out eight areas in which

13

A Countercyclical Adventure

93

the committee felt immediate changes in the tax law should be made.

As might have been expected, the statement repeated the committee's well-known plea for a substantial reduction of individual income rates in the higher brackets, again mainly on the theory that money thus released would remove the heavy burden on "effort, talent, enterprise, and investment." It repeated CED's call for a tax credit in place of exemption of interest on future state and local securities, and for steps to remove "double taxation" of dividends. Turning to consideration of the major loopholes in the Revenue Act, it would tighten tax compliance by recipients of interest and dividends through withholding of the tax, at the source "if necessary." It urged better measures to prevent taxpayers from "disguising their personal expenditures as business expenses."

With most of these proposals there was little general quarrel. CED's strong sentiments for reforms that would increase business investment struck a responsive note within the Administration. There the "new economists" were already busy with plans of their own.

Because of the trend of thinking by Administration policy makers, especially in the Treasury, the section of the statement of most immediate importance was that which dealt with depreciation allowances for tax purposes. The committee took a strong stand on this, even as it had in 1954 when the Revenue Act was last changed in this respect.

The CED formula called for greater flexibility for business in determining depreciation allowances than it then enjoyed, even giving this priority (for the time being) over reduction of the corporate income tax. More liberal depreciation allowances would have a more stimulating effect, it said, on investment expenditures per dollar of taxes deferred than lost by a corporate tax cut.[1] In addition, the committee urged that profits on the sale of depreciated assets be taxed as ordinary income to the extent of the amount previously deducted. This would prevent abuse of present, or even more liberal, allowances. Under the 1954 law the entire profit was taxed as a capital gain, including the amounts already deducted through depreciation at ordinary income tax rates.

The key paragraph in the statement, important in the light of later events, was:

---

[1] Taxes are not lost, only postponed.

The high tax rates curtail the funds available to business from internal sources and reduce the expected rate of return on investment. In view of the great importance of increasing our growth rate, an effort should be made to moderate these effects of the high tax rates. The most direct method of accomplishing this objective is to permit taxpayers to write off the cost of investment at a faster rate.[2] *This can be done in any one of a number of ways—for example, through an initial allowance of, say, 10 per cent, or some other percentage, of the cost of the asset (with the remaining cost amortized according to one of the methods available under present law), or by adding to the list of allowable depreciation methods the declining balance method at three times (instead of just twice) the straightline rate.*

Throughout the business community the acceleration of depreciation allowances had became an obsession. It was a hangover from President Eisenhower's last years. One of his parting abjurations, expressed in his valedictory Budget Message, was a proposal for more liberal and flexible depreciation allowances "contingent upon changes in the taxing of gains resulting from depreciable property." Now the new Administration—although it was Democratic and thus automatically and traditionally suspect of being anti-business—was determined to do something for business, and the economy as a whole, along these lines.

The necessity to do this was deepened by the fact that, since 1958, the United States had been beset by a new and disturbing problem—a deficit in the balance of international payments large enough to cause worldwide concern. This focused attention upon the apparent need to encourage American firms to bring their plants and equipment up to date, so that they might be more competitive with foreign industry, especially in West Germany and Japan. American modernization, the convincing argument ran, was needed to produce goods for export to reduce the growing payments imbalance.

In April President Kennedy sent a special economic message to Congress outlining certain "urgent and obvious" tax adjustments (like CED, he promised major tax reform later) that he felt were of immediate necessity. Not for a long time had business been

---

[2] Emphasis added.

offered as much as Kennedy wrapped up in this package. His proposals startled the business community.

This innovation called for allowance of a tax credit of 15 per cent of all new investment in plant and equipment in excess of current depreciation allowances, and of 6 per cent of such investment below that level but in excess of one-half of current depreciation allowances. This preferential treatment was to be available to partnerships as well as to corporations. It was limited, however, to spending for new plant and equipment with a life of six or more years and which had to be located within the United States. Investment in residential construction or by public utilities (except transportation) was excluded.

It was estimated by the Administration that this plan would cost the federal government $1.7 billion in revenues. Accelerated depreciation, it said, would cost twice that much. To recoup this loss it was proposed to tax the undistributed profits of American subsidiaries operating abroad and by discouraging other overseas "tax havens." It also would impose a 20 per cent withholding tax on corporate dividends and taxable interest from bonds and savings accounts, and it would repeal the $50 exclusion and 4 per cent tax credit of dividend income. Except for repeal of the dividend income credit, these ideas were by no means inimical to CED's stated policies. It also would limit business expense account deductibility, again as CED suggested. And, once more from the CED book, it would revise tax treatment on the sale of depreciable property to take account of accrued depreciation, limiting capital gains treatment to excess of sales price over original cost.

President Kennedy said these proposals would bring benefits through increased expenditures in capital goods and industries, new employment in them, and more jobs in consumer and service industries because of the increased demands of these additional workers. But when the proposals went before the House Ways and Means Committee, they ran into rigorous opposition. Wilbur Mills, the Chairman, whose dream was to reform the tax law by broadening the tax base, was against the investment incentive measure. Many business leaders, lobbyists, and special interest Congressmen, opposed one or another specific ingredient in the package. Business was particularly vocal in opposing the investment tax credit. It preferred the depreciation allowances it had enjoyed since 1954, especially if acceleration were to be added. Among those who took this stand was the CED statement's chief author, Howard Petersen.

Mr. Petersen's testimony was of more than passing interest, for a reason not connected with the investment tax credit proposal. Taking advantage of previous testimony by Secretary of the Treasury Douglas Dillon and Walter Heller, then Chairman of the Council of Economic Advisers, and the stand of the Joint Economic Committee, he became among the first private citizens to support a tax cut as a stabilizing measure needed at that time.

"The time may have arrived," he said, "when we not only can stand, but may require, permanent tax reduction. . . . Certainly we can take seriously the possibility . . . that a permanent tax reduction is required. Consideration should be given to doing it now. There may be no reason to defer for a year the benefits of tax reduction, in the form of accelerated recovery and higher employment. In fact, this may be the time when we most need these benefits."

But as for the investment tax credit—which Mr. Petersen called "the most novel, the most arbitrary, and the most objectionable feature of the proposals"—he would have no part of it. "We believe," he said, speaking for CED, "that the proposed investment credit involves too much arbitrary inequity, and the liberalization of depreciation charges is a better-balanced approach to the encouragement of investment."

By midsummer the Mills committee had not reported a bill. In late August, with Congress chafing for adjournment, it concluded it could not write a bill acceptable to itself (or at least to Mr. Mills), let alone the country. Whereupon it postponed further action until 1962.

In his January messages President Kennedy urged reconsideration of his 1961 proposals, especially the investment tax credit and the provisions to close tax loopholes. Those who expected quick congressional response were disappointed. The Kennedy "package" became the subject of lengthy, partisan debate at a time when the nation was undergoing a period of threatening economic uncertainty. The second Kennedy year had opened with most economic signs pointing to rapid recovery from the inherited recession. This encouraged the Administration to project a budget surplus for fiscal 1963. But this optimism was to last only until mid-year, when the indicators began flashing danger signals. At this time Washington was echoing with suggestions for a "quickie" tax cut to combat the threatened economic decline.

The Mills committee went stolidly ahead. In March it had partially rejected the President's proposals. Instead, it sought an 8 per cent investment credit, subject to an annual limit of $100,000 applicable to all qualified investment, without regard to current depreciation charges. Soon thereafter it cut the credit to 7 per cent, limited to the first $25,000 of tax liability plus 25 per cent of additional tax, with different qualifications. In spite of the tactics of Republican leaders, who focused their fire on this section of the entire bill, it passed the House late in March, with only one Republican voting in its favor.

In the Senate the bill ran up against the powerful opposition of such Senators as Byrd, Gore, Williams, and Curtis. Ironically they called it a measure that would be of little or no use as an economic tool for stabilization. They denied its stimulative qualities. But at long last it was passed and sent to conference, becoming law with President Kennedy's signature on October 16, 1962.

The tax investment credit scheme that he got was not quite what he had asked for. Gone was the 15 per cent he had first suggested, and changed indeed were the qualifying phrases. Historians now hail it as one of the great economic victories of his Administration, which it indeed may have been. Although at the time he looked upon it mostly as a stepping stone for the then unrevealed tax reform program he intended to propose to the next Congress, President Kennedy had indeed got what he had once referred to as "the centerpiece of [his] proposals."

As far as the record shows, CED did not carry on any further attack on the investment tax credit once it had become law. Although it issued no statement to this effect, the committee must have been happy at a move by the federal Treasury that accompanied the investment tax credit. In July, the Treasury revised its schedules for depreciation of equipment and machinery, known as Bulletin F, that had been on the books unchanged since 1945. This helped to answer the widespread charge by many businessmen, and CED, that the time schedules for writing off some 5,000 depreciable items were so out of date that they discouraged the replacement of obsolete equipment. The new schedules consolidated most items into fewer than 100 categories and they cut, or accelerated, the average depreciable life of manufacturing assets from 19 to 12 years. This made it possible for firms to recover tax-free the entire cost of capital outlays over a much shorter period. During the first year when these schedules were in operation it was estimated that they amounted to a temporary business tax cut of some $1.5 billion.

Both the law and the revised depreciation schedules stayed on the books and became a significant part of what may well be called the "businessman's bill of rights." No open attempt was made to disturb them. It was almost universally agreed that their creation was one of the most important economic innovations of the postwar era. But that they could be used for economic purposes other than stimulation of investment was something that nobody considered.

Then, suddenly, in September 1966, they took on new meaning and became a tool in the renewed fight against the inflation which followed the boom that got its first spur by the action of the Kennedy Administration in 1961–62.

Pressures mounted in 1966 for a tax increase to help contain the boom that monetary policy was seemingly unable to slow down. In answer, President Johnson asked Congress to suspend the investment tax credit for 16 months.

This was an historic event. Never before had a President of the United States recommended a change in the tax laws—one which amounted to a tax rise—for the sole purpose of *restraining* a business boom. President Johnson made it clear that this was the purpose of his proposal. He denied explicitly that he was seeking more revenue. He openly and frankly urged the change as an implementation of what Eileen Shanahan of *The New York Times* described as "the cornerstone theory of the 'New Economics' which holds that tax changes provide the fastest and most effective way of altering the course of the economy." He was openly using tax manipulation to affect the economy. President Kennedy, of course, had a similar purpose in mind when he presented his 1963 tax-reduction proposal, but that was a measure deliberately designed to *stimulate* the economy. President Johnson went a big step farther. What, in effect, he was asking was a tax raise, albeit a limited one. And no one had ever done that before.

As Max Frankel summed up President Johnson's reasons in *The New York Times*, this unprecedented action was necessary in order to "slow down the rate of corporate expansion, ease the demand for loans, halt the rise in the cost of living, regain the confidence of the financial community, and restore calm in the stock market." This, of course, was quite a load for any one measure to carry.

Business, as we have seen, had turned a cold eye on the investment tax credit when it was proposed. Now it rushed to its defense, as if it were its most precious right. One argument, not quite accurate, was that it had never been meant for a countercyclical weapon. But the outcries fell on deaf congressional ears. Chairman Mills, who had been reluctant to support the measure three years earlier, sped it through his committee. It was debated in both Houses and in an amazingly short time (which goes to show that Congress can move quickly in adjusting taxes when it wants to) the suspension act was passed. Announced on September 8, it became law on October 21, 1966. It was scheduled to be in effect for sixteen months, or until January 1, 1968.

The overheated economy did cool off, quicker than had been expected. To what extent this was due to the suspension of the investment tax credit the magicians of the dismal science have not yet figured out. But in the opinion of the Administration it was substantial.

In the midst of the debate over President Johnson's 1967 proposal for a 6 per cent income surtax increase, it was decided once again to use the investment credit as an economic tool. This time the purpose was to restore investment incentives in a mildly slumping economy.

On March 8, 1967, President Johnson told the nation that the time had come to restore the sixteen-month suspension of the 7 per cent investment tax credit, then less than six months old. He recalled that at the time of its passage he had told the nation that, in the event of any change in the economic situation warranting such action, he would not hesitate to take it. Once again—this time to the cheers of most of the business community—Congress acted swiftly. Had it not been for political interference in the form of extraneous amendments this would have broken a record for using fiscal policy as a countercyclical tool. Whether the timing or even the economic condition called for this action remains for historians to decide.

Postponement of consideration of the first Kennedy tax bill until Congress reconvened in January 1962, gave everybody time needed for some serious fiscal thinking. While President Kennedy, harried by grave problems of international concern, and his economic advisers worked hard preparing the Administration's first full round of January messages, the Committee for Economic Development was laboring on one of the most highly effective pronunciamentos in its history.

Fiscal and Monetary Policy for High Employment, a timely and pertinent document as events were to prove, was made public in Washington on January 21, 1962, sandwiched in between President Kennedy's State of the Union and Budget messages, and his *Economic Report*.

This CED statement was written as a long-term rather than as an ad hoc policy prescription. As such it is of more than passing value, for it reveals certain advances in CED's evolution. It clarifies the committee's approach, for one thing, to deficit financing and it refines its stabilizing budget policy in several particulars. It adds understanding to the continuing discussion of

14

The Great Tax Cut

wage-price policy and the meaning of high employment. It has cogent things to say about the use of public works as an antidote for recession.

On the whole, this clearly written document carried not only a considerable amount of economic information, thus adding to CED's reputation as an objective educational organization, but it had an appreciable effect in creating the climate in the business community which made possible the historic tax cut of 1964.

The statement was made public in Washington just two days after President Kennedy had publicly given up the hope, expressed shortly after taking office, that his budget would be "strictly in balance." He now estimated that the fiscal 1962 budget would be $7 billion in deficit, but he optimistically predicted that there would be a surplus of at least $463 million in fiscal 1963. Commitments for the growing defense program and for new ventures in outer space made it impossible, in his opinion, to cut expenditures and still maintain, as he insisted upon doing, a reasonable and progressive domestic program.

In order to meet his optimistic projections the President offered a program to cut the distressingly high rate of unemployment, spur economic growth, and strengthen his own machinery for stabilizing the economy. The CED statement touched upon many parts of this program.

Among the Presidential suggestions was one taken from the Commission on Money and Credit which would give him temporary power under certain economic conditions to cut taxes. Although CED had earlier come close to endorsing a similar proposal it now only gave it fainthearted support. It was with President Kennedy on his request for liberalizing unemployment insurance. As we have seen, it both agreed and disagreed on details of his investment tax credit and depreciation allowance program; and, as we shall see, it was wholeheartedly in favor of his proposed Trade Expansion Act. Among other measures that it found meritorious (in this and other statements) were the manpower retraining act and an increase in postal rates.

Much of the document is devoted to a restatement of CED's policies as they had developed in recent years. It reviewed, without suggesting changes, the committee's stands on growth, productivity, investment, wage-and-price policy, and other subjects to which it had long devoted attention and on which its positions were now well known.

It then turned to what was being widely and avidly debated—

the President's tax and expenditure program. Although details for 1962 were not available when the CED statement was written, the trend was clear. Lacking specifics, the committee sternly urged the Administration to fall back upon the rules of the stabilizing budget policy—to cut taxes if the budget revealed a high employment surplus, to raise taxes if enlargement of the surplus were required and if expenditures could not "wisely be reduced." However, in the light of history, the statement's comments on a possible depression were of most significance.

In the section devoted to this possible contingency the committee made it clear that, although the automatic stabilizers on which the CED budget policy so firmly rested had in the past proved themselves to be "powerful and effective," there was no sound reason to believe that they would "always suffice."

Should that occur, then "deliberate enlargement of the federal deficit, over and above the deficit that automatically emerges in recession periods, comprises the chief tool that is available." When such action became necessary, the statement continued, the most efficient method to enlarge private spending is through a temporary tax cut, quickly imposed and for a limited period.

It is a tribute to the educational prowess of CED, to the work of the Council of Economic Advisers, to the Joint Economic Committee, to the economics profession as a whole, that such a statement —which would have been rank heresy two decades earlier—was received with utmost calm by most of the nation's press. In the hundreds of newspaper editorials and comments which this statement engendered, hardly any singled out this defiance of the Puritan ethic for adverse criticism. Deficit financing as the chief weapon against depression had become—or almost become—the conventional wisdom of 1962.

Within six months of the time CED issued this sober and reflective statement a disturbing deterioration of the economy had set in. In turn this had set off a wordy controversy over what to do about it. Many excitable statements were bandied back and forth between the White House, the Council, and the Treasury, and from invited and uninvited outside forums. What caused most of the excitement was what happened on Wall Street. This, at least, is what caught most public attention. It started May 28, when the New York Stock Market underwent the sharpest one-day decline since the memorable disaster of 1929. Was another economic holocaust at hand?

Since President Kennedy had only recently emerged from his

embroglio with United States Steel over the "inflationary" price rises, he was a ready scapegoat for those who had lost money on Wall Street. After all, he had shown himself in that battle as being "against profits and free enterprise" (in Theodore Sorensen's words) and so they blamed him (another "that man in the White House") for what they scornfully called the "Kennedy market." This, of course, was nonsense. The stock market had been declining (as it possibly should have done) for some time before Mr. Blough went to the White House with his new price tag on steel. But to be accused, for this or other reasons, of being anti-business irked the intuitively conservative President who was at this time eager to "improve his image" in the business community. He felt he needed its help and that it needed his, especially at a time when economic danger signals other than the stock market were flashing. He had no desire to have a recession named after him. And yet, as things stood, a recession was a distinct possibility.

Soon the President was being inundated with suggestions from all sides. By the end of May, Walter Heller, Paul Samuelson of M.I.T., Hubert Humphrey (then majority leader of the Senate), Secretary of Commerce Luther Hodges, and many other advisors, both in government and out, were voicing advice. Most of them wanted him to rush to Congress and ask for a "quickie" income tax cut ranging from 5 to 10 per cent. Douglas Dillon wanted to wait and see, and it was his counsel that prevailed.

President Kennedy, torn in two directions, let politics—or, if not politics, then the political process—decide. He felt that if only Congress would act on the investment tax credit and other fiscal proposals then pending, and then wait for his promised comprehensive tax reform measure, all would be well. He did not want to kill the chances of reform by asking for a tax cut now—that should be saved as "sweetening" for the more important requests that were in the offing. He seemingly knew what he was doing, and he was doing it in no little degree because stolid Chairman Mills had told him the "quickie" tax cut had no chance of passage. After all, as Sorensen quotes him as saying, "Wilbur Mills knows that he was chairman of Ways and Means before I got here and that he'll still be chairman after I'm gone—and he knows I know it. I don't have any hold on him."

But this political awareness did not force President Kennedy to foreclose on the possibility of tax cut in the reasonably near future—if conditions convinced him that was the proper action to take. On August 13 he went before the people on television with an otherwise unimpressive mid-year *Economic Report*. In it his final words were a promise of a permanent tax cut bill in 1963 and a further promise that, if things really went wrong, he would not hesitate to call Congress into special session to pass a temporary tax reduction measure. He said, in words of more wisdom than he may then have realized, that a tax cut "could not *now be either justified or enacted*." "Those opposed to the temporary tax cut agreed with his judgment that it could not be justified," Sorensen has said, "and those favoring it accepted his judgment that it could not be enacted." And thus the matter was temporarily left to rest.

The year 1962 was one of the busiest and, in many respects, one of the most important and productive in the Committee for Economic Development's first twenty years of policy making. During that year, while President Kennedy and *his* advisors worked overtime and committees of Congress struggled with a wide variety of economic problems, the policy makers of CED and their advisors produced five statements that not only attracted national attention at the time but that added measurably to the intellectual quality of the national debate.

None, however, captured the imagination of the national press as completely as did *Reducing Tax Rates for Production and Growth*. In previous years several CED statements, often by chance, had appeared at propitious moments in history and, as this book has shown, had an immediate effect on national thinking although they had been originally issued with long-range changes and reforms in mind. This one started out as the others had, but midway in the subcommittee's deliberations it was aimed at a specific target, which it hit on the bull's-eye. Work on this statement was done under the driving leadership of Frazar B. Wilde, then chairman of Connecticut General Life Insurance Company, who only recently had returned to active participation in CED following his three-year chairmanship of the Commission on Money and Credit. It was to lead him, and the committee, into the heat of the battle over what has gone down in history as the Great Tax Cut of 1964.

Although, as we have seen, there had been skirmishes over the tax cut issue ever since President Kennedy had taken office, nothing decisive had been done. The program which he had offered in 1961 was still being ground out in the Mills committee and was not to become a part of the Revenue Act until autumn. The abortive drive for a "quickie" tax cut had died out and there was uncertainty about what the President would offer for the next year, although he was committed to a program of tax reform that would include some form of an across-the-board tax cut. On December 14, 1962, the picture changed.

On the afternoon of that day President Kennedy flew to New York to deliver one of the most carefully considered speeches of his Presidency. It was to be before the Economic Club, a conservative organization of businessmen generally described as being of the NAM stripe. In a way it was an unfortunate time for him to go to New York. No newspapers were being published there because of the extended printers' strike. But he must have had a premonition that his speech would be reasonably well received, that in this business-oriented audience he would find some friendly ears. For that morning *The Washington Post* had reported in large headlines on page one: "$11 Billion Cut in Taxes Urged by CED. Experts See Slash Aiding U.S. Growth. Economic Group Would Postpone Reform Legislation."

The policy statement on which this news story—and similar front page accounts in all the leading newspapers from coast to coast —was based had taken form during the summer, after the Mills committee had invited CED to present its views on the need for an immediate tax cut. CED declined the invitation then on the grounds that it was beyond the competence of the committee to respond to short-run changes in economic conditions. The fire engine theory, once again. It did, however, submit a statement summarizing past CED positions on tax and budget policy. It then decided to draft a new statement, as rapidly as was consistent with the CED process, that it felt would be helpful in 1963.

In this statement the committee attempted, as Theodore Yntema later put it, "to select and clearly indicate those few, feasible steps that we regard as absolutely first priority . . . and not allow our preferences to be obscured by other ideas and proposals that, while valid, are of lower priority." As he pointed out, discussions in the Wilde subcommittee made it clear that the first objective of fiscal policy was to raise total production, employment, and investment, at this time and over the long run as well. And this, as the 20 years' experience of CED clearly showed, called for a substantial reduction of individual and corporate tax rates *as soon as possible*.

The statement was ready for submission to the full Research and Policy Committee when it met in November in San Francisco. There the urgency of the situation was fully appreciated and it was decided that every effort should be made to release it before Congress reconvened. Advantage was taken of a by-law provision that cut the time for a vote by the whole Research and Policy Committee from fifteen to eight days. The statement, complete with memoranda of comment, reservation, or dissent, went to press December 7 and was ready for delivery to the Washington press corps on December 11. A press conference was held the following day. On December 14, the day of its release, few of the press accounts missed the significance in the fact that one of the nation's most influential business organizations had come, as Frank C. Porter said in *The Washington Post*, to "the aid of an embattled administration's plans to spur the flagging economy." One of the first to read it was President Kennedy himself. He was deeply impressed. While the plan that he was preparing for submission to Congress in January was different in many details, he recognized the importance of the CED proposal. At his personal request copies were sent to each member of Congress.

The proposal which the law makers read was for a two-part tax rate reduction amounting to a total of $11 billion over two years. The first part of the program called for a reduction of all individual income tax rates by 8 per cent of then current rates, with a proviso that no rate should exceed 70 per cent, plus a reduction of the corporate tax rate from 52 to 47 per cent. The statement argued that such a reduction would increase economic activity and thereby raise the national income. In the absence of such an increase in national income, the proposed reductions would cut revenues by some $6 billion. The rise in national income expected from the cut, however, would offset at least a part of the potential revenue loss.

The second part of the proposal was that Congress should hold planned federal expenditures for the fiscal year 1964 to the fiscal 1963 level. If this miracle should be achieved, it called for reduction of the individual income tax rate by a further 6 per cent of then current rates, and a cut of the corporate tax rate by another five percentage points, to 42 per cent. In the event of these rate reductions being effected, the maximum individual rate should be lowered to 60 per cent.

According to the committee's careful analysis the additional rate reductions which it proposed would reduce potential federal revenues by about $5 billion, an amount approximately equal to the increase in federal revenues per year. To the extent that the tax reduction raised the national income there would be a favorable effect on the budget position, the committee said.

The committee said that the first section of the two-part program should be enacted as soon as Congress returned and that it should be effective as of January 1, 1963. The second section should be enacted as soon as a congressional review of the President's budget "provides confidence" that fiscal 1964 expenditures (barring unforeseeable emergencies) would not exceed fiscal 1963.

The statement stressed the need for prompt action. This meant that the program should not be delayed pending action on other changes in the tax system, no matter how important or necessary they might be. Reform must wait. The tax reduction should not be considered an emergency action, but should itself be accepted in the nature of a long-awaited, long-needed major reform. The necessity of the hour was the stimulation of investment and growth in the American economy through reducing tax rates on profits as well as on individual incomes. Such a program, it said, would reduce revenue relative to expenditures, but it would also yield a balanced budget, given the revenues that would accrue from high employment. Thus it would, in the long run, lead the United States to a situation where there would be both high employment and a surplus.

A further proposal (that did not seem quite apropos to the existing situation) was to the effect that when the time came to return to other aspects of tax reform, consideration should be given to less dependence upon income taxes and greater reliance upon revenues derived from broadly based excise taxes. Of far greater significance and interest at the time were two answers which it gave to objections the committee knew would be raised against the proposal. First, it was not an inflationary plan. Since 1957, it pointed out, increases in the average level of prices had amounted to 1.5 per cent a year, an excellent record compared to that of other nations. "Moreover, the psychological atmosphere in the United States seems to have changed significantly in recent years. The danger that a small inflation would snowball into a large inflation is probably much diminished." Second, the plan was not inimicable to the balance-of-payments position of the United States. The reduction of rates would directly—and indirectly, by stimulating productivity—help American producers to compete in world markets.

President Kennedy did not reveal in detail to the Economic Club the plans he had for 1963. His purpose was to woo the enemy and prepare the way. Thus he said, shocking his Galbraithian friends, that the federal government should not "rush into a program of excessive increases in government expenditures" but should "expand the incentive and opportunity for private expenditures." Furthermore, it should be prepared to use tax policy regardless of the threat of a continued deficit. A budgetary deficit, he said, was more to be preferred than "a chronic deficit of inertia"; for a temporary deficit, resulting from a tax cut, would "boost the economy, increase the tax revenues, and achieve a future budget surplus." It is little wonder that he wanted the CED statement broadly circulated. Basically their economic policy was the same.

Exactly one month later President Kennedy unveiled his fiscal program in his eagerly awaited January messages. Although its core was tax reduction it was well wrapped in the skin of tax reform. It called for a net tax reduction of $10.2 billion. Through the lowering of tax rates it aimed at reducing federal revenues by $13.6 billion. Of this, $11 billion would come from individual income rate reduction and $2.6 billion from corporate income rate reduction. Certain reforms in the package would bring in an extra $3.4 billion in revenue, thus giving the net reduction of $10.2 billion.

In this Kennedy proposal the personal income rate schedule—then from 20 to 91 per cent—was to be slashed to rates ranging from 14 to 65 per cent, to be taken in a series of steps starting in 1963 and continuing into 1965. The corporate income was to be cut to a total rate of 47 per cent, 22 per cent of the normal tax and 25 per cent for surtax. As a part of the deal, corporate tax collections were to be speeded up, making them payable in the year they were earned. The bill also contained a reduction in capital gains taxes, a complex inheritance property tax, and other reforms in that area. Of importance to individuals was its scheme to limit total itemized personal reductions to those in excess of 5 per cent of income. And it contained at least a dozen other revisions, or reforms, of varying nature. Some had long been suggested by CED and other critics of the federal tax system.

Perhaps if President Kennedy had followed the advice of CED's 1962 statement, and had put basic tax reform aside for future consideration, and concentrated on tax reduction for production and growth, he might have achieved victory before his tragic death in November 1963. He insisted, however, that one went with the other. Thus great confusion and clashing of interests marked the stormy passage of the bill through the legislative process.

There was little agreement in Congress as to what reforms should have priority. Hearings before the Mills committee—whose chairman was committed to both reduction and reform—lasted for more than two months, and then the committee took five more months to put the bill into what it hoped was acceptable language.

There was of course a long and bitter debate over the question how taxes could be cut while the budget was in deficit and the national debt was soaring. All the myths that President Kennedy had once talked so eloquently about were restored to life in endless talk. As a matter of fact, this aspect seemed to dominate the debate. It was not until after President Johnson took up the torch, and at the same time offered his low budget for fiscal 1964, that a shift in thinking took place. Many commentators believe that this is what finally brought victory.

The Committee for Economic Development, of course, was barred by its own by-laws as well as by ukase of the Treasury Department from engaging in "lobbying" activities. It had made its position clear before the Kennedy proposals had been put on paper. Its firm stand for tax reduction was widely known and often repeated during the 1963–64 period, although it was obvious from the start that its two-part scheme stood no chance of being adopted. Messrs. Yntema and Wilde were called to testify before the House Ways and Means Committee and the Joint Economic Committee. In the spring of 1963, when the fate of the tax cut was in danger, a business group, headed by Henry Ford, II, and with Frazar B. Wilde playing a prominent part, formed a Business Committee for Tax Reduction. Several trustees of CED hastened to join with them. As free agents they worked out their own compromise tax plan, which differed somewhat from the Kennedy Plan and from the CED plan, but which was more nearly like the latter in that it, too, rejected reform in favor of reduction.

The important thing was not that the plans differed in details. Each was, after all, built on the original Keynesian model from which CED had derived its own theories as far back as 1944. But that each was aimed in the same direction—a deliberate attempt to manipulate the economy for the announced purpose of attaining high employment, high production, and sustainable growth—was a new departure. For the cream of American business leaders to espouse and openly fight for the application of a theory that less than twenty years before was believed to be the open door to socialism (or corporate fascism) signified an amazing change in the business mind. Business had, indeed, come of age!

President Kennedy and his advisors (many of whom had, in Walter Heller's words, "toiled like himself in the CED vineyard") were well aware of the important part which CED had played in creating the climate within which this "triumph of an idea," as *Business Week* described it, had burgeoned.

"Because of your concern for the public interest," President Kennedy said to the trustees of CED when they met in May 1963, in Washington, "it seems to me that perhaps more attention is paid to the deliberations of the CED than almost any other organization dealing with national problems. This is an enviable reputation, one which you continue to guard and, therefore, it has, it seems to me, been rewarded by the response which this organization receives from the public and from public officials." Then, following the spirit of a CED meeting, he proceeded to defend his program, especially his spending program which he knew was the part least acceptable to most businessmen. In an informal debate with trustees at the luncheon which followed his talk, he showed himself an able expositor of the New Economics—much of which, he candidly admitted, he had learned as Congressman and Senator from the philosophy of CED.

Looking back on the great tax cut debate, Frazar Wilde wrote: "No one would claim that the new tax bill is perfect. Everyone must admit, however, that on net balance it is a tremendous improvement over the former tax structure. No one would claim that CED is solely responsible for this constructive change. But no one who knows the whole story would doubt that the largest single force on the private front that brought about this change is CED. . . ."

At the time of the CED meeting the tax reform measure had passed the House. It now lay in the Senate Finance Committee, which held thirty-two days of hearings, and was still there when Congress adjourned in late December. In the meantime the dreadful event at Dallas occurred, throwing the awesome responsibility of the Presidency on the shoulders of Lyndon B. Johnson.

When Congress returned to Washington, President Johnson made it clear that he wanted the tax cut measure to be given priority. With almost unprecedented alacrity Congress responded. The tax cut became the law of the land on March 5. President Johnson said it was "the single most important step we have taken to strengthen our economy since World War II."

This year of the fiscal revolution was also an election year. President Johnson's open efforts to win friends in the business community paid off. Probably never before in history had as many businessmen turned from the Republican candidate to support the

Democratic nominee as did that year. Many of Johnson's business supporters came from the ranks of CED. This, of course, was not unusual. Barry Goldwater, as a Senator, had never been noted for his espousal of policies recommended by the committee. His was the voice of that very element which CED in vain had tried to win over to its modern economic philosophy. He showed no signs of understanding what CED had been preaching for the past twenty years. On the other hand, Lyndon Johnson did, as not only his taking up the torch for tax reduction showed. He had kept President Kennedy's counsellors, men like Walter Heller and Secretary Douglas Dillon, whose own philosophies were akin in so many ways to CED's.

President Johnson's first important speech made following the November election was to the CED trustees at their annual November meeting in Washington. Though not one of his most inspired speeches it had its value. If he did not charm his listeners, as President Kennedy had done less than a year before, he did convince them that he, too, was not without understanding of their economic aims. He talked at length of the need for federal frugality and the "continuing drive for economy and efficiency" so that the budget would "grow no more rapidly—and I would hope grow less rapidly—than our economy grows." He was well aware of CED's current efforts for improving management in government as well as its often repeated pleas for cutting unnecessary expenditures. But he warned against what he called "a stagnant budget," one which ignored the needs of the people for the sake of mere balance.

"The federal government must take into account the impact of its total spending and its taxing on our economic life, on markets, on jobs, on wages, on prices, on capital investment. The CED recognized this principle long ago. An ever-broadening consensus, conservative and liberal, labor and business, Republican and Democrat, now accepts it. The consensus recognizes that true fiscal responsibility will achieve a balanced budget out of the rising revenues of the healthy and prosperous economy."

But, the President added that budgetary balance would not be achieved by "reckless cutbacks" to fit the revenues of a "slick economy." And the places where he said the reckless cutbacks should not take place—education, vocational training, retraining, for example—were also areas where CED had already said that government—federal or state—should not be, as he put it, "parsimonious or prodigal with our public monies."

Thus business and the newly-elected President got off to a good start. In the ensuing months reams of newsprint recorded the ups and downs of this relationship. When he resorted to "jawbone" tactics to admonish business for raising prices, this relationship was recorded as down. It made good columns and Sunday features. But the record seems to show that President Johnson adhered, with as much fidelity as was politically possible in this democratic system, to the tenets of the not-so-new economics he had inherited from President Kennedy.

When the first research committee of the Committee for Economic Development gathered under Ralph Flanders' caustic gaze, its primary concern quite naturally was with the immediate and near future state of the domestic economy. As mentioned earlier, its initial venture was to formulate a postwar tax policy, thus launching CED's quarter of a century's deep involvement with national fiscal and monetary policy. But men like Paul Hoffman, Harry Scherman, Beardsley Ruml, by instinct and intellect, were not ones to be hedged in by national boundaries. Before World War II was won they spoke out in a bold attempt to set economic policy for America's peacetime place among the nations of the world.

In a plain and forthright paper, with its starkly descriptive title, *International Trade, Foreign Investment and Domestic Employment* (May 1945), the Flanders group wrote down certain principles that were to set CED's international direction and make its voice heard in the policy-making echelons of government through twenty-five years of extremely rapid change.

15

Beyond
The Water's Edge

Two simple sentences in that document tell the story:

"A restrictive course by America toward foreign trade is contrary to American interest. It will be followed by restrictions abroad."

"The United States has a major interest in the expansion of world commerce," the statement said. "We are a powerful industrial nation. We need vast quantities of goods and services of many kinds. We have a large margin of efficient, productive capacity which can be put to work making things for international trade. We can exchange these things with the people of other countries who, themselves, make other things available for trade—other things better or cheaper or different than we can or want to make."

Theodore O. Yntema, who helped write those words as CED's first research director, later gave this brief description of the committee's position:

"We have always believed that if competition is a good rule within nations it is a good rule also among them, that the international exchange of goods and services, no less than exchanges within national borders, benefits from competition."

In essence this was, of course, an old-fashioned, liberal, free trade position. As such it was not always a policy that was welcomed by some industrialists. From time to time it caused revolt even within the ranks of the committee. But, as Philip Reed has said, "Not only the principle, but also the practice of our first trade policy has stood the test of time."

The 1945 statement recommended:

1. The maintenance of dependable currencies and dependable relationships among currencies.
2. A substantial reduction in the restraints on world trade, including the reduction of both tariff and non-tariff barriers.
3. The development of rules of conduct for world trade.

In a long series of policy statements CED has tried to apply, with varying degrees of sophistication, those simple principles to the complex and worrisome problems of world commerce from the days of the Bretton Woods international monetary negotiations through the completion of the Kennedy Round of trade negotiations in 1967. On several occasions CED's impact has been, as we shall see, of no inconsiderable weight.

In 1943 the research committee had begun a long, arduous, and comprehensive study of postwar plans for international economic stability. The details of this exciting adventure have been told elsewhere, but they bear brief retelling here. The research committee engaged a group of able economists—Calvin B. Hoover, Jacob Viner, John Henry Williams, and Arthur Upgren—to prepare research papers for its use. The work of the two CED groups paralleled the meeting of international experts called together by President Roosevelt at Bretton Woods, New Hampshire.

Out of the long and difficult international sessions came the proposals for the International Monetary Fund (IMF) and for the International Bank for Reconstruction and Development, which has come to be known as the World Bank. The IMF was created to see that the currencies of the world were exchanged at a nearly constant rate, and through its pool of currencies to extend credit to member nations to cushion them against temporary imbalances in their international accounts. The World Bank, which was an afterthought to the real purpose of the conference, was set up to make reconstruction and development loans to member nations for economically sound projects which could not be expected to attract private financing.

When proposals for these two international institutions were made public they created much controversy. Most of the opposition centered around the question of whether the IMF—or Fund as it usually was called then—should be set up, or whether its proposed functions could not be performed better by the proposed World Bank. A well-organized group led by the American Bankers Association was convinced that, since the Fund involved the right of members to draw the currencies of other members, it would be subject to abuses which would result in unbalancing its accounts and freezing its resources as soon as its hard currencies, especially dollars, were exhausted. The Administration argued that any change in the proposals as written—and particularly placing the Fund under the supervision of the World Bank—would defeat the purpose of the Fund as an international institution for stabilization, and probably preclude any international agreement for a workable postwar financial system. At the very best, another prolonged international conference would have to be called to approve revisions demanded by the United States. This might well prove disastrous.

Just when a deadlock on the issue seemed inevitable, the CED quite literally intervened. Late in 1944 the research committee discussed the proposals in deadly seriousness, both at its own session and with high Washington officials and representatives of the adamant banking interests. Out of these talks there emerged a solution. Especially important was an all-day meeting in January 1945 of the research committee with most of its advisory board and such personalities as Harry Dexter White of the Treasury, Herbert Feis of the War Department, and L.D. Stinebower of the State Department.

The solution was a simple one. The bankers had contended that the Fund would become unbalanced and frozen because countries would improperly use their privilege of drawing other currencies from the Fund to tide them over temporary imbalances, and that in the end the credits extended would become stabilization loans. For this reason they wanted the World Bank's management to take over the stabilization function. The Administration, on the other hand, maintained that any country rightfully should have the privilege to exchange its currency through the Fund in order to correct temporary shortages of, say, dollars and that such transactions were not loans and should not be treated as such.

The CED proposal[1] was a synthesis of the two positions. It recommended that the World Bank be given the power to make both long-term and short-term stabilization loans when these loans could be justified and when they served to meet requirements outside the purposes of the Fund. It pointed out that the World Bank charter stated that the Bank was to be authorized to make loans for reconstruction, development, and "other purposes." All that had to be done was to make it clear, in the wording of the charter, that this phrase "other purposes" did include stabilization loans. Thus the position of the Bank would be protected and the danger to the Fund would be removed, for then the managers of the Fund could refer all inappropriate transactions to the Bank.

Secretary of the Treasury Vinson (who had succeeded Secretary Morgenthau after President Roosevelt's death) was to find the CED interpretation and proposal "constructive and clarifying." Indeed, within forty-eight hours after the statement's appearance, as Beardsley Ruml later recalled, "both the government and the bankers agreed that the CED proposal left very little in dispute."

The House amended the bill according to the CED suggestion. Late in June, President Truman, who had believed with the late President Roosevelt that both Bank and Fund were essential to postwar economic cooperation, singled out CED for praise for its part in saving the Bretton Woods proposals. On July 19 the

---

[1] Made public in March 1945, as a separate document; later (in May) it was incorporated in the policy statement, *International Trade, Foreign Investment and Domestic Employment.*

Senate ratified the agreement by a vote of 61 to 16, while President Truman was conferring with Churchill and Stalin at Potsdam.

The committee was soon to play another decisive role, this time in what was one of the most significant foreign economic policy decisions made by the United States in the postwar era—the launching of the European Recovery Program. The decision came in a period of political discontent, with the somewhat battered Truman Administration waging uncertain battle with the Republicans, who fully believed they would take over both Congress and the White House in 1948. While on the domestic front, strike-scarred and inflation-bent, there was turmoil, a certain amount of bipartisan cooperation existed in the area of foreign policy. Here Senator Arthur H. Vandenberg, a Republican, was the leader. He had worked closely with the Administration in forming the United Nations and on other international fronts. But as yet this bipartisanship did not extend to foreign economic policy, where isolationists such as Senators Robert A. Taft and Everett Dirksen held sway, impeding efforts to get through foreign relief and rehabilitation measures, and sniping at the Administration's liberal trade policy under the reciprocal trade agreements.

Western Europe, including Britain, went through the winter of 1946–47 on the verge of economic collapse; Russia was an enigma. Then late in the spring Secretary of State George Catlett Marshall stood up at Harvard and in a quiet speech outlined a plan for European recovery that was to make history. To Paul Hoffman and other trustees of CED it was obvious that carrying out the Marshall Plan was a matter of economic necessity, and that America's self-interest depended upon bringing prosperity to the war-ravaged world. When President Truman, at Senator Vandenberg's suggestion, created a President's Committee on Foreign Aid, Secretary of Commerce Averill Harriman was chosen as chairman. Five of the nine businessmen members, including Hoffman, were CED trustees; and many of its professional advisors had worked with these businessmen in the CED vineyard.

The Harriman committee was split over whether the American aid program should be envisaged primarily as a charity venture or as a cooperative effort to bring economic recovery. Hoffman and his confreres opted for the latter, as might be expected. Then the question arose as to whether aid should be given without promise on the part of the recipients to pattern their economic systems on the American free-enterprise model. Hoffman became the conciliator on this vital issue, finally winning the group around to saying: "While this committee firmly believes that the best method of obtaining high productivity is the American system of free enterprise, it does not believe that any foreign aid program should be used as a means of requiring other countries to adopt it." Socialist Europe and Labor Britain heaved a sigh of relief.

Early in 1948, soon after the Harriman committee reported, the CED research group issued *An American Program of European Economic Cooperation*, with Wayne Chatfield Taylor, former Under Secretary of Commerce, taking the lead. It was a sophisticated document which combined the consideration of economic necessity with political reality. It said that Congress should determine the broad basic policies governing the program and should delegate precise powers for their execution to the President. An administrative agency should be established to be headed by an administrator directly responsible to the President. This administrator and his key staff members should be appointed from among the "large number of able men who served our country during the war years and gained fruitful experience in dealing with questions similar to those presented by the program of cooperation." Furthermore CED proposed the appointment of a special ambassador to facilitate the operation of the program in Western Europe as a whole.

This was the administrative formula that was made public by the CED in the midst of hearings on the subject before the Senate Foreign Relations Committee. And it was the formula that appeared in the Economic Cooperation Act of 1948 when Senator Vandenberg presented the bill with the unanimous endorsement of that committee and when it was passed with substantial bipartisan majorities on April 3. Six days later, President Truman appointed Paul Hoffman as administrator of the Economic Cooperation Administration.

With Paul Hoffman gone from its councils, with Ralph Flanders now a United States Senator from Vermont, and with several other hardworking CED trustees and economic advisors plucked away by Hoffman to help administer the massive European Recovery Program, it might have seemed that CED had lost much of its strength. But its self-perpetuating, or self-renewing, board of trustees had no idea of retreat or withdrawal. Under the chairmanship of Walter Williams it continued its policy-making course in both the national and international economic field. Between 1949 and 1954, it produced three statements on international economic issues.

The first of these statements dealt with the ill-fated International Trade Organization (ITO), which was proposed by the United States and was to have been a specialized agency of the United Nations. The Charter of the International Trade Organization was negotiated at Havana in the winter of 1947–48, at a conference attended by 56 countries. Its acceptance by the United States was contingent on congressional approval.

The year 1948 being an election year, and the Havana Charter being a most controversial document, President Truman held it on his desk until March 1949. In June of that year, CED issued *The International Trade Organization and the Reconstruction of World Trade*. Nearly half of the 35-page document was given over to a detailed analysis of the ITO charter, supporting most of the 106 articles. Although CED found that the charter had several weaknesses, it felt strongly that its virtues outweighed its faults and urged its acceptance. Congress, however, ignored the matter in 1949. The following year, the House Foreign Affairs Committee considered it, listened among others to Fred Lazarus, Jr., one of the few businessmen to appear in ITO's behalf, as he set forth the CED position. But that was all Congress did. In 1950, the State Department announced that the charter would not be resubmitted. As a result, the less ambitious General Agreement on Tariffs and Trade (GATT) of 1947 became the focus of negotiations.

It was not long before CED again tackled problems in the international economic area. When President Eisenhower took office in January 1953 the European economic situation, to put it mildly, was greatly disturbed. Most alarming of the many pressing problems was the precarious state of once-proud Great Britain. Although it had been expected that the 1949 devaluation of the pound sterling would put Britain in a strong competitive position, the threat of financial disaster loomed up once more.

Hardly had President Eisenhower settled in the White House when Foreign Secretary Eden and Chancellor of the Exchequer Butler hastened to Washington, crying, "Trade not aid." They were met with a CED statement, *Britain's Economic Problem and Its Meaning to America*, a tough and pointed manifesto that spelled out what Britain had been and still was doing wrong. The product of a subcommittee headed by Gardner Cowles, the publisher of *Look*, and of the Research and Policy Committee under its new chairman Frazar B. Wilde, the statement committed CED even more deeply to a liberal trade policy.

The statement's complaints about Britain's economic policies, and about the attitudes of its government, businessmen, and workers, were incisive and valuable. But more significant was CED's concentration on the United States tariff and other protectionist commercial policies. United States policies, CED said, "were designed for a period . . . when the international economy was functioning well, when there was no iron curtain, when the competitive strength of foreign industry relative to American industry was much greater and when the world was far less dependent on American exports. . . . Today, these policies reduce the ability of other countries to earn the dollars they need to pay for American exports. Present tariff policies contribute to keeping these countries dependent on American aid, . . . add substantially to our tax burden, and lead to less efficient use of our resources."

The CED document called for further reductions in tariffs through an extension of the Trade Agreements Act, simplification of customs procedures, progressive removal of import quotas on agricultural products, and revision or outright repeal of the Buy American Act. Thus the committee took its stand and opened the way for an ever firmer affirmation of its liberal trade position.

The Trade Agreements Act was due to expire in June 1953. At their pre-inauguration meeting with the President-elect, the trustees of CED had placed the need for a "fundamental revision of United States commercial policy" high on its agenda. Responding to this and other suggestions from the liberal wing of his party, the President included in his State of the Union message a strong plea for a three-year extension of the Act.

Traditional Republicans were, of course, shocked. The Eisenhower-CED position went contrary to their party's traditionally protectionist point of view. Despite their opposition, Congress extended the Act, but only for one year. At the same time it created a Commission on Foreign Economic Policy.

Headed by Clarence Randall, of Inland Steel Co., this commission made its report in January 1954. Although it contained more than twenty-five dissenting footnotes by members, the report was a liberal document, calling for a three-year extension of the Act, Presidential authority to cut current tariff rates by 5 per cent annually, and to cut to 50 per cent of value all rates in excess of that. It would simplify American customs procedures, and by amending the "Buy American" law it would give the President greater discretionary powers. It rejected—but magnanimously published—a proposal by David McDonald, head of the Steelworkers Union, that would make federal aid available to workers, companies, and communities injured by changes in the tariff.

Only in some minor details did CED's policy differ from the Randall report. Nevertheless, CED felt that a clarification and extension of its own views was in order. But within the committee views on tariff policy ranged the widest spectrum. It has been recorded that the preparation of the resulting statement of November 1954, *United States Tariff Policy*, caused more blood, sweat, and tears within the CED ranks, and more consternation outside them when it was published, than any other CED statement up to that time.[2]

The statement proposed a five-year extension of the Act (or even a longer one) and proposed extending the scope of the President's authority to negotiate, giving him the power to trade tariff reductions for other trade concessions, or for measures that would encourage private investment abroad. It was widely praised editorially for its uncompromising statement: "As the strongest economic power in the free world, the United States has a special responsibility for liberalizing trade—the responsibility of leadership. The direction which our tariff policy takes will help to determine whether the free world moves ahead to widening markets or . . . in the opposite direction, toward intensified economic nationalism and political division." So persuasive were the arguments for free trade on the CED model that the U.S. Chamber of Commerce and even, to a limited extent, the NAM came to its support.

The prime author of the policy statement, *United States Tariff Policy*, was Howard Petersen, a New York lawyer turned Philadelphia banker, who personally guided it through subcommittee and twice through the Research and Policy Committee of CED before it was published. It might also be said of him that he became one of the prime authors of United States tariff policy itself. His hand was to be in its shaping from then on until the Kennedy Round of negotiations got under way.

Support for a liberal United States foreign economic policy

---

[2] See *Business Comes of Age*, pp. 180–183; and "Trade Policy: A Key to Free World Economic Strength" by Philip D. Reed, in *Taxes and Trade: 20 Years of CED Policy* (New York, Committee for Economic Development, 1963).

weakened after 1954 and the high hopes anticipated in the CED tariff statement did not materialize. In 1955, the Administration did manage to get the Trade Agreements Act extended for three years in somewhat diluted form, but meanwhile the foreign aid program had got into serious trouble. Appropriations were drastically cut and the use of foreign aid as a permanent tool of foreign policy for building a stable new world was under attack. In 1956 the CED, again under Howard Petersen's leadership, urged the Administration to expand its program of public assistance to underdeveloped nations while at the same time adopting measures that would help stimulate private investment in these countries.

"The revolutionary transformation through which Asia, Africa, the Middle East, and Latin America are now passing will have far-reaching consequences for the security and well-being of the United States and of western civilization," the 1956 statement, *Economic Development Abroad*, prophetically warned. It paid most attention to working out policies for private investment, but it pointed out strongly the need for government aid and investment. The following year, in *Economic Development Assistance*, another product of Petersen's subcommittee, CED boldly argued for increasing foreign-aid expenditures in underdeveloped countries by $1 billion a year. It said that it made this request "in full recognition of the need for economy in federal expenditures to prevent inflation, and to permit important tax reductions and tax reforms." It also supported the creation of a long-term development fund. Secretary of State Dulles used this statement as the basis of his testimony in behalf of the Development Loan Fund that was set up and which expended billions of dollars before it disappeared in 1961 as a separate institution.

Between 1954, when the statement on United States tariff policy was written, and the end of the Eisenhower Administration, CED spoke out on a change in the economic structure of the world that is still affecting the well-being of millions. Early in 1958 six nations—Belgium, France, West Germany, Italy, Luxembourg, and the Netherlands—established the European Economic Community, now known to all the world as the Common Market.

"The European Economic Community," the CED said in a policy statement which it issued the following year, "is one of the most important undertakings of the twentieth century and its establishment could be a watershed event in history. It could be the first step in a major new advance toward freer economic exchange, or it could be a step toward the creation of new regional barriers more dangerous and more durable than present barriers."

The European Common Market and its Meaning to the United States was written by a subcommittee headed by Thomas D. Cabot, Boston industrialist with long experience in foreign business. The statement was a sensible balancing of the hopes the Common Market had aroused and of the possible dangers that were inherent in such an undertaking. CED called upon the United States to take the lead in a world-wide movement for a general reduction of barriers to trade.

As one important step in this direction it called for the gradual elimination of such barriers between the Common Market and the rest of Europe. Although it looked skeptically upon the creation of other common markets by other regional groups, CED felt that such arrangements should be thoroughly explored, a theme it was to return to in later statements on Central America, Latin America, and the low-income countries in general. Turning inward, the statement looked at the United States' balance of payments, a matter that was beginning to be of particular concern.

> We [the United States] are not more immune than other countries from the law that a country that inflates more rapidly than others will meet trouble in its foreign trade and payments. For many years there was so much "excess demand" for our products that our export position was invulnerable. This is ceasing to be true. We shall have to pay more attention to keeping our town house in order, to restraining inflation and raising productivity.

This warning was written at a climatic moment in world history. The "postwar era" had already ended at home and abroad. The European nations and Japan had risen to positions of power in the markets of the world. Germany especially was on the rise to unprecedented prosperity. In Central America, South America, and elsewhere other groups of free-world nations were trying to hasten their rate of economic growth.

Colonial Africa was almost gone, replaced by a cluster of strange new nations with dreams of quick economic, social, and political betterment. Dissatisfaction with the past was spreading. In Cuba the bearded Castro had taken over. From Egypt in the Middle East and Yugoslavia in Europe to India and Indochina in the Far

East the grim choice of alliance with the West or with the East was a major issue. Soviet Russia and Communist China were picking their ideological ways through the underdeveloped nations of the free world. And in the United States doubt was arising as to the continuation of its world leadership, of its ability to correct its balance-of-payments problem and thus maintain confidence in the integrity of the dollar.

Against this background it became obvious, suddenly in a nation where the phrase "balance of payments" had not been heard for years by the general public, that elimination of the growing deficit was now a national necessity. Many economists and other observers of the economic scene, while admitting that in an over-all view of the state of the nation the balance of payments cannot be ignored, have felt that too great a stress was suddenly being placed upon it. After all, our international payments had been in deficit for all but one year (1957) for a decade.

In the late 1950's the CED took a middle-ground stand. But its leanings were definitely on the serious side. In 1959, when the payments deficit had reached about $4 billion, the Research and Policy Committee, then headed by T. V. Houser, arch foe of inflation, put a subcommittee to work on the subject. It was chaired by Emilio G. Collado, Treasurer of Standard Oil Company (New Jersey). Under his guidance three important policy statements were to be produced within the next three years.

The first of these documents was *National Objectives and the Balance of Payments Problem*. When the report appeared early in 1960 the committee felt there were time and opportunity, in spite of the serious deficit of the past two years, to find solutions to the problems in ways that would not call for reduction of United States military strength, or restraints on imports or foreign investment and economic assistance, but would depend on an expansion of exports of goods and services. At that time CED was certain that "an effective anti-inflationary policy at home and a non-discriminatory access to markets abroad" would allow American industry to succeed in restoring the United States balance to a sustainable position. It put forward a domestic anti-inflationary policy as "the first line of defense" against international imbalance, but it warned that "this policy by itself will not be sufficient."

It is essential that those particular industries whose products move in international trade compete effectively with for-

eign suppliers. This is essential not only to the national position of the United States; it is essential also to the wages and profits of the workers and investors in the industries concerned. In our economy we rely upon this self-interest to bring about the desired response. However, the degree of foreign competition we now face is new to business and labor in many industries and the need for more effective American competition is not yet sufficiently appreciated. . . .

The prosperity of investors and workers in many American industries will depend upon their labor costs and prices not being out of line with foreign costs and prices, on the suitability of their product to foreign requirements and on the vigor and appropriateness of their selling policies in foreign markets. A general policy of maintaining high levels of business activity in the United States cannot insulate particular industries from the pressure created by this dependence. The more rapidly American business and labor respond to this new situation the better it will be, for them and for the nation's balance of payments.

This stand, of course, brought the balance-of-payments problem squarely within the orbit of domestic economic policy which CED had been espousing right along, especially in such documents as *Defense Against Inflation*.

In this statement the committee also linked the international situation to its long-held policy regarding another major domestic problem, agriculture. In a rational pattern of world trade, it said, "our agricultural exports should be rising as Western Europe and Japan restore their trading position and improve their relative productivity in manufacturing. There are two main impediments to this development. One is our high [agricultural] price support policy—the clearest case of deliberately pricing ourselves out of world markets. The other is a worldwide policy of barriers to international trade in agricultural products, a policy in which we have acquiesced, and indeed taken the lead because of the need to protect our domestic price support programs."

The second statement, *The International Position of the Dollar*, published in May 1961, is memorable for the fact that it put the Committee for Economic Development squarely on one side of a major economic debate on whether the United States gold reserve ratio should be retained. This debate disturbed most bankers, many legislatures, and some economists and created unrealistic fears among the general public during the 1960's, a period in which a postgraduate course in monetary policy was almost necessary in order to understand the daily newspaper.

From 1913, that famous year in monetary history which saw the Federal Reserve System established, until 1933, when President Roosevelt took the nation off the gold standard, it had rightly been mandatory for Federal Reserve Banks to hold gold reserves against notes and deposits. But now with gold out of circulation domestically these high reserves were no longer necessary. As World War II approached, foreign gold began flowing to American vaults. The reserve ratio was nearly 90 per cent of combined note and deposit liabilities of all twelve banks by the end of 1941. But the wartime expansion of Federal Reserve credit brought this figure down, and by 1945 the reserve ratio was nearing 40 per cent. Prodded by the Truman Administration, Congress reduced the required minimum to 25 per cent on both notes and deposits of the Federal Reserve Banks.

By 1961, the gold situation had reversed itself. Instead of flowing in to pay for American goods and services, as it had in the early postwar years, gold was now flowing out and had been since 1958. Indeed, the outflow of gold associated with the payments deficits had cut the nation's gold supply to $17.5 billion. Of this, $11.5 billion represented the required reserve. Because this situation seemingly threatened confidence both at home and abroad, President Kennedy in February 1961 pledged that "the full strength of our total gold stocks and other international reserves stands behind the value of the dollar for use if needed." He did not, however, ask for drastic change in the reserve requirement law.

In May 1961, the CED subcommittee, which had been working for a year on *The International Position of the Dollar* and which had called in several European experts for consultation, reached the following starkly stated conclusion:

> *The requirement that the Federal Reserve banks maintain gold holdings equal to 25 per cent of their note and deposit liabilities should be abolished. There should be no doubt as to the availability of the total United States gold stock to meet international claims.*

That summer, the Commission on Money and Credit was to make the abolishment of the 25 per cent reserve requirement one of its major recommendations in its chapter on international monetary relations. The matter was kept in abeyance by the Administration, however, until 1965. Then the international monetary situation brought it again to the fore.

In January of that year Frazar B. Wilde, then chairman of CED, felt the time had come to "make it unmistakably clear that the whole United States gold stock is available to support the dollar." He thereupon wrote a letter to the trustees to this effect, repeating the arguments of the 1961 statement. The letter, made available to the press, was well-timed coming in the midst of legislative scurry over possible courses to be taken.

While there were screams from the right that any removal of the cover would be another step toward monetary irresponsibility that soon would lead the United States into an era of printing-press money, the climate was right for reform. Partly it was created by Britain's sterling crisis the previous summer and partly by President de Gaulle's announcement that France would turn in a substantial share of its dollars for United States gold.

In his *Economic Report* in February, President Johnson called on Congress to "eliminate the arbitrary requirement that the Federal Reserve banks maintain a gold certificate reserve against their deposit liabilities." Thus, he asked only half of what CED had suggested. Representative Patman was ready with a bill to this effect. The President said that he was not prompted by the existence of "any sudden emergency." Under the law the gold could and if necessary would be released "at any time in defense of the dollar." But he felt that confidence would be heightened by the legislative action. Congress followed his advice. On March 5, 1965 it passed the bill reducing gold reserve requirements from 25 per cent of note and deposit liabilities to 25 per cent of note liabilities. Congress had shown that when prompted by persuasive argument, it could move against an economic myth. And the CED policy makers could chalk off another addition to their list of contributions to economic rationality.

With completion of the 1961 statement on the dollar and the balance-of-payments problem, CED immediately undertook another study in this area. The plan was to devote attention to the longer-range problems and the evolution of the international monetary system. Instead the subcommittee responsible became involved for several years in further study of how the United States could bring its international accounts into balance. Finally, after exhausting two subcommittee chairmen, CED issued a statement late in

1966 covering both issues, *The Dollar and the World Monetary System*.

The statement again pointed to the importance of strengthening the nation's balance-of-payments position, stressing that this was essential to maintaining confidence in the dollar as the world's leading reserve currency and to assuring the continued strength of the international monetary system itself.

"Persistent deficits . . . and heavy gold losses in recent years," said the committee, "have led to questions at home and abroad about our determination and our ability to maintain the international role of the dollar."

In the recommendations, great weight was put on the need to reduce the "excessive" rate of domestic expansion that had begun in the second half of 1965 and was adversely affecting the country's trade balance. To deal with this situation the statement urged a budget surplus—to be provided by reductions in government expenditures but to the extent these were not adequate by a temporary tax increase—to reduce domestic demand, thus restraining cost and price increases and improving the competitive position in world markets. The statement also leaned rather heavily against the government program of voluntary restraints on private investment abroad. It called for freedom for capital transactions as soon as possible. These transactions, particularly direct investments abroad, contribute heavily to our international receipts through the income they earn and the large volume of merchandise exports they induce.

In other recommendations CED said that more effort should be made to economize and to be more selective in our overseas military and development aid expenditures. It concluded by endorsing current international discussions aimed at creating additional monetary reserves by supplementing gold and dollars with a new monetary reserve asset, preferably to be developed within the International Monetary Fund.

It might be added that the problems to which the statement addressed itself still remained unresolved in the summer of 1967.

Meanwhile the committee turned its attention once again to the complex subject of United States foreign trade policy. Six years had passed since its position had been so solidly laid down in CED's *United States Tariff Policy*, when in 1960 a new working task force undertook preparation of *A New Trade Policy for the United States*. This provocative and productive document was to take its place among CED's most persuasive statements.

President Kennedy was not overly concerned with either trade or the balance of payments in the early part of his campaign. But events caught up with him. By the time he moved into the White House his interest was deeply involved. Within a short time he was to issue several declarations, which fortunately were taken at face value in Europe's financial centers (including Zurich), in which he promised to keep the dollar "as good as gold." He gained much confidence from his appointment of Douglas Dillon as Secretary of the Treasury, and from his reappointment of William McC. Martin as Chairman of the Federal Reserve Board. His Administration took several actions, some good and some indifferent, cal-

16

Tariffs and Trade

culated to improve the nation's international economic posture. He soon was doing all in his power to educate the American people, businessmen, labor leaders, and citizens, in the vital need for the United States to increase its export trade as a first step toward stability.

Trade expansion was a major theme in his first State of the Union message, the subject of a special message to Congress, of talks to Democratic leaders, and of speeches. It was the reason why he reached into the councils of CED to take Howard Petersen to head a special organization in the White House to help shape new trade legislation, to promote the idea of trade expansion with skeptical congressmen, and to publicize it in the national press. According to his biographer, Arthur M. Schlesinger, President Kennedy also had to promote the idea within his own inner circles. There, many of his advisors resented his making an "entirely respectable, safe and overrated [trade] expansion bill" the top legislative priority of an Administration which they thought should instead be "staging a knock-down-drag-out fight over federal aid to education or Medicare."

The Trade Agreements Act was scheduled to expire in June 1962. Some kind of action had to be taken. Instead of asking merely for a further extension, as his predecessor had done, President Kennedy determined to ask, and fight, for an entirely new trade instrument that would give him much greater authority to cut tariffs. On January 25 he sent his proposed Trade Expansion Act to Capitol Hill.

The CED statement was not ready for publication until May. Meanwhile the House Ways and Means Committee was in the laborious process of filling six volumes (more than 4,000 pages) with testimony for and against what President Kennedy had said was "the most important piece of legislation before the nation this year."

Among those who went to Washington to speak their piece was T. V. Houser, chairman of CED. Although he had no printed CED statement to submit, he and his fellow committee members were in agreement with the President, and so he read into the record a detailed preview of what the forthcoming CED statement was to say.

When A New Trade Policy for the United States appeared it made an urgent plea that a new trade policy was necessary for several reasons. Foremost was America's interest in selling to the European Common Market, which was gradually increasing its discrimination against United States exports. But there were other reasons closer to home that called for new policy: rising production costs, excessive unemployment, unused productive capacity. The program which CED offered was aimed at increasing both exports and imports as a cure for these ills, but especially at increasing American exports in relation to imports.

In order to do this, said CED, the President should be given authority, for five years, to negotiate agreements for reductions of the United States tariff amounting to an average of 50 per cent in return for equal reductions by other nations. This authority would not limit the reduction of any particular rate, but if some rates were reduced by more than 50 per cent others could only be reduced by less than 50 per cent. This authority would be used in a two-stage bargaining process: (1) a general agreement to reduce tariffs to be reached among the bargaining partners; (2) detailed negotiations to determine how this general agreement would be applied to specific items.

The CED statement called for "hard bargaining" but stressed that this abjuration was not aimed at injuring trading partners. It was necessary to make certain what policies should be pursued that would genuinely lead to substantial general reductions in barriers to trade over a period of years. The size and rate of United States reductions should be governed by three considerations: (1) they should strengthen the United States balance-of-payments position; (2) they should minimize discrimination against the United States resulting from the difference between internal and external tariffs of the Common Market; and (3) the amount and speed of tariff reductions should be moderated when rapid cuts would result in hardship to an industry.

The President's authority should be large enough and flexible enough to permit "effective" bargaining, but it also should be "sufficiently limited" to permit Congress to review his policy. The United States should bargain for the "largest and most valuable" concessions possible in return for such concessions as it had to give. The new trade policy should include liberalization of agricultural trade. It should bring about reduction of excises and other practices— known as non-tariff barriers—which discriminate against imports. (These, it said, were most prevalent in Europe.) The United States should retain its right to defer or even withdraw concessions agreed upon should they prove to cause serious hardship in the United

States not otherwise remediable, even if concessions would have to be made in other rates as compensation to the foreign suppliers affected.

Tariff concessions made by any country in agreement with another should be extended to the rest of the world under the most-favored-nation principle. Barriers to imports of commodities that are of great importance to underdeveloped nations (such as coffee, tea, etc.) should be reduced while quantitative restrictions by the United States (on lead, zinc, petroleum) should be gradually eliminated, as should similar restrictions by other nations. Finally, agreements with other major industrial countries should be reached on a number of policies affecting the United States balance of payments—sharing the cost of mutual defense, aid to underdeveloped nations, and limitations imposed on private foreign investment in the United States.

The Trade Expansion Act became law in October 1962. It had been adroitly managed by Howard Petersen and by no means impeded by CED's statement, which received wide attention throughout the country. In spite of the welter of words and the lobbying of countless interests, the act was not far different from the bill the President had sent to Congress early that year. It was perhaps his greatest legislative triumph. Its essential similarity to the liberal trade philosophy expressed in the CED document, issued at the height of the debate, did not go unnoticed. But the 1962 Act was not as inclusive as the CED proposals. Moreover, President Kennedy's "adjustment assistance" clause, designed to provide federal aid to firms and workers damaged by increases in imports, was decidedly contrary to CED thinking on this score, which favored general rather than restricted assistance.

In the conduct of trade negotiations, the Act empowered the President to reduce duties on United States imports by 50 per cent of 1962 levels. This power was to continue until June 30, 1967.

Under special authority, the President was authorized, over a period of five years, to reduce to zero the tariffs on articles in any broad statistical category in which the United States and all countries of the European Economic Community together accounted for 80 per cent or more of the aggregate free world export value of all articles in such category. However, since Britain was not admitted to the Common Market, this 80 per cent provision became irrelevant.

The President was also empowered to cut or remove tariffs on agricultural products if necessary, to maintain or expand United States farm products. And he was empowered to eliminate tariffs on any product currently dutiable at a rate of 5 per cent or less. Under the Act he could withdraw concessions to any country maintaining unreasonable restrictions against United States exports and he could restrict imports if they threatened national security.

The President was not, however, made subject to congressional scrutiny, as CED had suggested. Instead he was called upon to submit a list of articles to the United States Tariff Commission, which, after hearings, would advise him on their probable economic effects. The office of Special Representative for Trade Negotiations was created, as was a cabinet-level Interagency Trade Organization.

When CED first turned to the problems of international trade and tariffs in 1945 it said, "Restrictions to world trade prevent the free flow of goods, services, and capital from where they are available to where they are needed. . . ." Two years later the General Agreement on Tariffs and Trade (GATT) came into being, and by 1962 five rounds of tariff negotiations had been conducted under its auspices.

In 1962 CED said: "The program we suggest here for basic revision of the trading relations within the free world would be a step toward the kind of world we would like to see. It would be a world in which the economic, cultural, and personal relations among people are less divided by national boundaries."

In 1964 it began to seem that movement toward the erosion of economic boundaries to the free market which had contributed so much "to the efficiency and growth of the American economy and has so much more to contribute when its limits are expanded," was really under way. In the spring of that year, after many pauses and some disappointments, the trade ministers of the nations belonging to the General Agreement on Tariffs and Trade met at Geneva to begin the sixth round of tariff negotiations, the round named after President Kennedy.

As events moved in this direction, trustees of the Research and Policy Committee of CED met several times with members of counterpart organizations abroad in an effort to arrive at an understanding among them of the direction the Kennedy Round should take. In the course of these debates at home and abroad CED worked out its own national policy statement. Its definite purpose was to influence the outcome of the negotiations. That it did have its effect seems apparent.

The policy statement, *Trade Negotiations for a Better Free World Economy*, was released in Washington and in Brussels at the same time. It attracted wide attention in the American and European press. Indicative of the reputation of CED at this time was the fact that the Common Market authorities for the first time extended their hospitality to a private organization for the purpose of holding a news conference. Also, the conference was held under the sponsorship of the Association of European Journalists, an equally unprecedented gesture. The statement is also interesting because it contained statements by the German, French, and Italian groups of the European Committee for Economic and Social Progress (CEPES). These organizations were patterned after CED.

The gist of the statement was that the United States should take what the press called a "hard line" in the Kennedy Round of negotiation. It suggested that if the Common Market did not find itself ready to make meaningful tariff cuts (at least an average of 30 to 35 per cent) the United States should strike tariff bargains with the European Free Trade Area, and with Canada, Japan, and other willing GATT nations. A long and carefully documented statement, it was, or as *The Washington Post* said, an "indispensable guide to the disputed issues of the Kennedy Round."

The issues were to be disputed through many prolonged sessions. In the end, most observers agreed that the negotiations were generally successful. The spirit of CED's stand on tariffs seems to have prevailed.[1]

The long and arduous Kennedy Round of negotiations began hopefully, but was soon beset by troubles. It is too early in history

---

[1] CED made an extra, valuable if indirect, contribution to the negotiations by publishing, as a supplementary paper in 1963, *Comparative Tariffs and Trade: The United States and the European Common Market*. In this 1,000-page, oversized document were detailed, for the first time anywhere, present and projected United States and Common Market tariffs based on the complete Brussels Tariff Nomenclature—factual data of vital importance to all who had to deal with the rapidly developing commercial relationships of the western world. This overwhelming, computerized task was financed by CED. It was produced by a small staff under the direction of Frances K. Topping.

to recount all the ramifications, of de Gaulle's veto of Great Britain's entry into the Common Market or of the protracted, French-inspired split between Common Market partners over farm policy. This latter delayed the real negotiating until the spring of 1966, leaving the 50 countries involved, who represented nearly 80 per cent of all world trade, only a year to complete their bargaining. That they did so in May 1967, practically on the deadline imposed by the Trade Expansion Act, was hailed by most observers as little less than miraculous.

To a great extent this was accomplished through the efforts of William M. Roth, who was in charge of the negotiations for the United States as the President's Special Representative for Trade Negotiations. William Roth, who succeeded Christian A. Herter in this post, had been a trustee of CED since 1958 and a hard working member of its Research and Policy Committee.

The pact finally worked out at Geneva by Roth and others brought the 50 nations to agree to an average one-third cut in industrial tariffs, to some liberalization of trade in agricultural products, and to a program of food aid to the "hungry nations."

Although parts of some major industries—primarily of the chemical and glass industries, those same groups who had so bitterly objected to CED's first statement of tariffs—were angry at the results, the general conclusion was that Roth's game fight across the negotiating tables had resulted in important gains for the United States and other major trading nations. Not only were these reflected in sizable tariff reductions, but most duties were brought so low as to render them relatively unimportant as barriers to trade.

Most observers believed that these changes would materially aid the growth of world trade, and some predicted substantial price reductions to customers as the result. Even if the latter did not happen at once it was obvious that the Kennedy Round had staved off an incipient inclination in the United States to turn back toward protectionism. It also forestalled the probable division of the world into two trading blocs, with the United States and like-minded nations on one side and the European Common Market on the other. Thus it saved the most-favored-nation principle from disaster.

Where the Kennedy Round seems to have fallen down most egregiously was in its approach to the problems of the less-developed countries. These nations apparently were awarded few benefits of consequence. But, as *The New Republic* rather surprisingly observed, "anything contributing to the prosperity of the rich nations also helps the poor, in terms of world trade and their own exports."

In this area and in others the work of the negotiators for freer world trade was not finished at the close of the marathon Kennedy Round. That CED would continue to suggest policy toward this end goes without saying.

In the latter years of the 1950's, the Committee for Economic Development recognized the vital importance of adding a new dimension to its policy-oriented research in international economic relations. It was felt that more work should be done on international problems and that collaborative research with businessmen and economists in other nations would not only strengthen its studies but increase their impact. Only a matter of resources stood in its way. The Ford Foundation, however, came to its financial support in 1960 with a grant of $450,000, to which the Rockefeller Foundation added $50,000. In 1963, The Ford Foundation contributed to CED a matching grant of $750,000 over four years. With this help the CED within the next several years developed a more substantial and more broadly based international program, the beginnings of which have been indicated above.

In 1960 CED was convinced that revolutionary changes in international economic relations were already in progress. It also believed that in the industrialized nations, as it had proved within the United States, one major potential for economic development lay in the articulate leadership of business-like CED organizations.

17

Cooperation for Progress

Although CED itself apparently had no ambitions to become an international organization, it deeply felt that its own methods or "process," if applied by similar groups in the world's key industrial nations, might make a significant contribution to better international understanding. Having proved at home the educational value of policy-making derived from objective research it assumed that similar mobilizations of key leaders from business and academic life in Europe, Japan, Latin America, and elsewhere, might contribute to establishing eventually "the kind of world we would like to see"— which someday might even become a global common market.

CED's hope was that through "counterparts" it might create a continuing, research-based dialogue with business leaders around the world from whose thinking might come lasting policies that would increase economic strength and unity within the free world. If CED's programs and publications had, as President Kennedy said, "helped bring about a fundamental change in the economic understanding of the nation in general, and its business community in particular," why could not this be extended to other nations?

And so CED reorganized itself to the extent of making its international program a much more extensive and cooperative venture than would otherwise have been possible. It encouraged the strengthening or creation of counterpart organizations in France, Germany, Italy, Sweden, Japan, Australia, Latin America, and elsewhere, and also measurably increased its own research program. It contracted for dozens of research papers by economic experts at universities in many parts of the world on a wide variety of subjects affecting its expanded plans for future policy statements. Some were published. It made arrangements with these groups to distribute CED's publications and undertook to distribute their papers in the United States. CED's "international library" has undoubtedly helped countless students in their quest for information on the world economy.

It would be impossible to try to follow all the activities which the expanded international program has engendered. Some highlights directly linked with policy statements will have to suffice.

A 1961 policy statement, *Cooperation for Progress in Latin America*, saw the beginnings of the research-based international dialogue in the developing nations of Latin America and other low-income areas. This statement was an attempt by CED to reconsider with respect to Latin America our foreign economic policy, including development-assistance policy, in the light of changing world conditions. To help in this reappraisal, CED invited the participation at the decisive stages of its discussions of several distinguished Latin American business leaders, economists, and a former government minister.

CED completed its work on this statement just before President Kennedy sent his Alliance for Progress program to Congress. The parallels between the two were striking, no doubt in part because some of CED's top advisors for this project also were members of Kennedy's "Alliance" task force.

The statement, in its first recommendation, stressed that "the greatest economic resource of any country is its people," and said that the United States should follow up promptly and fully its promise to provide an initial contribution of $500 million for a special inter-American fund for social development.

Other recommendations called for improvement of conditions of rural living and land use; improved education to hasten the economic and social progress of Latin America; urgent attention by the United States to ways in which the Latin American countries might be assured of a rising trend and a greater stability of exports earnings; support for movements toward economic integration to achieve the benefits of larger markets and increased competition; an increased flow of public funds from the United States, some of which should be used to assist the development of local private enterprise in Latin America; an effort by the United States and Latin American governments to enlarge "in all feasible ways" the mutually beneficial activities of the United States businesses there. In its final recommendation, CED urged the United States to give more attention and more weight to such inter-American agencies as the Inter-American Development Bank, the Inter-American Economic and Social Council of the Organization of American States, and the United Nations Economic Commission for Latin America.

CED next embarked on an intensive study of economic development in Central America, where five countries by this time had launched the now promising Central American common market. This region was selected because of its importance to the United States politically, because it is small enough to be examined in detail with available CED resources, because its problems are representative of problems encountered in other parts of Latin America and elsewhere, and because of its many "encouraging qualities which distinguish it from other areas, particularly in the scope and nature of self-help efforts to promote development."

Also, it seemed useful for CED to stimulate local businessmen in Central America to recognize, study, and help solve their national and regional problems. It was hoped, moreover, that insofar as this statement would be read generally in Latin America—it was printed in both English and Spanish—it would promote understanding of North American attitudes.

The statement stressed many of the same problems and opportunities for development covered in the earlier statement on Latin America as a whole: education and research, agricultural progress, taxes and finance generally, and international trade. However, it was directed mainly toward the technical-economic aspects of the development problem of Central America, putting less stress on the "political and social variables in the development equation."

CED devoted substantial resources to this project. A senior member of the research staff spent full time on it, and he and the subcommittee had the benefit of seven special research studies. Members of the subcommittee working on the project spent time in Central America examining its problems. Assisting in this study was a committee of Central American businessmen and economic experts who participated in CED meetings in New York and was host to a CED delegation in San Salvador.

In 1964 the CED subcommittee on development policy began an ambitious project on the internal policy aspects of development in the low-income countries. The work—involving separate studies of fifteen developing countries in Latin America, the Mediterranean region, and Southeast Asia—culminated two years later in an influential statement, *How Low Income Countries Can Advance Their Own Growth*.

During its preparation, CED developed ties with the Inter-American Council for Commerce and Production (CICYP), and drew, for the seven Latin American country studies, on the economists selected by CICYP's national sections in Argentina, Chile, Colombia, Mexico, Peru, and Venezuela. Moreover, the CED publication, which was issued in English and Spanish editions, included a separate CICYP statement, *Economic Development of Latin America*. Contacts between CED and CICYP were maintained by joint meetings (in Caracas, New York, and Mexico City) and by meetings of CED staff with several of the CICYP national sections in their own countries.

Four of the other studies—those on Malaya–Singapore, the

Philippines, Taiwan, and Thailand—were supplied through the Japan Committee for Economic Development (Keizai Doyukai) and the Committee for Economic Development of Australia (CEDA).

This statement, the first in which CED concerned itself solely with the internal aspects of economic development, has had wide distribution in the United States and abroad. Moreover, there is evidence that it has influenced thinking in the State Department's Agency for International Development and in the White House. Especially important in this respect is the stress given to the need for a strong private sector in the developing countries, and to the important supporting role that private foreign investment can also play. As congressional support for government aid has weakened markedly in the past year, the Administration has increasingly taken the view that unlike public assistance which is now subject to quite strict limits, private foreign investment is limited only by the extent of the opportunities for profitable investment in the low-income countries.

The statement emphasized that a major lesson could be drawn from the recent experience of a broad range of low-income countries. The lesson was that in the successful countries which had been experiencing sustained rapid growth, the "people . . . not only wanted development very much, but wanted it strongly enough to do what was required to get their economy started and to keep them going." According to the statement, there are four key areas responsive to internal policy which afford the low-income countries the greatest opportunity for promoting their own growth. A country's performance in these areas largely explains its relative success or failure in development.

In testifying almost a year after the statement was issued before the Subcommittee on Foreign Economic Policy of the House Committee on Foreign Affairs, Emilio G. Collado identified the four areas in this way:

> *Most important, is the prevailing over-all "climate" for private enterprise and initiative, for this obviously affects foreign as well as local private enterprise.*
>
> *The second involves matching human with physical resources—for example, adapting education and technology to the needs of development and checking population increases that are economically harmful.*
>
> *The third concerns the more efficient use of physical ca-*

pacities—such as providing adequate economic infrastructure facilities and balancing progress in industry with the necessary progress in agriculture.

The last major area is that of implementing appropriate fiscal and monetary policies which will avoid inflation and encourage domestic saving and productive investment.

In the statement, Mr. Collado told the subcommittee, CED recognized the need for public assistance from abroad and for measures on the part of the United States and other high-income countries that would expand the export earnings of the developing countries.

While CED was carrying out its work on development problems with the help of business groups primarily in the low-income countries, it moved into a new phase of collaboration with its counterparts in Western Europe and Japan. Out of this came CED's first joint policy statement in May 1965, East-West Trade: A Common Policy for the West. This study, undertaken by a subcommittee headed by Howard Petersen, also extended CED's international work into a new area.

From its beginnings early in 1964 this study was envisaged as a cooperative effort between CED, the three CEPES groups, the Keizai Doyukai, and—as far as they felt able to cooperate—Britain's Political and Economic Planning (PEP) and the Swedish Studieförbundet Näringsliv ochs Samhälle (SNS). It was agreed among the cooperating groups that the East-West trade study would be more closely collaborative than the model set by 1963 study on Japan in the Free World Economy or than any joint CED-CEPES effort up to this time.

The research side of the study was conducted by an international research steering committee to which each of the groups named an expert. During the process of this study, working papers were prepared by CED and four of the other organizations. Interspersed with CED subcommittee meetings, there were joint meetings in Paris, Tokyo, Rome, and Washington. In the end CED, the three CEPES groups, and the Keizai Doyukai adopted a common policy statement which each issued as its own. While representatives of the five organizations were gathered in Brussels for the press conference, they held a discussion on the subject of East-West trade with M. Jean Rey, then vice president and now president of the European Commission of the European Common Market.

For CED, the issuing of this joint statement involved authorization by the Research and Policy Committee to open up a policy statement for the first time to possible footnotes or reservations by other national groups. Some of these appeared in *East-West Trade*.

During the course of this study, Western Europe's trade with the Soviet bloc was expanding rapidly and the United States abandoned its aloofness from this trend to make a large sale of wheat to the Soviet Union. The basic question examined in the statement was whether more "normal" trade relations could be established with the East and whether this could be done in such a way as to serve Western economic and political interests. Because of the character of the centrally controlled communist economies, and the nature of postwar political relations between East and West, there remained serious doubts about the merits of trying to normalize trade with the East. The statement examined this question from the standpoint of Western interests and supported expansion of East-West trade. However it suggested guidelines under which Western nations might hope to realize the kinds of economic benefits they expect in trade among themselves, and opportunities through trade to improve political relations with the Eastern nations.

Four guidelines were laid down:

REALISM. Looking at conditions in the East as they are, varying from place to place and time to time, and adopting Western policies to the best view of the actual conditions.

SELECTIVITY. In view of differing economic conditions and practices, and political attitudes of the several Eastern countries, the West should differentiate its policies in line with these differences.

FLEXIBILITY. Western policy should be adapted to developing experience and therefore be kept fluid.

COOPERATION. Because of the uncertainty about the problems that could arise from the expansion of East-West trade, prompt exchange of necessary information between the Western nations should be carried out through a special committee of the Organization for Economic Cooperation and Development (OECD), to which a consultative group from business should be attached.

Among the most important specific recommendations were that Western nations had set a limit to terms of credits that might be given to the East (with CED calling, in a separate position, for a five-year limit); that members of the North Atlantic Treaty Organization (NATO) and Japan should continue their present military embargo and that there should be a limit to the export of high level non-military technology and know-how; that in most cases trade would have to be conducted through agreements between pairs of Eastern and Western countries, and therefore these agreements should be for limited periods.

In June 1967 CED published another joint policy statement in collaboration with the same groups, but this time on the trade problems of the low-income countries—in short, on what has come to be known as the UNCTAD [1] problems. In this new cooperative effort, CEPES, rather than CED, took the lead in sponsoring the study. The responsibility for drafting it was in the hands of PEP's director, John Pinder. In the end, the collaboration worked smoothly and all seven organizations joined in issuing the statement under the title, *Trade Policy Toward Low-Income Countries*. Again in this statement any differences, and they were fewer than in *East-West Trade*, were noted in the body of the text, or in special footnotes.

Trade Policy Toward Low-Income Countries proposes a broad program of further trade liberalization on the part of the industrialized nations. It suggests that this program first be coordinated in the OECD and then launched at the second UNCTAD conference to be held in 1968, with subsequent negotiations taking place in GATT.

Among its recommendations are the following:

That in the area of primary products, which account for more than four-fifths of the exports of the low-income countries, the high-income countries progressively eliminate their import and consumption taxes on tropical products which they do not produce themselves; reduce domestic subsidies and price supports for agricultural products imported from low-income countries; over a transitional period eliminate their tariffs and quotas on those raw materials and foodstuffs that are not subject to domestic market management.

That barriers to the export of manufactures from low-income countries be reduced, with emphasis on those products which offer the best opportunities for export—such as those resulting from the early stages of processing of raw materials and from labor—intensive industry, including assembly processes and the manufacture of parts.

That the high-income countries should not expect from the proposed trade liberalization immediate reciprocity on the part of the low-income countries, but that GATT be charged with the task of ensuring eventual reciprocity.

---

[1] United Nations Conference on Trade and Development.

With respect to strong pressures from low-income countries that industrial nations extend them generalized tariff preferences on manufactured exports, CED suggested that if such preferences are to be extended, they should be limited in scope and duration. And for this problem again, it was recommended that a special GATT committee offer its advice on the issues involved.

The statement also pointed out that regional trade groups among low-income countries may be required to provide a market sufficiently large to enable these countries to achieve economies of scale in manufacturing. It pointed out that regional trade groups which reduce barriers to trade among low-income countries and promote competition in the area thus provide a substantial stimulus to the development of efficient industries in the region. To assist developing countries which are particularly subject to sharp declines in their export earnings, CED suggested that over the long run these countries should diversify their economies and reduce their dependence on the export of a limited number of primary products. But in the meantime, it recommended short-term assistance to compensate for shortfalls in export earnings, such as that provided by the International Monetary Fund. This assistance could be usefully complemented by long-term assistance such as the proposed World Bank's scheme for supplementary finance.

The statement stressed, of course, that the benefits which will accrue to low-income countries as a result of any special trade liberalization steps taken by the high-income countries ultimately depend on domestic policy actions taken by the low-income countries themselves. Unless these policies are such as to promote international competitive strength, liberalization measures by the United States and other high-income countries clearly would not be much benefit.

In the summer of 1967, CED was preparing for a study of nontariff barriers in cooperation with the six organizations involved in *Trade Policy Toward Low-Income Countries*, and to this group was added CEDA. Initial discussions had also been held with the Keizai Doyukai and CEDA for a joint research project on the opportunities and problems facing private development efforts in Southeast Asia. As this new work began, however, there was no certainty that either project would result in a joint policy statement.

CED has long regarded its efforts to encourage such groups abroad as important. But experience has shown that these efforts seldom bear fruit except over a number of years, and then sometimes turn out to be virtually fruitless.

It is difficult for groups abroad, even those in the industrialized countries, to adopt CED's business-academic structure and the committee process by which CED trustees reach a consensus. It is only recently that the CEPES groups have begun to function effectively by CED standards. As a counterpart, PEP in Britain has suffered from lack of meaningful business participation. Australia's CEDA is still developing business support and participation on a scale to make it effective. In the developing countries, the difficulties naturally have proved much greater.

Probably the strongest of CED's counterpart organizations within its own country and internationally is the Keizai Doyukai. This "CED of Japan" owes its origin to some unidentified general in the American Occupation Forces who urged upon Japanese business leaders the kind of open partnership between business and academic leaders to modernize Japanese business thinking about its role in public policy. CED's relationship in the group was one-sided for a number of years, consisting mainly of occasional visits by members of Keizai Doyukai to CED when they came over on special trade or productivity missions. Finally in characteristically bold Japanese style, the Keizai Doyukai invited a high-level mission to Japan in April 1961 for a two-week period to do an intensive study of the Japanese program for urban and regional development. This mission, headed by CED's chairman, Donald K. David, included Thomas Roy Jones, Alfred C. Neal, and Paul N. Ylvisaker, then of The Ford Foundation and an advisor to CED.

There were two dramatic consequences following from this first of what was to be a continuing series of visits and exchanges. Keizai Doyukai was instrumental in setting up the Japan Center for Area Development Research, which has brought together the leading planners and regional economists from Japanese universities and institutes. As a research adjunct to the business leadership, the Center has become a highly influential body in Japan.

A second consequence was the joint CED-Keizai Doyukai policy statement on the position of *Japan in the Free World Economy*. In the end, CED and Keizai Doyukai each published its own statement based upon joint research and discussion. Its main thrust was that Japan was a leading industrial nation, that it should dismantle as quickly as possible its most protective barriers to international trade and payments, and become a full-fledged member of the International Monetary Fund's full convertibility group. The CED statement also urged that discrimination against Japanese products, especially in Europe, be eliminated as soon as possible. The CED collaboration with the Japanese resulted in their establishing relations with the various CED counterparts in Europe who were subsequently invited to a conference in Japan. While some Japanese referred to the CED proposals ruefully as like "the second visit of the black ships," Japanese foreign economic policy has continued on a liberal trend. As noted elsewhere, the Keizai Doyukai has been fully accepted as a working partner among the counterpart groups and pulls more than its weight in the international discussions in which CED is involved.

Very early in its history CED took under consideration one of the truly pressing social, economic, and political problems of our time—agriculture. Indeed, its interest in raising productivity and free markets made a study of agriculture an imperative. For a century and a half the "farm problem" has agitated the nation. The halls of Congress have reverberated to countless speeches on a countless variety of solutions. There have been plans and plans—especially since the collapse of farm prices after World War I— to save the farms, the farmers, and the American way of life. Billions of dollars have been spent to carry out these plans. But the farm problem has remained and will probably be with us for years to come.

In the 1950's a midwest economist said: "It is all right to dream dreams about the opening of a new West. It is all right to help farmers save their land, providing it is worth saving. But until such time as it is no longer necessary to spend annually great sums of money to support farm prices, it behooves us to consider the interrelated mat-

18

Farms, Shops, and Labor

149

ters of farm production, conservation, and reclamation with a minimum of sentimentality and a maximum of cold calculation."

It was with "a minimum of sentimentality and a maximum of cold calculation" that the businessmen of CED first looked at farming in a 1945 statement and continued to look at it in three later statements, all based on the economically sound, but highly unpopular, assumption that there are too many resources, especially human resources, in agriculture.

The first CED statement on agriculture might be dismissed here as an assessment that had meaning only as World War II ended, when food shortages and rationing were still a part of daily life. However, it is of more lasting value for two reasons. First, it was a good rationalization of why a group of businessmen, primarily industrialists representing many of the nation's largest industries then concerned mostly with ways to maintain high production and employment, should be deeply interested in the fate of farming. Second, and of greater importance, it contained a convincing argument that the heart of the matter lay in the overcommitment of human and material resources to the production of food and fibers.

In 1945 CED pointed out that "agriculture is in fact a cluster of industries," some of which are rising while others are falling. "There are national economic questions related to agriculture that have had less public discussion than the price and marketing problems of agriculture. The problems involved in maintaining the soil and its fertility and in correcting over-population in certain farming areas are two such matters. Both represent social costs and consequences to the nation that do not permit of further negligence."

The answer to these questions, as CED saw it, lay in the "farm-product demand-supply relationship." This could be righted only if every one involved realized that "an excessively large labor supply, an increasing rate of output per worker, and a slackening in the rate of increase of demand" created "an imbalance, with depressed conditions and low earnings per worker the result." In other words, the *"excess of human resources* [1] engaged in agriculture is probably the most important single factor in the 'farm problem.'"

A decade later the farm problem was still not "solved." (It probably never will be, although electoral reapportionment may help to solve it more quickly than would have been thought possible be-

---

[1] Emphasis added.

fore the Supreme Court decision.) A subcommittee, headed by that redoubtable midwesterner J. Cameron Thomson, whose banks depended upon high and steady farm income, undertook a new study that was ready in January 1956.

The document, *Economic Policy for American Agriculture*, took a philosophical approach. It concluded that America's farmers were not receiving their money's worth from the huge subsidies they were getting from the federal government. Despite these huge expenditures, they did not share adequately in the national income because of too much crop production, too much income instability, and too many low-income families.

To deal with production—the problem of surplus crops—the committee recommended a combination of continued price supports for wheat, corn, and possibly cotton, at gradually reduced levels, coupled with a program to pay farmers to take some land out of production. Government rental of this land, primarily wheat acreage, would be geared to bringing production into balance over a transitional period of perhaps five years.

To deal with the instability of farm income the committee recommended moderating extreme price fluctuations through a system of flexible price supports, or income payments, and a storage program, all of which would protect farmers against sharp and temporary swings of prices and incomes.

To alleviate the problems of about 1 million farmers trying to exist in areas of persistently low incomes, the committee urged stimulation of the very outmigration that was already taking place. To accelerate this process it asked for the government to supply increased information about available jobs in urban areas, to give financial aid to families who were willing to move, and to subsidize the location of new industries in rural areas to provide employment in the towns that otherwise might disappear. For those farmers who insisted on remaining on their low-income farms aid should be given in obtaining larger farms—if they were competent to manage them—through special credit arrangements. Such sons of the soil should be helped in running the farms they would not desert through training in the use of the newest farming techniques.

On a broader level CED also asked for a nonpartisan federal Agricultural Stabilization Board to determine broad agricultural policies and to help protect such decisions from short-run political demands. After all, the committee said, there was a national moral responsibility, with broad historic backing, to do something for the farmer. The costs of necessary readjustments in the farming industry should be shared by the country as a whole.

When the statement was disseminated throughout the farm belts of the nation, it received generally favorable comment. The most pointed criticism was directed against its insistence that small and unprofitable farmers should leave the land. This led to the perhaps not unjustified charge that CED would substitute the "corporate farm" for the family farm as the major answer to agriculture's plaints. This misconception stung Mr. Thomson, who denied it most vehemently in a statement issued in 1957 at a time when the farmers' economic situation was becoming increasingly insecure because of the inability of the Administration's farm program to stabilize, support, or protect farm income and prices.

In the heat of July 1962, when too much corn was slowly ripening and too many hogs were growing fat, the CED issued a fourth statement on the parlous state of agriculture. This statement, *An Adaptive Program for Agriculture*, came the closest of any CED document issued up until then to call for a return to laissez-faire. Its impact was unforeseen by the committee, although the latter knew that what it had to say was indubitably going to bring strong reactions for ideological and political reasons, if not because of its economic direction. It appeared at a sensitive time.

Congress was still struggling with President Kennedy's farm program, which called for imposing permanent and extremely stringent controls—some said the most stringent in history—over the production and marketing of feed grains, wheat, and dairy products, in the hope that they would force prices up by limiting supplies of the selected products. Congress was in the process of rejecting major portions of this program when the CED offered its new program. That it was a challenge to most programs that had come to the attention of that body in recent years is revealed by its greeting on Capitol Hill.

The CED statement was indeed a bold departure from the "commodity approach" that had been at the heart of most recent discussions of public policy for agriculture. Instead of confining itself to a discussion in terms of production and consumption of crops, the statement expanded into a general analysis of the use of all economic resources affecting agriculture.

The adaptive approach, as CED termed its conception of the farm problem, sought to achieve adjustment to economic reality without imposing hardships. Its programs to promote adjustment were cushioned by programs to soften the transitional effects upon people and property.

The adaptive approach called for "action by government with the free market, not against it." It sought to achieve the results of the free market "more quickly and easily, rather than to keep these results from occurring." The adaptive approach would work by permitting full production, rather than by limiting production. The adaptive program, when applied to a particular industry like farming, can be ordinarily temporary. The protectionist approach (which is what then existed under the government's program) works in opposite directions and generates the need of its own "indefinite continuance."

By the protectionist approach CED meant, of course, the use of federally-funded programs to sustain incomes in an industry where incomes that could be earned by selling products in a free market had declined. Agriculture was the leading case of this kind. But in order to get out of this bind meant meeting other problems: displacement of workers by technological improvements, increased competition from imports, and depression caused by the exhaustion of natural resources. Under these circumstances it was apparent that the farming industry was using too many resources.

Summed up, the committee said, the roots of the farm problem lay in a combination of five conditions: (1) swiftly rising productivity, (2) declining use of labor relative to capital, (3) the slow growth of demand for farm goods, (4) the low response of demand to price changes, and (5) the inadequate flow of resources, especially labor, out of farming. This left two choices. The government could devise a "leakproof control of farm production," or it could adopt a program that would "induce excess resources (people primarily) to move rapidly out of agriculture." The adaptive program was designed to do the latter.

The statement blurted out the truth. There were too many farms and too many farmers, a truth—as more than one commentator pointed out—that farmers in general were aware of, some dimly and some vividly. They had shown their awareness by leaving the farms in droves. In 1929 there were 10,450,000 persons employed on farms. By 1961 this number had shrunk by nearly one-half, to 5,463,000.

But even this high rate of migration and retirement was insufficient to compensate for the sensational increase in farm productivity brought about by better seed, more fertilizer, surer crop protection, and improved methods of planting, cultivating, and harvesting. By offering fixed prices for what farmers grew, regardless of whether the market could absorb it or not, official farm policy had curbed out-migration. A sane farm policy called for encouragement of their leaving in even greater numbers and for diverting marginal farm land and whole farms to other uses, thus reducing farm production to a volume that the market needed and could support.

The CED policy to correct these deficiencies was simple and it was offered in clear, straightforward prose. The first cure, it said, was to discourage excessive production by abandoning unrealistic high support prices. This should be done abruptly, bringing prices of wheat, corn, and cotton at once in line with actual demand. Drastically reduced income would result; but this reduction would be salutary for it would strike directly at the main incentive—to grow too much of the price-supported crops and too little of other things, especially livestock. To cushion the blow to producers the CED would establish a simple system of sharply graduated income payments for farmers. But these would end entirely within five years after they were put into effect.

The CED farm plan not only would discourage excess production by making expansion unprofitable, but it also would offer a range of inducements for marginal farmers to get out of farming entirely. These inducements, which would come out of federal funds, would take the form of more accessible education and vocational training, improved placement service for nonfarm employment, and even the underwriting of the cost of moving from the farm to the seat of new job opportunities. The plan would expand the soil-bank program and put it on a whole-farm basis. In wheat and grain producing areas it would offer powerful inducements for converting farms back into grassland. It would, in the end, "achieve adjustment to economic reality without imposing hardship by means of programs that promote adjustment but cushion the effects upon people and property." It was, in brief, practical and humane.

The CED "5-year plan to take 2 million farmers off the farm," as the newspapers headlined it, was consistently praised by the big city press. *The Baltimore Sun* said it broke "the conspiracy of silence as to the true nature of the farm program." The *Chicago Tribune*, never too friendly to CED, liked it because it called for a halt to federal interference in agriculture. *The Wall Street Journal*, however, complained because it would create another new federal agency to administer its proposed gradual reduction of crop supports. It remained, perhaps, for the Halletsville, Texas, *Tribune* to set forth best the genuine fears the statement was to arouse in rural America: "Our farms would be depopulated, our towns turned into ghost towns. We would return to the slavery times of big plantations. What has been built up on our farms and in our homes would all be doomed."

At the time the statement appeared, the Kennedy Administration itself was internally split—between Baltimore and Halletsville, as it were—as to the proper approach to the farm problem. Among its policy makers were several like Walter Heller who, being economists, saw great merit in the CED proposals. But they were then in the minority. The farmers of America are still a great political force, and the almost universal approval of the CED plan by the big city newspapers was not as compelling as the plaintive cries of the family farmers, their congressmen, and their newspapers. Fully aware of this situation and yet alert to President Kennedy's then evident wooing of the business community as represented by CED, Secretary of Agriculture Orville Freeman felt obliged to take the report with unusual seriousness. He called a press conference at which he said:

"I urge a careful study of the CED Five Year Plan—a careful evaluation of its methods and potential results, for farmers, for wage earners, for tax payers, for our urban population, yes, and for the representatives of industry who developed it and placed it before the public. . . ." He then predicted flat rejection by the farming community.

Senator Hubert Humphrey had another idea: "All the things that the corporations think farmers ought not to get fills an 80-page, dollar-a-copy printed report. So perhaps it would be only fair for farmers to scrounge up a few hundred thousand dollars to make a report on what they'd recommend for corporations. Things, perhaps, like doing away with subsidies for big business, cutting tractor prices by a third, lowering interest rates one-half, unlocking interlocking boards of directors, putting business on the free market so that it could be competitive at home and around the world. In other words, if corporation chiefs claim to know what's best for farmers, we're sure farmers have some appropriate suggestions as to what would be good for corporations. What do you think?"

The Chairman of the House Agricultural Committee, Harold D. Cooley of North Carolina, called the statement a "staggering blow to agriculture." It would, he said, open the way to a system of huge farms "run by corporations and tended by wage hands." Aghast at such a prospect, he announced that his committee would hold hearings to determine how CED had arrived at its startling conclusions.

The hearings opened on August 6 in Washington, in an atmosphere decidedly unfriendly to CED. The congressional committeemen could not understand why a group of businessmen should be concerned about farmers. They seemed to suspect the existence of a big business conspiracy behind the document, even going as far as to suggest that CED was trying to depopulate the farms in order to create a cheap supply of unskilled workers for their factories! Representative W. R. Poage of Texas (who succeeded Cooley as chairman in 1966 when the North Carolinian was retired by the voters) called the report "hogwash." In spite of this, the CED witnesses stuck to their main principle that "concern with the problems of agriculture is a logical part of concern with the whole economy." This concept the congressmen seemed to find difficult to comprehend. The hearings lasted seven days, with nearly 70 witnesses testifying or submitting statements totaling 407 printed pages. Many were highly critical of the CED plan. But public exposure through heavy coverage by the press brought to the CED's adaptive program more widespread publicity than any statement it had previously published.

Down in Kentucky one avid reader was an organizer for the relatively new National Farmers Organization (NFO). He found it ready-made for his purposes. At that time the NFO was conducting a membership campaign among small farmers to get them to join in signing collective bargaining contracts with food processors and other buyers of farm products. The NFO wanted its members to pledge not to sell farm products below contract prices, regardless of the market. The organizer took one look at the sponsors of the CED statement—an officer of the Hormel meat packing firm, the Grain Board of Trade, and the Jewel Tea Company—and another look at the headlines saying CED planned to "drive 2,000,000 farmers off the land in five years."

"Those monkeys who wrote the CED proposal are serious and they are going to put you off your farm unless you stand up and fight. Along with 2 million farmers they will also set the stage for destroying thousands of small businesses and communities. . . . CED officials are advocating the endangerment of the very backbone of private enterprise, the family farm."

So ran the declamatory oratory of the NFO. News reports of the attacks spread—in newspapers in Maine, Vermont, Ohio, Nebraska, Kansas—but they attracted biggest headlines in the middle west. They inspired even bigger headlines when NFO farmers discovered that the chairman of CED, Mr. Houser, was the head of Sears, Roebuck and Co. and the chairman of the Research and Policy Committee, Mr. Yntema, was a top official of the Ford Motor Company. They turned their protest into a boycott of Ford and Sears, those idols of the American farmer, and began picketing the local Ford salesrooms and turning in their old Sears Roebuck catalogues all over Iowa and Nebraska. In Corydon, Iowa, a caravan of 200 cars circled the Ford dealer's block. One placard read: "This is no boycott, but a protest against CED."

Sears found that the wives were shopping while the men were driving around in their tractor-parade protest. Some wives asked for the return of the current Sears catalogue, given up by mistake. Soon, even NFO farmers went back to driving to their nearby Sears outlets in their Ford cars. The NFO, however, continued to grow. It went on holding hogs and cattle off the market, spilling milk, and otherwise trying to force prices up on the market. And CED continued to stand by its 1962 findings.

In 1965 President Johnson created a National Advisory Commission on Food and Fiber whose task was to develop farm policy and a program for the future. According to William M. Blair, veteran farm reporter for *The New York Times*, the commission (whose report was to be ready for submission to the President in the summer of 1967) divided "along the classical lines characteristic of panels that have sought solutions to farm problems." On the majority side were producers and some economists who saw the need to continue support programs for the indefinite future, although they would set the level of supports at, or slightly below, world prices in order to assure "orderly marketing practices." They would make up the difference between the world price level with direct federal payments to wheat, grain, and cotton producers. This was in tune with the Johnson Administration's efforts to raise farm income to the level of nonfarm income, its supporters said.

The minority (the commission split 16 to 13, according to Mr. Blair) seems to have taken *An Adaptive Program for Agriculture* off the shelf and resubmitted its findings as its own program. It would, as CED had suggested, phase out price support and control programs hoping to eliminate them over a five-year period by cutting subsidies in each year. This action would—as CED had consistently asserted— enable a return to a completely free market and make it easier for producers, too small to compete in modern agriculture, to emigrate from farming to other pursuits. Apparently there was discord between the two sides regarding the ease and rapidity with which agriculture can adjust to continuing technological change, with the minority clinging to the CED's adaptive program in this respect. Both sides, however, stressed the need for a program in education and placement to make it easier for the small producers to leave the land.

There was further evidence that American agriculture was destined to progress along the lines predicted in the three major statements on farming issued by CED. In the summer of 1967 an article in *The Wall Street Journal* presented convincing evidence along this line. "Some farm economists," John A. Prestbo wrote in "Farmer Brown Inc." [August 9, 1967], "say the recent growth of corporate farming is just the start of a broad-scale conversion of agriculture to a profit-oriented industry. They foresee the day when the old family farm will fade into extinction and corporations will mass produce the nation's food as efficiently and impersonally as they today produce its autos and vacuum cleaners. Federal farm planners say privately that eventually the U.S. will need only about 500,000 farms, compared with today's 3,176,000 and that the future farms will be big, factory-like operations."

Mr. Prestbo listed several large corporations—some allied to the food industry, others seeking profitable diversification—that were already acquiring vast acreages, the most modern equipment, the latest chemicals, and entering farming with adequate financial backing to make these new corporate farms an industrial success. Was not that really what CED had been advocating over the years?

During World War II, when CED was working toward policies for peace, much attention was paid to helping small businessmen plan for a prosperous postwar era. From its headquarters in New York it sent out countless pamphlets designed for the use of local enterprises—small factories, shops, and stores. Throughout the country many of the most ardent members of the local "little CED's" were small businessmen in small towns and cities.

In his manifesto, *Economics of a Free Society*, founder William Benton had paid the small entrepreneur this compliment: "Essential to a system of free enterprise is a climate in which new, small, and independent business can be conceived and born, can grow and prosper. New, small business is the bulwark of a system of free and private enterprise."

In Europe and in Asia and on the high seas many an American soldier or sailor dreamed of starting his own business on his return.

Such aspiration was a part of the American way of life. There was much ferment in Congress and elsewhere in the transition period that small business, as well as labor and agriculture, should be encouraged by the government, and the lot of the small businessman made easier.

In CED councils there was little inclination to single out small business, as such, for preferential treatment. It was the committee's intention to make policy to benefit no single segment of the society; its guide was what is good for society as a whole.

In the course of its work it realized that there might indeed be *special* problems facing small business to which its more general policies did not specifically apply, or which they did not cover. Congress was facing considerable pressure in this direction. CED may well have felt a slight embarrassment at the charges, sometimes leveled against it, that it was too greatly oriented in the direction of big business.

The question of business size and power, and the role of the corporation in society, had been a great American puzzlement since late in the nineteenth century. In this nation "bigness" has long been a moral, as well as legal, question. The Sherman and Clayton Acts and other legislation to keep "big business" under control made this manifest. Reams of books have discussed the matter. Gardiner Means (a CED staff economist for several years), his collaborator, A. A. Berle, and scores of other thinkers had contributed to the never-ending debate. David Lilienthal, a CED trustee and former head of TVA and of the Atomic Energy Commission, wrote extensively on the subject of the corporation in America. As late as 1967 John K. Galbraith was to make it the basis of a book, *The New Industrial State*.

Both small business and big business might be expected to come within the CED purview. In its twenty-five year existence CED never took up the issue of bigness squarely. The whole question of corporation size and monopoly power, which it might have been expected to examine, has escaped its attention over the years. Although from time to time it has suggested that a thorough re-examination of the anti-trust laws, especially in their failure to relate to union power, should be undertaken, it has gone no further. In its important statement, *Defense Against Inflation*, CED said: "The laws to maintain competition in business need to be more vigorously enforced and constantly reviewed to assure their effectiveness."

In 1947 CED published *Meeting the Special Problems of Small*

Business. In essence the document lent moral support to the small businessman—employing 250 or fewer workers. It was especially concerned with the difficulties the small businessman had in getting adequate equity financing. Long before such institutions were set up under the Small Business Administration, CED supported federal creation of new private capital banks for this purpose. These were to be chartered under control of the Federal Reserve System in such a manner as to avert direct government loans or guarantees of loans. The Small Business Administration eventually established in 1953 was in close keeping with the 1947 proposal of CED and included provisions for setting up investment banks to aid new and small businesses. However, the committee can take little credit. This was the last CED had to say officially about small business as such.

In a way, however, CED did return to the subject of small business investment companies. In 1966, a Small Business and Venture Capital Study Center was set up in New York, with Thomas Roy Jones, long the treasurer of CED and a consultant to Schlumberger Limited, as chairman. Other CED trustees who served on this study group were Robert B. Anderson, former Secretary of the Treasury; Alfred C. Neal, president of CED; C. Wrede Petersmeyer, president of Corinthian Broadcasting Corporation; and Joseph C. Wilson, chairman of Xerox Corporation. CED and the Fund for Adult Education supported the group with small grants. Its report, a review of recent developments in venture-capital financing and an examination of the effectiveness of SBIC's and other sources of equity capital and long-term credit in meeting the special needs of small and new enterprises, was published by the Study Center in 1967.

It is not surprising that CED should eventually turn its attention to the touchy problems of collective bargaining. In 1947 a bitter debate over the Wagner Labor Relations Act was at its height and the Taft-Hartley Act was in the making. This was the climax of a thirty-year struggle which began with the passage of the Norris-LaGuardia Act in 1932 and was quickly followed by the National Industrial Recovery Act and the National Labor Relations Act (Wagner Act) of 1935. These laws, which established the right of workers to organize and bargain collectively, had paved the way for the tremendous and sometimes violent strides organized labor had taken during the late 1930's and during World War II. In 1930 less than 7 per cent of the labor force was unionized; by 1947 the number had risen to 25 per cent.

With the general acceptance of the right to organize had come a lessening of violence as unions and management in thousands of concerns both large and small had come to terms over conditions of employment. Union power had become a fact of life. At the end of World War II (as CED roughly summed it up in a later policy statement), "Some unions had gained power to close down a whole industry, or any part of it, by a strike, and by threatening to do so could gain wage increases without significant restraint by competition from other workers not represented by the union."

In many firms and industries unions had obtained contracts which required union membership as a condition of employment, depriving some workers of freedom to choose whether or not to belong to a union and restricting employment opportunities by limiting union membership. A union representing employees in one firm could use its powers there, through a secondary boycott, to force organization of other firms. In some cases union policies were "dominated by entrenched leadership that neither represented nor solicited the wishes of the union membership."

During the year 1946, when CED was preparing its paper *Collective Bargaining: How to Make it More Effective*, the nation experienced several strikes affecting the national interest. This was the year when President Truman unconstitutionally seized the railroads and the courts assessed a $3.5 million fine against John L. Lewis's coal miners. The Republican-dominated 80th Congress was more than ready to listen to widespread complaints that the public was "fed up" with ruthless labor leaders and that "something must be done about it." President Truman invited Congress to revise the Wagner Act drastically, which it proceeded to do.

Compared with demands from other organizations, notably the National Association of Manufacturers, which stretched its power so far as to have its lobbyists actually draft important sections of the new labor bill, the CED statement was a mild, evenly considered document. CED's main points were:

1. Government should not intrude in the collective bargaining process, for such intervention leads to "determination of contract terms by government edict."

2. The labor act should require unions as well as management to bargain and it should give management full freedom of speech.

3. A federal Mediation Service should replace the old conciliation service, with a single director responsible to a Labor Management Council, appointed by the President on advice of the Secretaries of Labor and Commerce with the consent of the Senate. This serv-

ice should foster state and local mediation, furnish mediators where requested, and encourage voluntary arbitration in contract making when parties disagreed. The Council should report annually to the President on the state of industrial relations.

4. No strike or lockout should be allowed until 10 days after a request to strike had been made to the Labor Mediation Board. This provision should be compulsory.

5. The Wagner and Norris-LaGuardia acts should be amended to allow courts to enjoin violation of the proposed mediation.

6. There should be compulsory arbitration of contract violations by either labor or management.

7. Foremen and other supervisory personnel should be made legally exempt from union membership as a part of management.

8. Secondary boycotts by minority unions should be forbidden.

9. The Clayton Anti-trust Act should be revised to bring unions within its scope when their actions "stifle competition."

10. There should be no legislation providing for "super-boards, compulsory arbitration, government seizure, or other coercive devices," for such devices, even in strikes affecting the national interest, "will retard, not advance, the development of collective bargaining and to that extent will jeopardize the maintenance of a free economy."

When the Taft-Hartley Act was passed over President Truman's veto, it was a much tougher law than CED had recommended. The CED proposal for nongovernmental intervention and no "super-board" was rejected. The system of the Presidential board, the intervention of the Attorney General, and the 80-day cooling off period for strikes affecting "national health and safety" became the law. The National Labor Relations Board was reorganized, partially as CED had suggested. Its general counsel was given broad powers. The United States Conciliation Service, which dated back to 1913, was abolished and a new independent agency, the Federal Mediation and Conciliation Service, was set up to mediate major strikes. Secondary boycotts, sympathy strikes for union recognition, and jurisdictional strikes were prohibited. The closed shop was also forbidden. The former prohibitions fitted into the CED pattern, but the latter had not been on the CED list of reforms.

In its 1947 statement the CED promised that sooner or later it would make a "comprehensive study of the development of sound labor-management relations" and that, among others it would tackle "such questions as industry-wide bargaining, the closed shop, secondary boycotts, and the monopolistic power of unions." Passage of the Taft-Hartley Act apparently took care of many of these worries. But the "monopolistic power of unions" continued to badger the thinking of many CED trustees.

It was undoubtedly the statement *Defense Against Inflation*, with its plea for the use of the productivity level in determining wages and prices, and its assertion that this principle would be more easily followed if organized labor was brought under the anti-trust laws, that inspired the next move in this direction by the committee. In October 1958, J. D. Zellerbach, former head of Crown-Zellerbach who had resigned as national chairman of CED to become United States Ambassador to Italy, urged the Research and Policy Committee to undertake a thorough examination of national labor policy.

Perhaps because it realized that any study of industry's and government's relations with labor might be disruptive of its own councils and become one of the most difficult of all topics in which to maintain objectivity, the CED trustees abrogated their responsibility for the first time and turned the task over to an independent group. A labor study committee made up entirely of experts in labor relations and known formally as the Labor Policy Study Group was carefully chosen and given complete freedom from CED to pursue its own studies and reach its own conclusions. The CED financed the group with some outside foundation help. Its fundamental purpose was to produce a report that would set forth appropriate public policies for collective bargaining. Its chairman was Clark Kerr, then president of the University of California.[1]

This distinguished group produced an able and conscientious report after some 15 months of arduous endeavor. As the group

---

[1] Members of the Study Group: Clark Kerr, Chairman, President University of California; Douglass V. Brown, Professor of Industrial Management, Massachusetts Institute of Technology; David L. Cole, Practicing Attorney and Arbitrator, Paterson, New Jersey; John T. Dunlop, Professor of Economics, Harvard University; William Y. Elliott, Professor of Government, Harvard University; Albert Rees, Professor of Economics, University of Chicago; Robert M. Solow, Professor of Economics, Massachusetts Institute of Technology; Philip Taft, Professor of Economics, Brown University; George W. Taylor, Professor of Labor Relations, Wharton School of Finance and Commerce, University of Pennsylvania.
Members of the Staff: George P. Shultz, Director, Professor of Industrial Relations, Graduate School of Business, University of Chicago; Abraham Siegel, Associate Director, Associate Professor of Industrial Relations, Massachusetts Institute of Technology; David Burke, Staff Associate, University of Chicago.

said in its foreword, the report reflected the views and experiences of each member, with which they were all in general accord. The same could not be said for the board of trustees of CED, however. Their disagreement with the report led to considerable discord within the committee. This later led to a determination on the part of CED to abandon the procedure of turning over difficult problems to outside groups, however "independent" they might be. It also led to the production of a CED statement on national labor policy which, in the opinion of many, added little to CED's reputation for objectivity.

The so-called Kerr report lived up to its authors' obligation to produce an independent report setting forth a consensus of their own views. The 160-page report touched upon almost every aspect of labor policy and though—as the CED statement did in 1947—it accepted collective bargaining as a part of the American way of life, it was neither pro-labor nor anti-labor in its over-all views. It stood pretty much for the status quo. Indeed, in some quarters, it was regarded as regressive, in that its major theme seemed to be the great need to halt the drift toward excessive regulatory detail that had the support of many who, whenever there was a strike or whenever there was a lockout, cried, "There ought to be a law!" It would be impossible here to summarize all its recommendations but some highlights are worth recording.

National policy with regard to the obligation to bargain in good faith, the report said, had "developed into an unwarranted intrusion into the business of the parties and a source of voluminous and wasteful litigation." The subjects to be covered, the procedures to be adopted, and the nuances of strategy involved in bargaining should be left to the parties themselves. The prime responsibility for reaching agreement and for moderating disputes should be left to the parties themselves. The government's role should be to assist the fulfillment of this obligation primarily by providing mediation service of a high quality. This, again, was what CED had said.

The Kerr report took the stand that procedures for dealing with emergency disputes affecting the national interest had been too frequently used in the past. The threat of an emergency was too often used and the actions of the President were too predictable, it said, in its recommendation for less interference by federal authority. More active work should be done by the Presidential emergency boards, which should often step into the situation before a strike has occurred. It had little to say in support of the Railway Labor Act, often looked upon as a model for emergency disputes.

Of special interest here is the Kerr report's observations on the relationship of collective bargaining to inflation. To a great extent it rejected the CED supposition that wage settlements were an important factor in producing and sustaining inflation. There were many other factors that had to be considered, although there was a possibility that creeping inflation might stem from unrealistic wage increases. Among the other causes were possible biases in the government's price indexes which did not take properly into consideration improvements in the quality of the products and services used. Others it suggested were: the "exploitation of old monopoly positions" by industry; the "rigid adherence by management to fixed wage-price relationships"; downward inflexibility of some prices in markets where demand was "weak"; and the "bidding up of salaries of managerial, technical, and scientific personnel not covered by collective bargaining."

The report pointed out that only about one-third of the wage and salary workers in the economy were covered by collective bargaining and questioned whether this small number necessarily "set the pace" for the rest of the work force. However, it refused to recommend establishment of federal machinery to regulate or review wage or price determinations resulting from collective bargaining, again following the CED prescription. Nor did it think well of "appeals for voluntary restraint." But it did suggest that more attention should be paid by business, labor, and government to the economic impact of collective bargaining, and proposed an annual labor-management conference on the *Economic Report of the President* as an aid to exchanging ideas and analyses among the groups. With this CED could have no quarrel.

The report showed an awareness of the great power exercised by both labor and management and, although it made several concessions to the rights and interests of the latter, it was adamant in its belief that organized collective bargaining was a necessity for the general economic peace and stability of the nation. And it was in this realm of union security that it caused its sponsors the most difficulty. "The federal laws (regarding labor) should be revised so that its regulations on union security apply in every state." It then went on to say, almost at the end of the statement:

> *Nineteen states have adopted so-called "right-to-work" laws which . . . restrict union-employer negotiations of . . .*

union security provisions. We believe that management and labor should have the right to bargain over and negotiate for a union shop. Because our national labor policy is predicated on the trade union as the exclusive representative of all the members of the bargaining unit and because we feel that the participation of all members of the bargaining unit would improve the quality of such representation, we urge the elimination of the right of states to go beyond the restrictions contained in the federal law.

At the same time the Kerr report suggested that the "conscientious objector" to union membership be allowed to retain his job. It supported the "agency shop" system whereby the non-union worker would retain his job as long as he paid his dues to the union that had been legally elected as bargaining agent for the employees.

The reception of this report was in accordance with the biases of the recipient. On the whole it was calmly received and caused little if any commotion. But soon the brief passage about the right-to-work law attracted the attention of the head of a semi-moribund National Right to Work Committee. This group had been created some years before to propagandize for the passage of such "right-to-work" laws in the various states and even to get similar legislation on the federal books. The lobbyist quite naturally refused to take at face value the CED disclaimer of responsibility for the ideas expressed by the independent task force. Seizing his opportunity he turned the CED-supported document neatly into the basis of a national campaign to revivify his own committee. He quickly won the open and vocal support of the NAM, which charged CED with being at least a traitor to its trust. As a result, several financial contributors withdrew their support. The right-wing press was strident in its attacks on CED. CED's chairman and its president, and every trustee were soon deluged with letters. Many CED trustees were deeply disturbed by the uproar. In time, a labor policy subcommittee under the leadership of William C. Stolk, then chairman of the board of the American Can Company, was recruited to prepare CED's own statement on national labor policy.

The report of the subcommittee, duly approved by the Research and Policy Committee, was published in March 1964. It was a mixture of approval and disapproval of the Kerr report. In tone or substance *Union Powers and Union Functions* was not one of CED's happiest productions. It was against violence—which, the record shows, had been singularly absent from the domestic scene in recent years. It was for injunctions against unions in cases involving strikes in alleged violation of a labor agreement. It supported the lockout, as did the Kerr report. It wanted stiffer penalties against the use of secondary boycotts, already illegal. It said determination of the form and content of collective bargaining should be left to the parties and not be interfered with by government rules. It supported the Taft-Hartley provisions for government intervention in national emergency disputes, but it sternly argued against government intervening in "every situation where it considers the public interest to be involved"; and it chided the National Labor Relations Board for inefficiency. As might have been expected, of the ten major recommendations presented, one caught the headlines:

> *Every worker should have the right to decide freely to belong or not to belong to a union. . . . The rights of some workers to effective representation by a union are not abridged by the failure of other workers to join. The rights of the employee who does not want to belong to a union have already been substantially abridged in the interests of labor relations stability; to go farther and compel him to belong to the labor organization is an unwarranted denial of his freedom.*

Up until this reversal of the Kerr philosophy, the CED had seldom been singled out for attack by organized labor. In fact, if the columns of the AFL-CIO's monthly economic reports were a criterion, the committee had held the respect of most unions which, while often in economic disagreement, nevertheless recognized the intellectual honesty of CED's statements. Now it unleashed a barrage of press releases against the Stolk report. Indeed, as one commentator said, there was only one recommendation in it that labor could accept, and that was its stand against racial discrimination.

But none of these suggestions touched upon what CED said was "the major source" of excessive union power. This was "the combination of employees—all employees or any group essential to continuing operations—of many competing employers. . . . The power that workers get from unified organization of an entire industry is the power to pass on increases of labor costs to consumers of the product."

Perhaps the calmest and best criticism which the policy statement engendered was contained in a footnote by Allan Sproul, with which William Benton, chairman of Encyclopaedia Britannica, Inc., asked to be associated:

> I recognize that this policy statement represents a sincere effort to suggest means of relating union powers to union functions, so that what has proved to be beneficial in this relationship will be preserved and what has proved to be detrimental may be altered. The possibility of bias in approach has been recognized and an attempt has been made to temper its effect. Nevertheless, the statement has the aspect of a presentation of grievances by the business community which it represents, which may well harden rather than soften the "adversary position" in labor-management relations which the statement itself deplores. This danger is increased, in my opinion, by the inclusion of sections in the statement which give expression to individual views which were not able to achieve group consensus, but which will almost inevitably be interpreted as reflecting a climate of discussion.
>
> On broader grounds, the narrowness of the frame in which the statement has been cast has deprived it of a measure of constructive quality, in that it does not attempt to focus attention upon changes in laws and practices, involving both business and labor, which might improve the competitive workings of our economic system. And it dismisses too cavalierly the interest and role of government in labor-management relations, quite apart from specific labor disputes, leaving a void with respect to the coordination of wage-price policies with fiscal and monetary policies designed to promote sustainable economic growth, which is one of the critical issues of our time.

A few years later Theodore O. Yntema, then chairman of the CED Research and Policy Committee, commented on the reaction to the statement:

> A common reaction has been surprise—surprise that an organization usually considered "liberal" had come to conclusions about labor policy that are generally considered conservative. . . . There should have been no surprise that CED, having championed freedom and competition in international trade and domestic agriculture, should come out for freedom and competition in labor markets. Neither should there have been surprise, after all we have said about equal treatment

under the law, that we should seek to apply this principle to the labor law.

The subject of labor power will continue to plague CED, the economics profession, business as a whole, and labor itself, for some time to come. It may well be that, as CED continues to study ways and means to "improve the workings of our economic system," to quote Mr. Sproul, through better "coordination of wage-price policies with fiscal and monetary policies," it will come up with better answers than the Kerr committee or CED itself has thus far been able to do.

When economists assemble their facts and figures in orderly array, the problems they seek to solve fall into clearly defined categories; but the world they are trying to explain is not a neat or orderly place. Policies based on theories seem simple and operable. The nation to which they are directed appears to be an entity, one place where one policy can or should prevail. In many respects this is true, but only partly so. National policy must be decided upon with the needs and aspirations of the individual citizens of 50 different states always in mind. And the policies of the 50 states must take into consideration, along with the states' obligations to the nation itself, the needs and aspirations of the people living in the cities, the counties, the towns, the villages, and the farms. Somehow, all of these must be brought together and made to fit into a national pattern—a political, economic, and social design that has meaning and purpose for all the people in the United States.

In recent years there has been a resurgence of concern for what we call the federal system, which is supposed to hold us in political unity: nation, state, city,

19

Problems of Megalopolis

170

town, and crossroads. Among these we are supposed to divide properly the problems and costs of self-preservation. Much nonsense has been said and written about federalism and much that makes good sense. Some talkers and writers have preached the virtues of nationalism or statism; others have called for the preservation of the innocent virtues of home rule. The spirits of rustic Thomas Jefferson on the one hand and urban Alexander Hamilton on the other have been endlessly invoked. And the nation has grown smaller in distance and time, and the fields have shrunk, and the pavements grown, and bigness has come to prevail.

America, once a nation of farmers, never ceases to be amazed and skeptical when certain facts are recited. The rural image as well as the Puritan ethic dies hard. It is difficult to believe that two-thirds of all Americans today live in metropolitan areas, holding 70 per cent of the nation's industrial jobs. It is difficult to believe that there are 142 more metropolitan areas than there are sovereign states, and that one-half of the national wealth is concentrated in them. It is difficult to realize that there are 80,000 separate political jurisdictions that are presumed to be necessary to maintain the nation's social order, health, and intellectual welfare. It is not pleasant to know that many of these Americans live amidst, or are threatened with, decay, pollution, dirt, noise, traffic, and the greyness of economic distress.

The Committee for Economic Development began to study the implication of these facts in 1957.[1] Since then it has devoted considerable time, money, effort, and talent to trying to solve these seemingly insoluble problems. In order to do this its trustees created two new organizations within the framework of CED. One, the Area Development Committee, was started in 1957. A few years later the Committee for Improvement of Management in Government was organized. The purpose of each was to study certain defined problems, reach conclusions, and make recommendations within its own scope of competence. Publication of the results, however, rested with the approval of the Research and Policy Committee, the same as with all CED statements on national policy.

The Area Development Committee first distinguished itself with the publication in 1959 of two brief but brilliant supplemen-

---

[1] Not insignificantly, after a reorganization of its own structure and the acquisition of a new chairman (the late J. D. Zellerbach) and its first president (Alfred C. Neal).

tary papers originally prepared for its own internal use. At that time Raymond Vernon was director of a massive study of the New York metropolitan region. He was also an advisor to CED. The gist of his findings were set forth in his study, *The Changing Economic Function of the Central City.*

This paper raised fundamental questions about the progressive downgrading of urban values, especially in those "grey belts" of urban decay that lie between business districts and surrounding suburbs, and where the economic function of the city was most rapidly changing. Of particular interest to the CED group was Raymond Vernon's comments on the "inescapable political fact" that, although city and suburb are inseparable segments of larger social and economic organisms, they are "separate entities in the taxing, regulating, and spending sense." In its future studies of urban-metropolitan problems CED was to explore this aspect time and again. Also of significance were Mr. Vernon's strictures concerning the costs of transportation and the tax structure, wherein he compared the lowness of transportation costs with the off-setting economic costs brought about by traffic congestion. This, too, was to ensnare the CED policy makers.

Robert Wood's paper, *Metropolis Against Itself*, was also based on the New York Metropolitan Region studies. In it, the M.I.T. political scientist and author of the deservedly popular book, *Suburbia*, examined the ways in which the essentially service-oriented governments can come to grips with metropolitan problems.

The existing patterns of diversity and autonomy, Wood said, may be able to maintain law and order, but they cannot make policy. He pointed out the incongruity of having both large policy governments and small service governments, and said that metropolitan areas must decide between the values of autonomy and diversity and coordination and region-wide acceptance.

Throughout this century, people have debated the question of whether or not the American political system could countenance an unbridled laissez-faire economy—whether it did not have to intervene by selective measures to redress the balance of competition, at times to preserve it, and at times to guide it. But in the modern metropolitan region, the question is reversed. The issue is whether or not a modern economic system, requiring positive stimulation and selective aid and direction by public authority, can tolerate an unbridled

*laissez-faire profusion of governments which systematically avoid
any responsibility for these matters.*

The committee's contribution to this debate was published
in the summer of 1960. It was entitled *Guiding Metropolitan Growth*.
Its outspoken ideas stemmed considerably from the dual Vernon-
Wood thesis. Perhaps *Architectural Forum* was not overly exagger-
ating when it said that, "in a quiet, academic way," this small booklet
was a "revolutionary document." To political and economic students
of urban affairs of course it was not. But seldom had a business-
oriented organization entertained its basic ideas. It frankly implied
that the heart of metropolitan decay lay in the unwillingness of
governments to meet their responsibilities. It was equally severe in
laying much of the blame for this state of affairs on the intran-
sigence of business leadership. The great need was first for governments adequate in scope and power, and then for intelligent
planning, programing, and budgeting on the local level to meet the
increasing demands for public service.

As described by the committee, a metropolitan area was a
single economic entity composed of many political and geographic
units. The CED statement did not say that this entity should
merge into a large single government, but it was adamant in its
belief that it should so reorganize itself as to be capable of planning on an area-wide metropolitan scale. This should start from
all-inclusive economic base studies, which would include careful
analysis of the economic and demographic forces that influence the
volume and pattern of its income-generating activities. Knowledge
of the base was essential to a meaningful understanding of public
policy designed to retain, expand, or attract private investment that
would create opportunities for employment.

While the committee supported continuance of federal urban
renewal activities at the 1960 level, it felt their over-all value should
be reappraised. It urged the Administration to "give special preference in financial and administrative assistance to communities where
workable program and renewal planning are carried out on a metro-
politan-wide basis." This principle later was incorporated in the
Housing and Urban Renewal Act. Furthermore, it viewed the
federal role as setting the stage for private development and providing financial assistance "only to the extent required to permit the
private real estate market to function effectively."

Many commentators felt with *The Washington Post* that the

CED took "too narrow a view of the public responsibility for curbing and wiping out blight." They agreed with the *St. Louis Post-Dispatch* that what really was needed was the application of federal help on a much greater scale. However, a careful reading of the press comments on this statement reveals that its discussion of economic base studies on a metropolitan scale struck a ready response across the country. This was especially true in regions where the suburbs and cities had long been in conflict over plans for their mutual development, or where old industries had departed, leaving labor and business problems behind. There the pragmatic pronouncements of the CED document had a lasting effect. Citizens and officials in areas as varied as Burlington, Vermont, or Evanston, Illinois, found much substance in it.

The blight of metropolis was not the only disturbing aspect of modern life which CED, as an organization concerned with economic development, felt obliged to face. Six months after President Kennedy took office the CED issued through the Area Development Committee its statement, *Distressed Areas in a Growing Economy.*

"For several years," Chairman T. V. Houser wrote in his foreword, "the Committee for Economic Development has been concerned about the problems of local and regional economies. Quite a number of our local economies have not only failed to keep pace with the growth of the nation, but have actually moved backward while the nation was moving forward. High and persistent unemployment in such areas has caused prolonged human suffering and extensive economic waste."

The philosophy behind the statement had been expressed by CED in earlier statements, notably in *Meeting the Special Problems of Small Business* (1947) and in *Economic Growth in the United States* (1958). In those studies CED had listed certain elements which it felt were essential to the growth of the United States' productive capacity and standard of living. One was the importance of the free enterprise system, which was "animated by opportunities for profit and the danger of loss." Its great attribute included decentralization of economic initiative and opportunity for the birth of new enterprises; a belief in the survival of socially useful enterprises and the weeding out of the socially useless; the importance of the quality of business management; the quality of the labor force; the diffusion of education; the maintenance of a high degree of mobility of both capital and labor; and the importance of the specialization of occupation.

"All these observations," the report said, "are particularly relevant to the problem at hand. The recommendations are an application of this broad philosophy."

In many respects the 1961 statement went farther toward approval of federal aid and expenditure, and the use of federal fiscal policy, to meet the problems of a distressed economy than might have been expected. Of the sixteen major recommendations to aid distressed areas which the statement offered, eleven asked for some kind of federal support, either financial or moral. In only one instance did the report come out flatly against direct federal expenditure. One proposal was particularly interesting, for it edged up to one of the political controversies of the 1960's.

Almost at the outset the report called for "a high level federal executive" who would have prime responsibility for coordinating the efforts of various existing federal departments involved with the problems of distressed areas. The report said:

> If the federal government is to make a major effort to help alleviate the problems of distressed areas, it must maintain a central point of leadership. . . . Currently, several federal agencies have programs which work with distressed areas as well as other areas. Some increase in these programs as they affect distressed areas is necessary. A high level federal executive with sufficient stature to deal effectively with the various departments and independent agencies can both promote and coordinate such an expansion of effort. He can also be a focal point for advice to the states and localities.

While the CED statement upheld the use of a surprisingly generous amount of federal aid for distressed areas it insisted that they should be carefully defined to eliminate areas that develop labor surpluses only during national recessions. Such areas needed no subsidy beyond that which the proper application of fiscal and monetary policy would bring with recovery. It suggested that the program to provide more adequate general education and training systems in states and localities with below average per capita incomes, which it had set forth in an earlier policy statement, *Paying for Better Public Schools*, might be extended to distressed areas. Federal advice to states and depressed localities, and additional federal financial assistance for vocational training in distressed localities, should be provided. It went even to the extent of urging the training of qualified students away from home if the locality could not provide adequate schooling. This, of course, was in tune with its farm program, in which it had offered similar suggestions in order to make the migration from non-economic farms easier on those forced to leave.

The report called for the payment of unemployment insurance benefits to workers undergoing retraining. In distressed areas this should be provided by the federal government. Some such system as this was needed to maintain mobility of the labor force. After all, many job seekers had to cross state lines to find work, and they should not have to suffer undue hardships in the process. The statement, however, stressed that, wherever possible, development programs and land use plans should be local in origin and financing— although those living up to reasonable standards might well be given government financial assistance.

Among other suggestions was the locating of permanent federal government facilities in distressed areas so long as the area could meet the requirements of economy and efficiency. But CED rigorously opposed outright federal grants for private capital construction. Instead it offered its own loan program, which it presented in detail.

In essence this called for each of the twelve Federal Reserve Banks to establish a Federal Reserve Development Corporation, whose purpose would be to assure adequate financing for sound business ventures and necessary public facilities in distressed areas. These corporations would supplement and sometimes provide additional backing for existing state and private financing programs. Alfred C. Neal, CED's president, who had had wide first-hand experience with such local problems during his years with the Boston Federal Reserve Bank, later made a cogent plea for this system before the Senate Banking and Currency Committee. As he then recalled, CED had urged a similar program in 1947, when it proposed the establishment, within the Federal Reserve System, of capital banks for the sole purpose of financially aiding small business.

One section of the report moved away from close concentration on localized plans and programs into the realm of national fiscal policy. Earlier that year CED had issued *Growth and Taxes: Steps for 1961*, in which it had fervently supported more rapid depreciation allowances as a major incentive to business investment.

The committee now called for extending this special privilege to firms that would expand, or build new plants, or install new equipment in old plants in chronically distressed areas. It said that rapid amortization would be a spur to national economic growth as well as assistance to the depressed regions. Firms to which this privilege was offered would have an equivalent of an interest-free loan from the federal government for the period covered. This tax grant would be made available only for firms located within areas where a continuing labor surplus existed, and only where an *increase* in employment would result from expansion or from new plants or equipment.

This led Walter Wheeler of Pitney-Bowes, chairman of the subcommittee which prepared the report, to suggest that a tax credit might be given to any firm in a distressed area which increased its labor force. But it also led Allan Sproul to remark, "To begin spreading the advantages of fast write-offs to meet special situations, which lack the warrant of temporary emergencies, could contribute to misuse of the power to tax."

The imaginative idea seems to have died on the pages of the CED statement.

It is perhaps no exaggeration to say that not since CED wrote its original postwar tax plan had a working committee faced a more difficult internal problem than did the subcommittee which produced the next report on area development.

In his foreword to *Developing Metropolitan Transportation Policies*, Frazar B. Wilde said that the subcommittee worked for three years on the statement issued in the spring of 1965. Before that another group had worked equally long on transportation and had come to no conclusions. It is easy to understand. Nothing perhaps affects the everyday life of all people more closely than their daily means of transportation.

Everybody has an idea about what should be done about it —from banning all automobiles to shooting every featherbedding railroad union man. To get a group of businessmen (even when led by a university president) to reach a consensus was almost to ask the impossible.[2] For involved in the problem are not only the personal preferences but the deeply imbedded, divergent economic outlooks of the beleaguered railroad man, of the trucker, of

[2] The transportation subcommittee of CED was headed by John A. Perkins, then president of the University of Delaware.

the automobile manufacturer, of the highway builder, to name a few. Men in these walks of life do not look upon the world with equal vision or even speak the same language.

Despite this, the committee sweated out a statement which at long last managed to gain the approval of the Research and Policy Committee. Strangely enough, the result was not a statement of bland consensus; but neither was it as forthright as many once had hoped. In some sections it is difficult to determine its exact meaning. It is, perhaps, an outstanding example of the inherent weaknesses in any committee effort to reach a conclusion—a weakness which, it would seem, CED had long recognized and generally been able to overcome. In the end it seemed to make a point: that the future health of urban existence depends upon the development of mass transportation systems and less reliance on the use of the automobile.

One warning that most commentators, and they were legion, felt the statement issued was, the *Philadelphia Inquirer* said, "that if the cities failed to meet mass transportation needs, urban areas would deteriorate and federal intervention would grow." (Sometimes, reading the articles, one gets the impression that urban deterioration was more desirable than federal intervention!) The lesson that one writer found in the statement was that a way had to be devised to get people back and forth which would go beyond "the present antiquated method of allowing one 150-pound person to haul a ton and a half of metal, which consumes 300 square feet of space, with him when he goes to the center of the city." And *The New York Times* hailed the committee for having supported what that newspaper thought was the one way for future metropolitan development—establishment of "liberal financial and regulatory inducements to commuter systems," a prescription later to be followed, or at least advocated, by Governor Rockefeller and Mayor Lindsay of New York.

To many commentators the statement must have said more than it seemed to say. In footnotes, George Russell of General Motors disassociated himself from the report and Theodore O. Yntema of Ford Motor Company attacked it on the grounds that it was based on bad economics. From another point of view Philip Sporn of American Electric Power said that he did not think that the substance of the report did justice to the complex subject. He saw in it a "timidity in analysis, a lack of breadth in over-all pre-

scription for approach, and rather innocuous underscoring of bro-
midic apparencies." He added:

> *Nowhere is there a forthright statement of the fact that*
> *the condition of transportation in most of our metropolitan*
> *areas is close to complete breakdown; of the appalling waste*
> *in manpower, time, and energy that is being piled up every*
> *working day; nor that the basic difficulty is that the problem*
> *has rarely been tackled on the basis of a completely integrated*
> *view: embodying all areas comprising and contiguous to each*
> *community or groups of communities; all needs of all segments*
> *of the people in their business, home, and recreational ac-*
> *tivities; utilizing all the available technologies including those*
> *sufficiently advanced but still in need of some final develop-*
> *ment; and supported and made feasible by all instruments—*
> *administrative, fiscal, and social-economic—for bringing into be-*
> *ing and operating in the public interest.*

What did the statement offer? It emphasized that transportation—roads, highways, streets, even parking places as well as mass
transportation systems—must be the concern of entire metropolitan
areas and not just of the individual localities. Major land-use and
transportation policies must be developed together. No decision
should be made that did not rest on a comparison of total costs
with total benefits from the proposed programs. Standards ordinarily used for decision-making for private investments were not
adequate for public decisions. A method should be devised that
would take into account all relevant costs and benefits, both direct
and indirect, economic and social, financial and nonfinancial. This
method should identify who would benefit and how much, who
would bear the costs, and how much they would be. It should measure the costs and benefits over the reasonable life of the project.
And it should apply this method to every alternative possibility so
that the ultimate choice could be decided on the value-judgments
of the whole community.

When it came to financing projects decided upon by this cost-
benefit analysis process it favored continuation of user charges for
highways (gasoline taxes) with the states returning to the municipalities more than they had hitherto done. For common carriers it suggested a fare level based on total benefits and costs of services, with
the municipalities sharing some of the costs. Business leadership

should show the way that would force a reluctant officialdom to move forward.

Although the statement met much opposition within the committee's own councils, and led the irascible *Wall Street Journal* to say that such a paper "neither helps toward solutions nor greatly enhances respect for the business community," many who were in a position to know regarded it as more than useful. Newspapers in many regions beset by crippling transportation problems—Utica, New York, Kansas City, Salt Lake City, San Jose, Salem, Oregon, to name a few—found it a useful document. In some instances it offered substantial backing for projects already under way; in others because it seemed to point the way for future solutions to jammed highways, human irascibility, and restrictions to local economic development.

The statement gladdened the hearts of planners everywhere, and became the basis for forward moves on comprehensive transportation systems in Seattle, Denver, and other major cities. It opened the way for CED's later attacks on the inadequacies of local and state governments.

A theme which runs recurrently through the policy statements of CED is an insistence that the interests of the business community, and the nation in general, require businessmen to take a more positive interest in public policy. "Business leadership" and "business responsibility" are oft-repeated phrases in the CED lexicon. With this has persistently gone the maxim that sound policies will mean little unless they are supported by good government management. In statement after statement primarily designed to improve the economic machinery, the CED has called for administrative reforms, even the invention of new tools, to make the machinery perform more effectively, efficiently, and economically.

The committee's preoccupation with the application to public administration of the lessons learned in private management led it early in the 1960's to undertake an unusual and interesting assignment, quite far removed from anything CED had hitherto undertaken. It might never have been tried were it not for the long presence on the board of trustees of one of its founding fathers, Marion B. Folsom.

20

Managing the Government

Mr. Folsom's career of public service covered three federal administrations. He had helped start CED, had headed its Field Division during the war years, had sat in President Eisenhower's Cabinet, and was now busily returned to active trusteeship of CED. His ventures in public administration in Washington were probably the most extensive of any CED trustee, although some forty members of the committee's board had served the federal government at one time or another. Among them were four former Cabinet members, three former undersecretaries, three former assistant secretaries, two heads of commissions, including the Federal Reserve Board and the Tennessee Valley Authority, eleven chairmen or members of federal advisory committees, seven directors of bureaus or chiefs of federal agencies, six special assistants to the President or to Cabinet officers, two former senators, and one former congressman.

In November 1961, a group of top officials of the Kennedy Administration, some former officials of the Eisenhower regime, private management consultants, and personnel directors, felt the time had come to create an organization, since none then existed, whose primary aim would be the improvement of management in government. The Carnegie Corporation promised funds. The group turned to Mr. Folsom for leadership because it felt his experience in both Democratic and Republican Administrations would help bring whatever reforms might come out of the venture to the attention of both parties. But Mr. Folsom felt there were already too many committees striving for attention. When he discovered that the group hoped to pattern itself after CED, however, he approached Chairman Theodore V. Houser, President Alfred C. Neal, and Research and Policy Committee Chairman Theodore O. Yntema and suggested that, as an effective organization, "we could put the prestige of CED behind the new organization." This was eventually accomplished.

The Committee for Improvement of Management in Government (CIMG) became a separate but nevertheless integral part of CED, consisting of twenty-five CED trustees and ten non-CED trustee members. It widened the scope of its own separate advisory board of technical experts to include political scientists, management consultants, personnel directors, as well as economists. Most of them had wide experience in government as well as in private enterprise. It was beholden to use the CED process of objective research and open discussion between members and advisors, and to bring "nonpartisan wisdom" to bear on essential problems of governmental management at all levels. Its public statements had to meet with approval of the CED Research and Policy Committee before they could be published.[1]

The first document which the adventuresome CIMG produced, *Improving Executive Management in the Federal Government* (July 1964), was exciting, controversial, and outspoken in its appraisal of the status of top-level personnel management in the federal government. It offered many business-like suggestions for institutional and personnel improvements. There had, of course, been previous studies with similar purposes in mind. Early in the New Deal, for example, President Roosevelt had created a committee, headed by Louis Brownlow (who was aided by Luther Gulick, now an articulate adviser to CIMG), to study federal administrative management and make proposals for modernizing the administration of federal personnel. This had been followed by reports and recommendations by the so-called Hoover Commissions in 1949 and 1955.

"These and other studies," the CIMG report commented, "recommended many means for correcting problems they identified, but often they proposed no mechanism for following through on their recommendations."

The CED-CIMG statement set out to do just this.

Within the inner circles of government, it was widely reported in Washington, the document created a furor of discussion. With the general public it brought decided reactions. To some observers it appeared to be advocating, at least by implication, the creation of a bureaucratic elite not in keeping with American democratic traditions. To others it appeared to have political implications, especially in certain proposals which, its critics felt, gave increased patronage power to a presidency already too powerful in this area. Others disliked its criticism of the Civil Service Commission, and still others feared that it would be wasteful of the taxpayers' money. If there were any justification for these objections, it can also fairly be said that none of them was its intent. Its constructive proposals, business-like in purpose and content, far outweighed its faults.

---

[1] The major financial support for the CIMG has been supplied by the Carnegie Corporation which contributed $500,000 in 1963 for a five-year period. Other financial aid was supplied by the Rockefeller Brothers Fund, the Kellogg Foundation, and the Edgar Stern Family Fund. Other foundations also contributed.

The statement was, indeed, sharply critical of the manner in which the federal government hires, promotes, and pays the 8,600 federal employees who may fairly be called the federal government's key decision makers. In order to correct the deficiencies of management inherent in this situation the statement called, among other things, for the establishment of a new Office of Executive Personnel in the White House. This office's continuing assignment would be the hiring, firing, or promotion of this elite executive group.

The key managers of the federal government are responsible for more than 5 million employees in the various agencies, the Foreign Service, and the armed forces. CED's investigations showed that, from a business-like point of view, bringing these under the "highly structured" rolls of the Civil Service Commission was a wasteful practice. This led CED to comment that the president of any large corporation with so little effective control over his key executives would be severely restricted in his ability to accomplish corporate objectives and to operate the business effectively and profitably. This situation would be remedied by the suggested "office of executive personnel."

This proposal, CED hoped, would help remove that excess of bureaucratic caution which impedes decision-making. The 500 or so political appointees at the top of the bureaucratic ladder would not come under this office. But it would take over responsibility for the 8,000 jobs just below the top, which are under Civil Service or one of its counterparts. The proposed office's acts and decisions would be subject to periodic review by a special board drawn from personnel or management experts.

Although the office of executive personnel has not yet been created, as a direct result of the CED suggestion the White House Staff dealing with high-level appointments has been strengthened under the direction of John W. Macy, Jr., of the Civil Service Commission, who undertook this internal reform in addition to his regular duties. The roster of available executive talent, those in the know have said, has been appreciably strengthened.

The CED statement, highly technical in its detailed survey of federal management policies, emphasized the need for creating incentives that would allow the civil servant to take as much pride in his work as his counterpart in private industry presumably enjoys. Not only would he be well paid but one who merited the distinction would be given a "supergrade" above the grades now attainable in Civil Service. Thus would competition and movement be introduced to the upper echelon. Under the proposal, the top officials could be moved from one area of an agency to another, or even from agency to agency, where their skills were required. They also would be allowed to move "laterally," that is, in and out of government for stated periods of time. CED thought that tours of duty with private enterprise might sharpen the abilities of civil servants, as its members had seen happen to their business associates who served with government.

This proposal to bring about better mobility within the executive branch led President Johnson to issue an Executive Order in 1966 which created an "executive assignment system" designed to place most highly qualified persons in appropriate supergrades.

The CED reforms—far too many and technical to be of general public interest—stressed the need, already recognized in the Foreign Service and some branches of the military as well as in private enterprise, for better management-training services for younger employees. It wanted schools set up within the agencies to aid in the advancement of personnel and the improvement of services.

The statement also called for better pay for civil servants, especially in the middle and top ranks, saying that it was vital if topmost efficiency were to be obtained. It wanted servants in the so-called GS-16 rank and above placed under presidential direction as to salaries. It said the President ought to be able to raise salaries in these categories without congressional sanction. At the same time it suggested substantial pay increases for Cabinet secretaries, heads of important agencies, and their top assistants. The Vice President would also get a raise.

Under Mr. Folsom's leadership the committee delved deeply into the bureaucratic maze. Although all its recommendations were not universally acceptable in federal ranks, the statement had considerable and almost immediate effect. President Johnson took steps to implement some of its provisions.

The statement was presented to President Johnson by Mr. Folsom and other trustees on the day it was made public. The President's interest in it was manifest and, of course, it was closely read by the "Men Near the Top" [1] whose careers might be affected by its recommendations. President Johnson shortly thereafter created

---

[1] This was the title of a supplementary paper by John Corson and R. Shale Paul, published in 1966 by CED.

a commission of five Cabinet members and five private citizens under Mr. Folsom's chairmanship, to recommend salary levels for high-level federal employees. Their recommendations touched upon the fact revealed in the CED statement that upper-level civil servants were paid far below comparable positions in private enterprise while lower-level civil servants were paid at or above comparable rates. The commission's report, presented unchanged to Congress by the Administration, contained most of the CED recommendations. Those asking for salary raises were adopted by Congress, which raised salaries of some upper levels between 20 and 40 per cent.

The federal budget, which was the third problem tackled by CIMG, [2] is an essential instrument for defining national purposes and achieving public objectives. CED had, of course, recognized from the beginning the importance of the budget process as an economic tool of the highest importance. Indeed, it had been a pioneer in setting forth measures for improving the process, but along different lines from those suggested in the 1966 policy statement, *Budgeting for National Objectives*, although both old and new proposals are interrelated.

Since its first important statement on fiscal policy in 1947 CED had been a foremost supporter of the use of what it then called the cash-consolidated budget rather than the administrative budget as the better guide to federal tax policy. This was because the cash budget includes everything that goes into the administrative budget but also includes important items excluded from the latter such as social security, unemployment insurance, highway funds, and other federal trust accounts. Although CED used the cash-consolidated budget in its statements on fiscal policy, it admitted this budget had its imperfections and early in the postwar

---

[2] The second policy statement by the CIMG under Mr. Folsom led the CED far away from familiar pastures. It was a purely political exercise only loosely connected with CED's long preoccupation with economic affairs. Nevertheless, *Presidential Succession and Inability* was a useful contribution to the history of the 1960's. Also, it was in keeping with CED's belief that the business community, like all good citizens, should involve itself in the affairs of government. And, from a business point of view, that the well being of the Chief Executive is a matter of concern to management. The statement played an effective if minor role in the eventual adoption of the 25th Amendment to the Constitution. Although its recommendations were, in several instances, different from those shepherded through Congress by Senator Birch Bayh, the essence of the two proposals was much the same.

years promised to seek a more perfect measure of the economic impact of federal finance.

For some time the Department of Commerce had been collecting national income and output statistics. When properly put together the federal budget could be cast in income and product terms. Primarily the difference between the two methods lies in the ways in which they measure the direct effects of federal activity on aggregate private income. But the national income budget has a better timing mechanism than the cash budget. It includes, for example, corporate profits taxes at the time the liability accrues rather than at the time the government receives payment. It also excludes expenditures of loans, mortgage purchases, purchase of land, and other transactions that are exchanges of existing assets rather than additions to private income. Thus it is a better analytical tool and one more suited for computing the full employment surplus, which is at the heart of fiscal policy.

In 1962, in its policy statement *Monetary and Fiscal Policy for High Employment*, CED adopted use of the national income budget at about the same time that the Council of Economic Advisers had opened up the subject for administrative consideration. The federal government now makes use of it as a better guide to the actual state of the economy as reflected through the budget than the administrative budget, which continues to be the guide for Congress in appropriating funds.

CED's campaign for the use of a more modern and more revealing budgetary system (begun, as we have said, in 1947) began to bear fruit in March 1967, when President Johnson created a special Commission on Budget Concepts. Composed of businessmen, economists, wall streeters, and congressional leaders, this group was enjoined to work out recommendations for a simpler presentation of the annual budget.[3] Much confusion had followed President Johnson's use of the national income and the administrative budget figures in the presentation of the 1968 (fiscal year) budget in January 1967. There was considerable criticism that President Johnson

---

[3] It included several CED and CMC trustees and advisors, among them T. O. Yntema, Robert B. Anderson, Secretary of the Treasury Henry H. Fowler, Budget Director Charles L. Schultze, Dr. Paul McCracken, and Leonard Silk of *Business Week*. David M. Kennedy, chairman of Continental-Illinois Bank and Trust Company, Chicago, a CED trustee, was its chairman.

was politically motivated in his use of national income account figures because they showed a $2.1 billion deficit—a lower figure than the administrative and the cash-consolidated budget figures revealed. One member of the commission said in *Business Week*, in August 1967, that the main purpose of the group was to eliminate the "gimickry and incredibility charges that have arisen as a result of budget presentations in recent years." This member strongly indicated that in January 1968, a new, simplified budget concept would be adopted—one quite close, it would seem to the cash-consolidated budget so long ago urged by CED.

The CIMG statement in 1966 was not, of course, concerned with this aspect of budgeting. It was concerned with reform of the budgetary process itself. And this, too, was a matter in which CED had pioneered.

In 1955, in its provocative policy statement *Control of Federal Government Expenditures*, it turned its attention to the vexing problem of efficiency in government operations, with particular stress on finding better procedures (which, of course, was now in the province of CIMG).

In an ad hoc statement on tax and spending policy, published as early as 1949, CED had said that a major function of the budget was to enable the voters to understand the choices that were open to them. Sensible choices, it said, can only be made in terms of government "functions." Budget representation should focus attention on functions by bringing together related activities and by summarizing these activities in categories that would aid citizens to make intelligent policy choices. The 1946 Legislative Reorganization Act had taken some steps in this direction. The resultant "legislative budget," which had a brief life in Congress, had broken up expenditures into broad categories such as national defense, international finance, and veterans' services. But CED wanted to go farther by splitting broad functions into activities, and activities into projects.

The first Hoover Commission had suggested this type of procedure, which it called a "program budget." Thereafter, several studies were made in this field. One in particular was David Novak's study for the RAND Corporation, which showed how this system could effectively be applied to the Department of Defense. In 1955 CED urged its adoption on a widespread scale and was later to return to its defense.

Some federal agencies, in the meantime, developed their own versions of program budgeting, hoping to bring to government techniques long used by successful business concerns in long-range capital planning and development of new products. The most sweeping application, of course, was in the Defense Department. Spurred on by the Defense Department's success, similar experiments were introduced into a few non-defense agencies.

In the summer of 1965 President Johnson ordered all departments and most agencies to use this new and, as he called it, "revolutionary" system of planning, programing, and budgeting. This meant that each was to define in advance the major objective, or program, it wished to pursue, to apply systematic analysis to alternative ways in which this objective might be obtained, and to plan its spending not only on an annual (fiscal year) basis but for the long run. In this regard CED warned, as had President Johnson, that "too much should not be expected too soon." But, when the system was refined and improved it should be of great value for, as CED said in *Budgeting for National Objectives*, "it permits and encourages the informed and expeditious adjustments of programs and resource commitments to accommodate changed conditions, better information, and refinements in thinking." Moreover, one of the major values of program planning is that it encourages a more precise comparison of programs than can be achieved through traditional budgetary devices. This system "encourages comparisons throughout the budget year—as required for management decision —rather than limiting comparisons to the 'budget season.'" Thus it calls for techniques such as cost-benefit and cost-effectiveness analysis which, as every businessman knows and a growing number of government officials are coming to know, is essential to the maintenance of sound business practices.[4]

All budgets—public or private—have common characteristics, and procedures found useful in any large organization can be applied elsewhere. The statement, while recognizing this, refused to fall into the common error of asserting that the federal budget can be managed in every detail as a corporate enterprise manages its

---

[4] In its 1955 statement, CED argued that budget process reform was impossible without reform within Congress. It then would create a "joint budget policy conference" within Congress, to consider the total size of the budget and relations between revenues and expenditures. It would require congressional committees to include estimates of *future* costs in their reports on authorization of new activities. It would give the President authorization to veto individual items in appropriations bills. And it would instigate a system of audits and reports to aid the President in improving efficiency in government activities.

budget. Public goals call for different policies and methods from those employed in profit-making. Political considerations influence public budgeting. Organizational patterns of the federal bureaucracy are not the same as those followed in private business.

"It is fortunate that both business and government have developed improved budgetary methods and mechanisms . . . new and sophisticated techniques of analysis and decision-making" that should make it easier for the government to meet "the growing requirements and responsibilities of a modern nation-state in the final third of the twentieth century."

In order to do this several "serious inadequacies" must be overcome. More attention must be paid to longer-range planning by both the executive and the legislative branches. Both have for too long a time put too much stress on details and not enough on the "broader picture."

Most spending plans focus on the 80-odd agencies reporting to the President and not enough on the functions they are supposed to perform or on the efficiency of the programs they are supposed to carry out. In congressional committees there has been more concern with "the numbers of people to be employed, the contracts to be let, the grants or subsidies to be given, and the things to be purchased," than with serving purposes or gaining results.

Organizational objectives have been too seldom defined in specific, measurable terms. The structural organization of the executive branch is not well adapted to current needs. Efforts at reorganization to conform more nearly with functional and other appropriate criteria have been sporadic, limited, and insufficient. The budgetary process should be used more effectively to improve operational effectiveness. Properly administered, it can achieve a more rational balance in allocating scarce resources among such competing fields as transportation, urban renewal, agricultural productivity, education, and even the exploration of outer space.

The five measures which the CED insisted would improve policy planning and program design provide means for effective control over budgetary execution, and bring about better management of operations, are important.

The federal budget should conform in every respect with well-defined broad national goals. The pervasive influence of federal policies and programs requires that conscious attention be given to formulating goals and setting priorities. A consistent set of plans is, of course, the responsibility of the President, but Congress also has its responsibilities in setting goals and priorities. Its recognition of this should be strengthened. Continuing recognition of this is at the heart of effective budgetary procedure.

The staffs of responsible departments and agencies should develop close working relationships with each other and with line management, under top-level leadership. This is also true in large bureaus and major subdivisions. In a recent directive President Johnson ordered that this be done. But as he said, its accomplishment "will require continuous and determined emphasis over a period of years."

The Bureau of the Budget in its role as a presidential staff unit should expand its efforts in reviewing broad program alternatives, coordinating functions scattered among separate agencies, giving attention to administrative reorganization, evaluating program achievements, and appraising and improving agency management performance. Its staffing and internal organization should reflect the scope and difficulty of these assignments—particularly with respect to executive branch reorganization. The Bureau must enlist the best personnel in the nation "with breadth of vision, practical wisdom, and creative initiative." And there should be mobility. The Budget Bureau should bring able recruits in from other agencies and from outside the government, while sending qualified and experienced persons out to strengthen weak spots in the departments.

Congress has an important role in the budget process. In carrying it out effectively it should assume more responsibility. This would require creation of an effective forum to consider broad fiscal policy and to examine the budget as a whole. This of course was a repetition of policy in this area long held by CED. Longer-range authorizations should be substituted in many instances for the annual measures now in use. Emphasis in appropriations should be shifted to functions and programs from the agency-object approach. Appropriations subcommittees should be set up on a functional basis. Public attendance at their hearings should be permitted whenever practicable. The report of the Joint Committee on Congressional Reorganization in 1966 reflected several of the recommendations made in the CED statement. A bill to effectuate this report passed the Senate in March 1967 and was pending in the House as this book went to press. However, this bill does not go nearly as far as the CED statement or the Joint Committee's report in changing prevailing congressional patterns.

The General Accounting Office (GAO) should conduct a

government-wide annual financial audit in accordance with present law, as urgently recommended by numerous advisory commissions and study groups. This audit should be comparable with those made for business concerns by private accounting firms and by GAO for governmental corporations.

Most journalistic reaction to the statement—one newspaper said it "hit with a thud louder than that of the voluminous budget itself"—was focused on the somewhat iconoclastic suggestions that there should be greater congressional debate on over-all budgetary policy questions, that authorization of funds should be for three to five years instead of for one, as at present, and that the President be given authority to withhold appropriations when and if they proved not to be essential. The proposal to open the budget sessions of subcommittees of the House Appropriations Committee to the public and the press (including television) of course struck a responsive journalistic response. All these ideas were elaborated upon in the body of the "lengthy, well-documented, and even dispassionate critique," as the *Los Angeles Times* described the essay.

But, as *The Christian Science Monitor* sighed, after praising the substance of the report, "Only if there is strong citizen demand can the President and Congress be expected to carry out such a revolution."

The seeds that were sown back in 1958, when Robert Wood was explaining the political realities of urban existence and Raymond Vernon was trying to bring some order to the metropolitan chaos, came to flower in the summer of 1966 when CIMG-CED published *Modernizing Local Government*.

In this statement CED came closer to the problems of people—their daily lives, their hopes and frustrations—than at any time in the committee's history. The paper dealt with things close to home. Other CED statements, of course, had tended in this direction—when CED moved into the distressed areas, when it tackled the transportation problem, when it examined the costs of public schools, when it offered its program for improving the conditions of the poor through better education.

Modernizing Local Government, as its title indicated, had to do with one's own neighbors—the appointed and elected persons in county, town, and suburb who are responsible for keeping down the crime rate, collecting the garbage, assessing the property, and making out the tax bill. Realistically it was based on the assumption that

21

Revitalizing Federalism

most of the nation's average local governments were in a mess and that something had to be done about it if the affluent society was to solve some of its worst social problems.

The statement was only one of several CED papers to be published in the 1960's dealing with the federal system under which the United States has managed its political business since 1789. Two other important contributions in the field of federalism were to follow. One was to deal with the role of federal tax policy as it affects the 50 states, and the second was to carry on from the local governments to the functions of the states themselves. Together they form an interesting and imaginative contribution to the political and economic knowledge of the contemporary scene.[1]

These guidelines to efficiency in town, county, city, and state and to more effective fiscal relations among them, bring into focus most of the advanced thinking of political scientists and at a time when almost every edition of the local paper brings fresh evidence of the need for governmental reform. The states need to modernize their constitutions, rearrange their tax systems, give more authority to cities and towns that are geographically expanded to cover their problem areas, work in better harmony with their neighbors, and through efficient reorganization and recognition of their own resources place less reliance on federal assistance for the accomplishment of their purposes.

The most startling assumption in *Modernizing Local Government* is that the number of local governments in the United States could be reduced at least 80 per cent. This drastic movement, if it occurred, would cut the actual number from 80,000 to 16,000. It would help considerably in bringing about the curtailment of overlapping layers of government, found in most states, which are one of the greatest detriments to efficient management of public affairs and therefore an obstacle to political, social, and economic progress.

At the same time CED would confine local popular election to what it calls "members of the policy-making bodies of government." This would eliminate some 500,000 unpaid or elected offi-

---

[1] *Modernizing Local Government* and *Modernizing State Government* were the product of the Committee for Improvement of Management in Government. *A Fiscal Program for A Balanced Federalism* was prepared by a subcommittee on federal-state-local fiscal relations of which Jervis J. Babb was chairman. All three were issued by the Research and Policy Committee.

cials from their outworn and useless jobs, from "fence-viewers" and "measurers of lumber" upward.

The CED program would also ban the election of all administrative department heads. It would either elect or appoint a single chief executive to take charge of all administrative agencies. A single executive can coordinate and can be held responsible for setting goals and measuring results; multiple executive responsibility to voters promotes conflict and waste in administration. CED hoped that this change would lead to personnel practices based on merit and professional competence. In all sections of the nation, except New England and in the great megalopolises, it would make modernized county governments the chief governmental agency of rural, urban, and most metropolitan communities.

When local governments reached this state of grace, the CED formula would give them broad, up-to-date legal powers to plan, finance, and execute programs suited to the needs, interests, and desires of their citizens. In order to reach this level most of the 50 state constitutions—which probably need revision, anyway—would have to be revamped to provide for necessary boundary revisions, extension of legal authority, and the elimination of useless government units. Finally, the plan called for the revision of the terms and conditions of federal and state grants-in-aid so that they would be aimed at encouraging the modernizing of local governments.

In presenting its evidence to support these conclusions the 78-page document had little that is kind to say about existing forms and conditions of local and even state governments. Only by concerted efforts of combining the resources in business, labor, civic, and other groups will the myriad local governments be able to "move toward the imperative institutional changes" necessary to make them "the efficient organizations that modern life demands." If they do move in this direction, then, says the CED paper, they will be able to solve their problems in the American way—with less reliance on "the pervasive presence of the national government."

But this will not be easy, for "the nation's courthouses and city halls have often seemed to lack the vision and dedication—as well as the financial resources—to diagnose conditions, devise solutions, and make vigorous response. New functions needed to meet new situations are neglected by most local units, and old functions are conducted without benefit of new techniques. By default, initiatives have commonly been left to more resourceful federal forces. Cast in an archaic mold, unable to cope with new issues, many—if not most

—local governments are centers of strenuous resistance to change of any kind."

Furthermore, the costs are exorbitant. Direct expenditures for all municipalities—counties, New England towns, townships, and special districts—rose from $20.1 billion in 1952 to $45.1 billion in 1962, or 124 per cent. The statement says they will probably double again by 1972.

Following these gloomy facts the rest of the statement is an orderly exposition of a detailed program designed for modernizing local governments.

Of considerable interest and value are its animadversions on the growing trend of local governments to depend on the federal government for financial aid. Between 1952 and fiscal 1964 federal aid to local units had quadrupled. Federal aid to the states—the next subject in this area to be reviewed by CED—also nearly quadrupled, permitting the states in turn to increase their support to localities. State aid to local units has continued to exceed state receipts from the federal treasury, but the net difference has grown quite slowly in recent years. Federal aid to states and local units combined will increase again, by 50 per cent, from fiscal 1964 to fiscal 1967. There is no visible prospect of significant future deviation from established trends.

Federal leadership in dealing with national problems at local levels has been beneficial in many fields. But it is time for the citizens of the 50 states "to take stock of their systems of local government in relation to urgent present and prospective needs. This involves more than an assessment of current performance. It also demands a judgment of future capabilities in planning and executing activities essential to healthy community development. As we approach the twenty-first century, weaknesses in eighteenth and nineteenth century forms must be corrected—or new systems created—if local government is to survive as a vital force."

This report has been widely circulated, and has had significant impact in many states, including West Virginia, Minnesota, North and South Dakota, Washington, Pennsylvania, Maryland, Connecticut, Florida, New York, and Rhode Island. (Maryland, New York, Pennsylvania, and Rhode Island, it is interesting to note, had Constitutional Conventions under way in 1967.) A series of articles in *The Reader's Digest* based on the CED document brought its proposals to national attention in the summer of 1967.

Organizations that were clearly influenced in their activities and which assisted in the circulation of CED's, basic ideas include: the National League of Cities, the Council of State Governments, the National Association of Counties, the National League of Women Voters and several of its constituent bodies, the American Farm Bureau Federation, the Governmental Research Association, the U. S. Chamber of Commerce and its constituents, the National Municipal League, the Municipal Finance Officers Association, the American Institute of Planners, and the American Society for Public Administration. In addition, the Chamber of Commerce started an action program in 1967 to encourage state and local chambers to press for improvement of state and local government. In May 1967, the Chamber published a brochure on this subject, including a section on "how to do it," entitled *Modernizing Local Government.*

Civil Service Commission Chairman Macy, in a letter to Alfred C. Neal, president of CED, said this statement ". . . has played a critical role in the development of the Administration's proposal, the Intergovernmental Manpower Act of 1967, . . . designed to assist state and local governments in improving their staffs and strengthening their systems of personnel administration."

Before CED went on to cope with the political and economic murk hovering over the state capitals, and to examine the states' relations to the 80,000 political entities that are their creatures, it paused to look at the pressing problems of federal-state fiscal policy.

The fiscal relationship between Washington and the state and local governments has been a political and economic arena splashed with the blood of many conflicts from time immemorial. Especially since the New Deal the federal government has assumed an ever-growing concern with state and local affairs. It has grown closer to the people, has sought to discover and further their aspirations and needs in the interest of their general welfare. As our society has grown more industrial and more urban the costs of maintaining an orderly existence have increased. No longer have towns and cities and even the states themselves been able to meet these costs from their own resources. Hence the great revival of interest in what has been called fiscal federalism—a sharing of costs throughout the combination of political entities that make up our federal system.

In a *Fiscal Program for a Balanced Federalism* this problem is made clear. "The committee decided," Emilio G. Collado, executive vice president of Standard Oil Company (New Jersey) and chairman of the Research and Policy Committee, wrote in his foreword, "that a most urgent problem of fiscal federalism is to strengthen the financial capacity of the states, which in turn would strengthen their capacity to help their local governments. . . ."

The thrust of the statement is to provide a fiscal program that would, as far as possible, lessen the reliance of state and local governments on the Treasury of the United States. It therefore makes five major recommendations:

1. Since local governments cannot meet the full cost of public services from their revenue sources, states should help equalize and improve the ability of their local units to pay for education and welfare through direct expenditures or grants-in-aid.

2. State governments should improve the administration of the property tax—the source of nearly 90 per cent of local tax revenue—and take steps to make it more productive. States should also increase the relative importance of state sales and personal income taxes.

3. A system of uniform regulations establishing equitable and clear limits of tax jurisdiction upon interstate businesses by individual states should be enacted by Congress if it cannot be assured by a compact of the states.

4. The national government through Congress and the Bureau of the Budget should establish procedures for a regular review of its grant-in-aid programs, in order to promote the efficient use of public funds and the beneficial participation in these programs by state and local governments.

5. When the budgetary situation permits a reduction in the federal taxes, it should be accomplished in part by giving individual taxpayers a partial credit against their federal personal income tax liability for state personal income tax payments.

These five recommendations are consistent with the arguments set forth in the CIMG-CED statements on modernizing local and state governments. They recognize the shift in power in the federal system to the national government and the growing interdependence among individuals, local communities, and the various regions of the nation. They acknowledge that with the growth of the nation what once were local problems are now matters of national concern—as Harlem, Roxbury, and Watts confirm. Thus CED aimed its program at cooperation among all levels of government, but in ways whereby the states would re-establish their powers and responsibilities under the Constitution.

Since the state governments and their local units account for two-thirds of all general expenditures for civilian domestic public services, these powers and responsibilities are immense. But, as CED says, for too many years the states and their local units of government "have not been performing as effectively as they should. State and local governments are for the most part poorly equipped to cope with the problems of the last third of the twentieth century." Demands for improved public services have accelerated beyond the "apparent capacity and will of state and local governments to provide them effectively." The result has been for the national government, with its superior revenue resources, to assume ever greater responsibility.

"The gap between state performance and responsibility could widen during the next decade as state and local governments grapple with increased demands for better education, better housing, better transportation, and less air and water pollution. If states are to perform more effectively they must strengthen their capacity, and that of local governments, to raise the revenues needed to meet these demands."

The statement declares that this revenue should be raised by improved state tax structures which would call for more equitable and uniform state-wide assessment of property for tax purposes. Greater reliance should be placed on the use of the personal income tax as well as on broad-based general retail sales taxes. A reformed tax system in most states would eliminate some of the need for turning to the federal government for financial aid.

Most interesting of CED's recommendations were those in this federal-state area, where the committee rejected the most widely publicized plan for sharing federal revenues with the states. The scheme whereby a specified percentage of federal tax revenue would be returned to the states in the form of general untied assistance grants met its disapproval—despite the fact that its authors, Walter Heller and Joseph A. Pechman, former member of the CED staff and presently a tax expert for the Brookings Institution, were advisors to the subcommittee. Instead, CED proposed revenue-sharing in the form of crediting federal income taxpayers for part of the personal income tax they would pay the states. This would presumably encourage the states to make greater efforts to raise their own tax revenues in the form of income taxes—a revenue source largely preempted by the federal government.

The main objection to the CED tax credit plan, duly noted in several dissenting footnotes, was that it would "coerce" the seventeen states that do not have personal income taxes into accepting a tax system hitherto found repugnant to their citizens.

In its next statement, on *Modernizing State Government*, CED made many proposals pertinent to the state of the union and of the states in 1967. They can be summed up as follows:

1. Practically every state should re-read and probably rewrite its constitution in the light of present day political and economic needs. Limitations to "constructive legislative and executive action" should be deleted. Modernization of local government in both rural and urban areas should be their goals. "Appropriate inclusions are a bill of rights, voting qualifications, provisions concerning political parties and elections, relationships between state and local governments, broad structural patterns for each of the three branches of government, the scope of gubernatorial authority in legislation and administration, and the means of amendment. Most, if not all, other matters are properly extraneous to . . . [constitutions]."

2. State legislatures should not have more than 100 members in total. Smaller states would be better served by still fewer members. In all states, sessions should be annual, without time limitations for adjournment. Committees should be few in number, organized along broad functional lines, and supplied with strong staff support. Public hearings should be held on all major legislation. Legislators should serve four-year terms and receive salaries commensurate with their responsibilities and equal to at least half that of the governor—a minimum of $15,000 per year.

3. Governors, who should be the *only* elected official (except a jointly-elected lieutenant governor) of the states, should serve four-year terms, be free to seek re-election as often as desired, and given authority and responsibility "for development of long-range plans, program supervision, budgetary preparation and execution, and personnel management." No governor should get less than $30,000 a year, the same salary as a congressman.

4. Court systems should be modernized into a state system. In many states the number of courts and jurisdictions should be reduced.

5. Much greater use should be made of interstate compacts between adjacent states with common problems.

Efficiency, reorganization, modernization, simplification—these were the aims expressed in CED's national policy for a renewed federalism. All, or almost all, were controversial, and some were revolutionary. But all seemed to be aimed at CED's goals of the "attainment and maintenance of high and secure standards of living for people in all walks of life. . . ."

Education was very much in the minds of Paul G. Hoffman and William Benton when they walked the University of Chicago campus dreaming up the idea that they grafted in CED in 1942. The economic education of businessmen and of educators by a mutual association of ideas and purposes lay at the heart of the committee from the beginning.

Before the war had ended there were 2,947 "community CED's" spread in cities and towns across the nation. The efforts of the old Field Division had been directed toward averting postwar unemployment by stimulating advance planning at all levels in the economy. The efforts of the Research Committee, under the direction of Ralph Flanders, were directed toward the same end. Mr. Flanders's group did the thinking about the government economic policies; Mr. Folsom's group did the educating and selling, spreading the word that unemployment and depression need not follow the war if business as a whole did its share of planning in the right direction. Between

22

Fighting Economic Illiteracy

them they helped avert any postwar depression, for they were listened to at the grass roots.

By 1962, CED's Executive Committee had become concerned about the extent of penetration of CED's point of view in the business community as a whole. One result of this concern was the establishment of a "policy forum program" through which CED once again set out to reach the ears and minds of business executives throughout the country on a face-to-face basis.

The purpose of these forums was to bring together business leaders in a community to spend a day examining, criticizing, and discussing in depth a current national policy statement. Since the "policy forum" was organized many such meetings have been held. Such statements as *Union Powers and Union Functions, Trade Negotiations for a Better Free World Economy, Improving Executive Management in the Federal Government,* and *Educating Tomorrow's Managers* have been discussed. The problems of managing government—local, state, national—and even such esoteric subjects as the budget process, have a wide appeal.

Developing Metropolitan Transportation Policies, designed to be of interest and use at the local level, was the subject of lively meetings in Seattle, Washington, and Denver, Colorado, where local research and planning on the subject at the time had reached the height of local involvement. The *Denver Post* found Denver's meeting "one of the most stimulating such events ever held in Denver."

A most successful meeting was held at Rochester, N. Y., where *Raising Low Incomes Through Improved Education,* a statement discussed later, was vigorously gone over. This meeting drew more than a hundred businessmen, educators, civic and government leaders in that troubled city, who listened and discussed heatedly the pertinent ways of implementing locally the CED position that improved education of the poor and unskilled is a road to higher incomes. The *Times-Union* said, in a lengthy report, that "if the CED statement suffers a bit from overstating the obvious, it nonetheless provided a catalyst for ideas on ways to overcome barriers to improved education and higher incomes for the poor." The newspaper reported that as a result many local businessmen left determined to "help the unskilled fill those vacant jobs that limit production and profits."

But, CED has also been concerned with a less exalted form of education—that of the youth of America in the schools, colleges, and universities.

Long before the phrase became well known, CED was deeply

disturbed by the prevalence of "economic illiteracy" among the products of the American school system. It was often said that CED was concerned because whole new generations were growing up who could not understand what CED was talking about. There was more to this than a joke. We have already seen the great difficulty that not only CED, but all who were interested in promoting the so-called new economics, had in dispelling the myths of conventional wisdom about fiscal policy. As more than one witness has testified, the "selling" to the American public of even so palatable a notion as a tax cut as late as 1962 entailed a vast program of educating the general public that this was not a dangerous, or even an un-American, thing to do.

The orbiting of Sputnik I in 1957 dramatized the widespread neglect of modern education in the United States. The Soviet challenge put the nation on the path to redemption, as the vast sums of money that have been spent since then for education by federal, state, and local governments has shown.

Years before the first man-made moon took to the heavens, the clear danger posed by undereducation in specific disciplines had alarmed the trustees of CED. As far back as 1947 the committee started to pay more than token attention to it. In that early postwar year it launched a program that has continually moved forward and is still progressing, although its emphasis has changed in the intervening years. At first it was directed toward correcting the malfunctioning of the teaching of economics in the secondary schools, but later it spread in many directions, even to the uneasy task of instructing Russian economists on how capitalism works. It was contiguous to CED's major educational effort—the dissemination of information through policy statements, supplementary papers, research studies, which have long been widely used in American college classrooms.

During World War II, CED was, of course, less of a national organization than a loose amalgam of small organizations scattered in hundreds of towns and cities throughout the United States. When these and their parent, the CED Field Division, were dissolved and CED was reorganized as a research and policy committee, there remained a need for something to satisfy the local longing for what they had represented.

New vistas of opportunity and enlightenment had been opened by the autonomous CED's. This was borne in upon CED when colleges and universities began to request help in setting up regional or local counterparts of CED—town and gown organizations in which local businessmen and nearby academicians could gather together to study local or regional economic problems affecting their own lives. At the same time representatives of various public schools turned to CED for help in creating summer programs in economics for high school teachers and administrators, who looked forward to finding ways of improving economic instruction in their own bailiwicks.

In 1947 CED created within its own organization what it called the Business-Education Committee. This was a ready-made answer to the calls from businessmen and educators. From its beginning the Business-Education Committee found itself involved in experimental projects in two areas, the local business communities and the public schools. The committee set forth certain rules for its own guidance: it would foster but not try to dominate; it would furnish help, both financial and consultant, but it would insist upon local autonomy. Heading this committee was James F. Brownlee, who gave much time and effort to the project as well as to his work with the Research and Policy Committee, of which he was an able member.

A partner in J. H. Whitney & Company, investment bankers, Brownlee gave six years to the Business-Education Committee. He was the right man for the job. California born and Harvard educated, he had gone from the vice presidency of General Foods to serve in high posts in the War Production Board, the Office of Price Administration, and the Office of Economic Stabilization. Later he was to be chairman of the board of Minute Maid. He was able to recruit influential men and women from private industry and finance, government, education, and labor, to aid his cause.

In 1949 he brought some seventy-five businessmen and educators to a two-day session in New York to discuss the results of twelve experimental programs that had been going on in various parts of the country during the past two years. One of the projects was a workshop on methods of improving economic education in high schools. This had been held for three weeks the previous summer at the Riverdale school in New York and was to become a model for many subsequent workshops elsewhere. It was attended by seventy-one secondary school administrators and teachers, under the sponsorship of CED and New York University School of Education. In the workshop the attendees participated in day-long discussions of how the economy operates, what it produces, how the product is distributed, as well as more esoteric subjects such as productivity, high employment, fiscal and monetary policy. Along with all this went debates on how best to devise understandable methods of imparting some of this information in high school classrooms. The instructors at this workshop came from seven colleges, six corporations, three federal agencies, the Brookings Institution, and one library.

At the conclusion of the three weeks' work it was the consensus of the sponsors that the experiment had been successful and should be carried on elsewhere. As a result the Joint Council on Economic Education was established.

This independent organization of educators and laymen set out to improve economic education in the schools on a national basis. Its chief sponsor, CED, agreed to assist the national service program of the Joint Council, but regional, state, and local activities were to be autonomous and self-supporting.

Although it only touched the surface of economic illiteracy, the Joint Council's summer workshops reached thousands of teachers. Under its aegis, state councils on economic education were set up until, in the mid-1950's, more than fifty workshops were in annual summer operation. CED maintained a small staff to supervise the distribution of funds from its own coffers and from The Ford Foundation via the Fund for Adult Education.

While all this was taking place CED also established a series of what it called College-Community Research Centers. These were set up in the hope of extending the CED process to the regional and local level. In eleven of these centers, businessmen and other community leaders joined in research projects with faculty members of nearby colleges and universities. They turned their attention to projects ranging from a study of state agricultural problems in Georgia, to an examination of state resources in Colorado. In Iowa, under the guidance of Harold Brenton, a Midwest banker and a CED trustee, where they sought to create what Mr. Brenton called a "cross fertilization between the academic and the practical," they studied the need for bringing new industry to that predominantly agricultural state.

These centers were maintained under the loose supervision of CED, which had not been the case with the educational workshops. They, too, drew funds through CED from the Fund for Adult Education, but in addition they used matching funds raised on home territory. The centers were eventually phased into the current Policy Forum program, but between 1947 and 1957 some 3,000 businessmen participated in twenty-six centers. Their efforts resulted in more than eighty publications. These studies and reports were not always of tangible value, beyond the educational stimulus that they gave to the participants. A few of them, however, extended beyond local boundaries in their inherent interest. One or two attracted national attention, such as a Minnesota study on the effect of international trade on the Midwest, or a Southern California analysis of future resources in that burgeoning state. It is fair to say that this application of "cross fertilization" to local economic problems had a stimulating effect in many areas. It increased public awareness of important issues, and encouraged the understanding of the "new economics" in those years.

But, with the spread of prosperity, interest in these centers began to wane. In 1958 CED reorganized the system and, at the same time, expanded its business-education program along other lines. Under the revitalized committee, set up enthusiastically by that old CED warhorse, J. Cameron Thomson, new CED Associate Centers were established in several cities where CED trustees were available to sponsor and encourage a research relationship between leading businessmen and scholars.

These "little CED's," as they became known, were to approach their self-chosen economic problems, that were not necessarily local ones, in much the same spirit as CED did in preparing its own statements on national policy. They also were encouraged to study and discuss the policy statements of national CED committees in Policy Forums, on the theory that the resulting feedback would prove mutually stimulating and useful in the development of CED's nationally directed policies.

Through this method the first center to be established, in Dallas, Texas, produced a statement on the role of private investment in underdeveloped nations. A Boston center worked closely with CED's Area Development Committee on a well-received series of monographs on metropolitan area development. Some of these were found to be of great value to city planners far from the Bay State. Kansas City tackled the ticklish Plains States problem of wheat surpluses. Southern California, as might be expected, delved into the intricacies of defense spending. And, as we have seen, a New York group revived CED's interest in the problems of financing new and small business with a study of small business investment companies.

The year 1959 saw a reinforcement of the effort to improve the teaching of economics at the high school level, and even below. Although the Joint Council had been carrying on its summer workshops for teachers and a series of experimental courses for potential teachers—attracting that summer as many as 1,638 participants in 46 workshops—these efforts were obviously not widespread enough. The fact was that less than 5 per cent of the nation's high school students, and less than 25 per cent of its college students, were receiving any meaningful instruction in economics.

Better teachers and more adequate teaching material were needed almost everywhere. The impact of the work of the Joint Council, which CED continued to support until 1964, needed to be buttressed by developing more adequate teaching materials, if the dismal science were ever to be more palatable to young minds. Several of CED's top economic advisors, aroused by the failure of their own profession to cope with this situation, urged CED to sponsor the formation of a national "task force on economics." They had in mind an independent group, similar to the Commission on Money and Credit and the Clark Kerr Labor Policy Study Group.

The CED trustees accepted this challenge and asked the national organization of the economics profession, the American Economic Association (AEA)—which was headed by Theodore W. Schultz of the University of Chicago and long a CED advisor—to lend its support. As a result Mr. Schultz set up a task force of a distinguished group of economists headed by George L. Bach of the Carnegie Institute of Technology.

This task force was assigned to work independently of both CED and the AEA in drafting a statement that would define the "minimum understanding of economics essential for good citizenship and [that was] attainable by high school students." Working with George Bach were Arno A. Bellack of Columbia University, Lester V. Chandler of Princeton, M. L. Frankel of the Joint Council, Robert A. Gordon of the University of California at Berkeley, Ben W. Lewis of Oberlin College, Paul A. Samuelson of M.I.T., and Floyd A. Bond of the University of Michigan who was the executive secretary—all of whom had also had experience with the CED process.

Using the report which George Bach and his associates produced, a second group, appointed by the Joint Council, was put to work selecting, from the great mass of existing but often unreadable teaching materials, a comprehensive bibliography of economic studies that were suitable for use in the high schools. The program included the production of new teaching materials and the devising of a test of basic economic competence for students who were being graduated from high schools.

Economic Education in the Schools, the report of the Bach task force, was published in September 1961. It was followed, a month later, with the CED supplementary paper, *Study Materials for Economic Education,* which was the report of the Joint Council's materials evaluation committee. Together these two documents marked an important breakthrough in modern education. For the first time the basic economic concepts which can be taught in secondary schools were defined and a list of usable working papers was collected. According to Fred Hechinger, education editor of *The New York Times,* this CED-sponsored action made economics "the first of the social sciences to follow the revolutionary reforms instituted in mathematics and the sciences." From many quarters—from the *Catholic School Journal* to *Kiplinger's Letter*—praise for this accomplishment poured in.

There was praise, but there was also dissent.

The evaluation committee had examined 7,000 books and pamphlets on economic subjects. Out of these it had selected 97 items as appropriate to set before malleable high school students. On the recommended list were publications bearing the imprint of the U.S. Chamber of Commerce (7), the Committee for Economic Development (5), the AFL-CIO (4), the Federal Reserve System (4), the Brookings Institution (3), and the United States Government (9). Markedly missing was a single title published by the National Association of Manufacturers, which in the past had stirred up much discord among educators because of its conservative nature and its propagandistic approach to economics and history.

Whether it was piqued because of this omission or due to some other more deeply hidden cause, the NAM reacted violently to the two CED-sponsored documents, ignoring the task force's independent status. It mailed to its members a circular attacking the task force, the evaluation committee, and the CED. It followed this up with an attack on CED for having backed this venture in an editorial in its newsletter entitled, "Whom or What Does CED Represent?" The result was that several member companies of the NAM withdrew their financial support from CED, the first time this had happened since CED published its first policy statements on tariff policy, when a few financial supporters withdrew. (CED has since stated that most of the recalcitrants have returned to the fold.)

The NAM attack was spurred on, also, by *The Wall Street Journal,* which detected strong "leftish" leanings in the task force report and blamed this by inference on the CED. The *Journal* had seldom supported CED on its editorial page, although it had given it more than adequate and fair treatment in its news columns.

Irascible Lawrence Fertig, a financial and economic commentator for the Scripps Howard newspapers, also blasted off against the left-wing stance which he read into the statements. And on Christmas Eve, Donald I. Rogers, then financial page editor of the now defunct *New York Herald Tribune*, filled his column with a diatribe which condemned the two statements for "poisoning the schools."

Over the years the CED had been occasionally attacked for its "leftish" tendencies, but on most occasions such broadsides had come from sources with obvious right-wing axes to grind. Paul G. Hoffman had been the first chairman to be assaulted. He had chosen the policy of answering such attacks by silence rather than by angry retort. The Rogers attack, however, was so filled with factual error that CED Chairman Donald K. David, then vice chairman of the board of The Ford Foundation, felt constrained to call the editor's attention to them. Eventually Mr. Rogers retracted his remarks—when he found that the First National City Bank of New York was basing a course in economics for its executives and staff members on the two CED publications!

The Bach paper and its companion also contributed to journalistic history. *The Wall Street Journal's* attack stirred George Bach to write a long rebuttal, which the newspaper printed in full, along with another editorial. The combination—an unprecedented combination —filled the entire editorial page of the *Journal* except for one little corner left for its joke column, "Pepper and Salt."

As it had with the Kerr report on labor problems, the Research and Policy Committee completed its program by issuing its own policy statement on economic education,[1] in February 1962, entitled, *Economic Literacy for Americans*. A. L. Williams, then president of IBM, was chairman of the working subcommittee which prepared it. It leaned slightly more to the "right" than did the task force report, more heavily stressing the role of individual freedom and free enterprise in the American economy. In no other way was it a retraction of the gist of *Economic Education in the Schools*. By the time it appeared the task force document had reached a distribution of some 60,000 copies and the evaluation paper, a distribution of some 50,000. But CED's own statement, *Economic Literacy for Americans*, which the National Education Association, the National School Board As-

---

[1] This experience led CED to change its practice of publishing background papers prepared for its use before its own policy statement was completed. CED now issues such papers only after its own views are on record.

sociation, and many state and local school boards adopted, went on to become a "best seller," reaching a circulation of 128,752 copies by April 1962. In addition, kits containing 47 of the 97 recommended teaching materials (three newly published NAM titles were on a revised list!) were sent free to some 24,500 high school principals.

The excitement and the presumably effective results of all this spurred the Business-Education Committee to go even farther in the CED crusade against economic illiteracy. Out of it came the CBS College of the Air television study course on "the American economy." It made television history.

This course was a joint effort by the AEA, the Joint Council, the task force, and the Learning Resources Institute. Financial support came from The Ford Foundation and eighty-five corporations, the latter being mostly lined up in this endeavor by Herbert Malley, the director of CED's own fund-raising division. A brilliant economist with a "telegenic" personality, the ideal person to conduct the 160-lesson course was found in John R. Coleman, then of Carnegie Institute of Technology, now president of Haverford College. A "class" of one million viewers, avid to find some way of brightening up the dismal science, took the course—the largest television class ever assembled until then. Community and corporate viewing was arranged in many schools and offices. Five thousand two hundred viewers enrolled for credit at participating colleges. McGraw-Hill Book Company published a text book designed especially for this course. Hundreds of film reproductions of the course were later distributed for local use.

It takes little imagination to believe the boast of CBS that more teachers learned the elements of economics from this program than had ever before in the course of an academic year.

But for all this activity, important and productive though it may have seemed at the time, the scourge of economic illiteracy was unfortunately far from being wiped out in the United States. Economic myths and pre-occupation with the same Puritan ethic that had disturbed Walter Heller were hard to eradicate in a nation where some 90 per cent of its high school students received no formal education in economics.

Awareness of this dismal situation spread slowly, but it spread. By 1966 it had penetrated the consciousness of the United States Senate. Or, at least, the consciousness of Senator Russell R. Long of Louisiana. In that year he persuaded his fellow lawmakers to authorize a study of economic education by a subcommittee of the

Joint Economic Committee. Senator Proxmire of Wisconsin had replaced Representative Wright Patman as chairman of the Joint Economic Committee and thus Mr. Patman became chairman of the subcommittee on economic education. In the spring of 1967 the Patman subcommittee held hearings. They revealed what CED had long ago discovered and publicized—that most voters do not understand economics.

During the national debate over wage-price guidelines, Secretary of Labor Willard Wirtz had caustically commented on the lack of understanding on the part of the general public of the philosophy underlying the productivity-trend standard. He had blamed this in great measure on the inability of that massive organ of education, the national press, to express itself clearly on this subject. By inference, at least, he had damned the newspapers for not themselves employing writers sufficiently trained in economics to do their job. Now Senator Long put the matter clearly when he told the Joint Economic Committee, "The achievement of the goals of the Employment Act requires a widespread understanding of the implications of taxation, government spending, monetary policy, and other measures of our free enterprise economy." Both he and Representative Wilbur Mills recalled the difficulty in getting the public to understand the economic reasoning that lay behind the tax cut in the face of a large federal deficit in 1964. Senator Long cited the fact that most voters were even then finding "incomprehensible the Administration's action in suspending the 7 per cent investment tax credit in 1966 and restoring it in 1967."

After sixteen years of close association with CED, the Joint Council drew away in 1963. This came about as a result of a lengthy review by a special CED study group working with the Business-Education Committee, which decided the time was propitious for the Joint Council to carry on its work independently. The tie to CED, loose as it was, prevented the enlistment of enlarged support that the Council needed. A terminal grant from CED helped to tide it over the separation period, and the Council now supports itself and carries on its work on a larger scale. Of course, CED's involvement with education did not end with this occurrence, nor did it lessen its interest in economic education.

For a long time many trustees of CED had questioned whether the schools were offering the type of education that was best suited for students who expected to pursue business careers. Others had given this subject considerable attention. In the late 1950's, for example, it had become a serious enough problem for The Ford Foundation and the Carnegie Corporation to commission and finance important studies in this field. The resulting reports leveled serious charges against existing business schools and graduate schools of business administration. The principal points on which the two studies [2] agreed were that academic standards were too low, that too few top students were being drawn to business programs, that many specialized vocational courses were of doubtful long-run value, that teaching methods failed to develop either analytical or managerial abilities, that faculty quality was less than adequate, and that postgraduate programs were weak.

At CED's request, Leonard Silk, then senior editor of *Business Week*, was engaged to review these two learned tomes. He found fault with them, especially because he felt each had been written from too narrow a point of view, that of economics professors. They unfortunately were built on too little factual evidence as to what types of education actually did lead to successful business careers. Mr. Silk's study, originally done for committee consideration, was published in 1960 by CED with the title, *The Education of Businessmen*. This supplementary paper was not the only research CED conducted as its subcommittee on business education moved slowly toward a policy statement. Papers on the type of education needed for business careers were obtained from authorities in England, France, and Sweden, as well as in the United States. Interviews were conducted with chief officers of major corporations on the education, experience, and other qualities sought in prospective top executives. Deans of eighteen leading business schools joined the CED trustees at Aspen, Colorado, for a two-day conference, and inquisitive visits by members of the subcommittee were made to sixteen campuses.

The resulting document, *Educating Tomorrow's Managers*, was interesting and provocative, not only because of its "horse's-mouth" character. It was primarily a defense of education in the exact meaning of the word rather than of specialized education in a narrower sense. The major aim of colleges, it said, should not be to supply the business community with people trained to perform their first job,

---

[2] Robert A. Gordon and James E. Howell, *Higher Education for Business* (New York: Columbia University Press, 1959) and Frank C. Pierson, *The Education of American Businessmen* (New York: McGraw-Hill Book Company, 1959).

but to provide all students with a basic education that would serve the individual throughout his entire career. Out of every five college undergraduates, the committee found, one would major in business. This minority would be among the 26 million young people expected at that time to enter the labor force by 1970. From them would be recruited the 200,000 persons necessary to fill the "top" managerial posts in the United States. Thousands more would be needed for the lower echelons of business administration. All of these should be given a realistic picture, during their undergraduate days, of what to expect when they were graduated. Their education should be directed so that they might live "worthy" and "important" lives with a sense of "dignity, purpose, and self-fulfillment," whether they gained great wealth or not.

The education of the businessman, the report continued, should not end at either the undergraduate or the graduate level. Because of the need for a continuing, even life-long, process of intellectual growth, educators and businessmen should work together to develop managerial and leadership qualities. Achievement of this goal should be the responsibility of private enterprise.

In reporting the publication of the statement, *Business Week* said: "Last week CED shot an arrow into the air—this time a national policy statement entitled *Educating Tomorrow's Managers*. Not so high flown as other shafts aimed at the need for improved business education, CED's shot may prick the conscience and self-interest of management itself." That, of course, was the statement's purpose. In it CED was speaking to its peers.

Well aware of youth's oft-expressed antipathy to business, as frequently reported by pollsters on the nation's campuses,[3] the CED statement said it should be the concern of business itself to find ways of attracting the best students to its fold. This could be done only by recruiting better teachers and developing through research better methods of operation for the business schools everywhere. Managers of the schools should be aware of this. For only by developing sound, long-range programs in education and research, could business schools attract the financial help, from business itself, needed to do the necessary job. It was a matter of cooperation: business schools and

---

[3] According to a 1967 article in *The Saturday Review*, this aloofness to careers in counting houses or corporate stables is still a matter of deep dismay to management.

the business community should work together to develop a relationship comparable to that enjoyed by the best professional schools and practitioners in other fields.

CED's concern for the quality of education was not confined to the needs of the business community or to the high schools' need for better economic instruction. In the mid-1950's Beardsley Ruml had once asked CED how it could be a committee for economic development without being concerned with the state of the nation's public schools. Later Marion B. Folsom was to lead CED into further concern with the quality and availability of education as an important economic factor affecting the lives of everyone, from pre-school age upward. The postwar years had been critical ones, as far as the primary and secondary schools were concerned. In a dozen years public school population had increased by 11 million boys and girls. From 1947 through 1959 expenditures for public schools had tripled, from $4.3 billion to $14.4 billion. It was anticipated that the following decade would see a 50 per cent further increase in costs. The question that bothered CED—and millions of other American taxpayers—was, how to pay for the schools we need and want.

For two years a subcommittee headed by Ralph Lazarus, then president of Federated Department Stores, worked on this perplexing problem. The most difficult question that faced this group was how to strike the delicate balance between federal, state, and local responsibility and domain. This was a test of ingenuity for, as we have seen, CED had for many years skittered away from crossing the line of federal intervention. But, on the other hand, it had never stated that the federal government should not intervene with economic expenditures which the people in their collective wisdom desired. In a national atmosphere that, since Sputnik I and later revelations engendered by the revolution for civil rights, was sparked by an overwhelming demand for better schools and better-paid teachers, CED found a solution that it hoped would be acceptable to federalists and nationalists alike.

The statement, *Paying for Better Public Schools,* made clear that the brunt of the burden lay with the states, for historic reasons, if for no others. For a wide variety of reasons stretching back to colonial days the states themselves had divided responsibility for education into small units. The result was the school district. And this was exactly where CED now said reform should start.

The first thing to be done was to make mandatory in every state the immediate reorganization of small school districts into effective units of local government. An adequate school program, as the report made clear, cannot be conducted by a school system having less than 2,000 students. On the contrary, economic, social, and educational advantages continue to increase as the system reaches a minimum of 25,000 students. But, in 1957, some 30,000 school districts were operating with less than 50 students.

The revision of school districts would, of course, increase costs that would be manifest in increased tax rates. But the accompanying increase in efficiency of operation and quality of product should, in the long run, make the tax burden more tolerable. These costs should fall more heavily upon the state than on the community. States, therefore, should revise their tax systems to meet the situation. Upon assuming this responsibility the states should lay down minimum standards, equitably applicable throughout the state, through what is known as a foundation program—a minimum standard of educational competence.

But what if the states balked at such a program, especially on the grounds of inability to pay? Should the federal government step in with funds? It was on this primarily ideological thorn that the committee trod most gingerly. In the end it reached a compromise, but one that for a variety of reasons dissatisfied fourteen of the fifty-two trustees eligible to vote on the document.

The cause of this minor rebellion was simple. The statement proposed that federal grants for public schools should be made to those states where the income per school child was substantially below the national level. These grants should be allocated without any strings that even suggested federal control of educational policy.

"We find," the statement said, "that in most of the country additional federal school support is unnecessary. Hence we oppose federal grants to support schools throughout the country. However, we also find that some parts of the nation cannot, with any probable allocation of their own resources, support their schools at a level that meets the nation's requirements. Although we are reluctant to see further expansion of the federal role in education, we conclude that to secure adequate schools throughout the country it is necessary for the federal government to supplement school finances in states where incomes are lowest."

The footnotes of the dissenting trustees reflected within CED the same diversity of views that was prevalent throughout the country. Why, one dissenter asked, should citizens of one state help pay for the problems of another state, even if the latter was one of the underdeveloped Southern states? Others felt that it was unwarranted to divert federal funds to an activity that is a local responsibility, even if the activity "is clearly needed." Still others felt the proposal was merely an entering wedge to all sorts of other needless federal grants to states, which should pay their own way with their own taxes. But others stood with Beardsley Ruml, who said: "I believe the federal government has a responsibility to share in the support of schools throughout the country and that the goal of adequate education demands that it do so."

Strangely enough, neither the report nor the dissenters openly raised the question of integration, thus evading one of the tremendous problems of the vastly increased federal aid to public education that has come about since 1960. In those years the national trend seems to have been toward the philosophy expressed by Mr. Ruml, who made a strong plea for what he called federal *support*, rather than federal *aid*, for education.

> *Support implies interest and duty. Certainly we have a federal interest in making certain that our future citizens can communicate and can compute. These are the basics on which our society rests; and having a federal society as we do, a federal interest in the basics of education follows inescapably.*
>
> *A federal duty to support the public flows from both the national interest and from the fact that access to the growing income of the country is most direct and most equitably imposed through the federal income tax.*
>
> *The federal duty and interest in education are not qualified by the income of the child or of the state in which he lives.*

Despite the objections, the report made a good case for its limited federal support program. In many respects it was a bold move on the part of CED, for the report did indeed go farther than any previous committee document in its approval of the appropriation of federal funds for state and local use. As has been shown, this limited access of the states to federal funds was advocated to an even greater extent in later policy statements, especially those dealing with urban problems and the reorganization of state government operations. As of 1961 CED calculated that the total cost of its suggested program would be about $600 million annually, certainly not an overwhelming, disastrous amount.

The fact that the report was widely hailed in the national press and that the section on federal aid was generally considered one of its strongest features cannot have failed to encourage the "liberal wing" of CED. The report, as Ralph McGill said in his syndicated column, was historically significant because "for the first time in the nation's history" corporate business had formally revealed not merely "the great waste of young talent in inadequate schools" but had made a "major endorsement of federal aid to education." As *Time* magazine interpreted the statement, what CED was saying was, "Where the decentralized system cannot provide good schools, federal aid is an urgent necessity."

This money would go to those states where the "personal income per student in average daily attendance in public schools is below 80 per cent of the national average." These federal funds could be used for any item in the public school budget—salaries, current expenses, or capital outlays. They would be given without federal controls over curricula, the only conformance necessary being with the regulations established by the Office of Education for uniform reporting of average daily attendance and school finance. They would go only to *public* schools.

Three-fourths of the CED trustees voting supported this general program. Three wanted federal funds to go to *every* state, regardless of pupil income. Eight opposed any federal grants (beyond any existing programs), and one would confine grants to use for construction on a matching basis. Thus, as T. V. Houser later told the House Committee on Education and Labor, the proposal was not a compromise position. It was aimed, as he said, at alleviating the great geographic inequality of school expenditures, and to enable low-income states to finance public school education "at levels meeting a minimum standard of adequacy." While this would hardly meet Galbraithian standards of an affluent society, it was a creditable step in the right direction.

Furthermore, it was an equitable way of doing business. As T. V. Houser explained it to Congress, the people—and not the states—pay federal taxes. An individual with a $15,000 income pays the same *federal* tax whether he lives in New York or Mississippi. A "high-income state," therefore, is simply one where there are more rich people than there are in "low-income states." Thus the argument that the "richer" states would support the "poorer" ones is fallacious.

The statement also touched on another area where it said the federal government had a responsibility—research and development. It urged the United States Office of Education to do more research aimed at improving efficiency in education which, as Mr. Houser told Congress, "simply means getting the best quality of education possible for the money that is spent."

Thus the committee was, in a way, restating an old theme that it had been repeating from its early postwar days—that local, state, and federal government, along with individual citizens (and especially businessmen) have a joint responsibility. Together they can promote a school structure in which all schools can provide education at least at an adequate level and in which the stronger school units can forge ahead and, by their example, create new standards of excellence that will become new targets elsewhere.

We live, as we always have, in a changing world and one of the greatest changes of our time has been the rapid, even terrifying, automation of our society. But to CED automation has not been as terrifying as it seems to have been to many other groups deeply concerned with the general welfare. It early rejected, by inference at least, any suggestion that automation *per se* entailed insoluble problems and it would not listen to that school of thought which envisioned vast armies of unemployed fleeing before the monster machine. It had an answer to the threat of automation and that answer to a great extent was education.

Strangely enough, CED has never published a statement of national policy on automation. That, however, does not mean that it had not studied the problem at length and in depth. Among its subcommittees there had long been one with the awkward title of Subcommittee on the Adaptation of the Economy to Change. The chairman of this group was Marion B. Folsom, whose business career with Eastman Kodak and whose public career had culminated as Secretary of Health, Education, and Welfare under President Eisenhower, had brought him for many years close to the subject.

This subcommittee studied the whole field of industrial change for several months. The statistics which it gathered—at a time when the unemployment rate was around 7 per cent and when many people were concerned as to whether this rate might become permanent—revealed that unemployment was concentrated in the uneducated and untrained groups. For this reason the committee decided —and quite correctly, as later events proved—to develop a policy statement confined to showing the need for better education and training of low-income families. The result was the statement, *Raising Low Incomes through Improved Education*, issued in 1965.

In testimony to the Senate Committee on Manpower and Employment made back in 1963, Mr. Folsom had made several observations that take on added interest in light of the urban turbulence that swept the nation in the summer of 1967.

"Education," Mr. Folsom said, "has kept pace with the shift of demand toward more skilled workers sufficiently to prevent the accumulation of a growing proportion of unskilled people with relatively low incomes and higher risk of unemployment. But it has not caught up sufficiently to eliminate the pool of workers with productivity far below the average, incomes far below the average, and exceptionally high risk of unemployment."

This, of course, was the gist of the 1965 statement. Mr. Folsom stressed the need for better schools for children from poor and uneducated families, with smaller classes, better guidance, and "more capable and understanding teachers." He recognized the costs involved but said "it will be well worth the investment."

"It is time for the federal government to recognize the national interest in the improvement of general primary and secondary education. It should back up this recognition by providing federal financial assistance where it is not needed. . . .

"Federal funds spent on improvement and expansion of the education available to Americans is the best possible investment of tax money. . . . Federal aid will not relieve the states and localities of their financial responsibilities. It would . . . only emphasize the need for improvement of education that arises from technological change and our rising standards of economic and social performance. . . ."

Mr. Folsom challenged private enterprise to play its necessary part, and suggested that "business will find investment in the education and training of its employees of increasing value."

His words found an echo in the 1965 statement.

> Unless all the resources of our federal, state, local private-nonprofit and private-business education and training system are brought to bear, our educational goals will not be met. More than money is needed. To achieve our goals will require leadership, imagination, talent. It also will require better adaptation of our educational system to the needs and opportunities of the economic system and better use of the capacities of the economic system to help meet the needs of education. The federal government alone, for all its great financial capacity, cannot supply these requirements. One of the main purposes of

this statement is to urge greater efforts by states, localities, and private business to discharge their proper responsibilities.

The statement then offered a series of integrated recommendations, some new, some based on existing machinery, all reconciled to the increased role of the federal government. These recommendations follow in brief.

1. Education should begin at the earliest possible age, even before kindergarten. It should be provided for all children, but mostly those who suffer the disadvantages of being reared in homes and neighborhoods that generate little learning and even less motivation. Under the Education Act of 1965, the federal government was even then providing funds for this purpose, through what came to be known as the Head Start program. Continuation of this important process was so much a part of the over-all, day-by-day educational process, responsibility for it should not only be a part of the federal responsibility but means for its continuance should be assured by the states and localities.

2. States and school districts should modernize vocational training in the schools to bring it into line with occupational requirements where they can be foreseen, and to improve the ability of adults to adapt to unforeseen changes in occupational requirements. States that have not yet done so should establish adequate systems of conveniently available educational institutions beyond high school—junior colleges, community colleges, or technical institutes.

3. Programs for training and retraining adults, whether employed or unemployed, carried on by the states for many years, had then just begun to receive federal support under the Manpower Development and Training Act. These programs should be developed further, but with more financial support by the states for their expansion, the statement said. At the same time programs to eliminate adult illiteracy should be launched by citizens in communities throughout the nation. In view of the demonstrated returns to the efforts already made, existing programs for rehabilitating the physically handicapped should be expanded. States should appropriate the amounts required to obtain the federal funds allotted in the federal-state matching program. In federal programs for assisting economically distressed regions, such as Appalachia, more emphasis should be placed on financial support for the construction and equipping of needed educational and rehabilitation facilities. More use should be made of the capacities of business for training. Businesses should move systematically to foresee and prepare for changes in their labor requirements.

In general, the statement said, "it will be necessary to operate the educational system more efficiently, by better organization of school districts, quicker application of modern techniques, and more research to develop better techniques, in order to hold down the costs of the growing educational program and improve its quality."

The need for a comprehensive and independent study of the entire United States financial structure and its problems had long been apparent to students of the American economic scene. As far back as 1948 CED had called for the establishment of a temporary commission to study the possibilities of improving the structure and policies "of monetary, budgetary and related institutions." It had, of course, made piecemeal forays into these areas. But as the Federal Reserve Act was approaching its 45th anniversary, the clamor for an over-all examination grew stronger. There had been no such scrutiny since the Senate had undertaken one between 1908 and 1911, partly out of which the Federal Reserve System had emerged in 1913.

It is true that the Aldrich report had been born after a financial panic swept the country and at a time when the solidity of the banking system was in danger. No such critical situation existed when President Eisenhower suggested a presidential commission for this purpose in 1957. But the

23

A Look at Money and Credit

changes in banking regulations, the creation of a chain of federal financial agencies, the growth of commercial banking, the birth of new nonfinancial institutions, and the surge of personal credit facilities, did call for a new hard look.

For a variety of reasons, both good and bad, Congress rejected the Eisenhower proposal out of hand—and then could not agree on how to go about conducting its own investigation. President Eisenhower went to his friends in the business and banking communities, in the face of his congressional rebuff, suggesting that a privately endowed nonpolitical commission be set up. One of those whom he approached was Donald K. David, then chairman of CED and vice chairman of The Ford Foundation. After much careful preparation, aided by outstanding economic advisers, David induced the CED trustees to charter an independent group known as the Commission on Money and Credit and The Ford Foundation to furnish the necessary funds for a three-year study of the money and credit institutions and policies of the United States.

Although created under the auspices of CED, the CMC was wholly independent of the committee in every respect. Its 25-man board, however, contained six CED trustees and the chairman was Frazar B. Wilde, who resigned as chairman of the CED Research and Policy Committee to take that post. Besides these businessmen the board harbored bankers, representatives of labor and agriculture, lawyers, a professional economist, a former Federal Reserve Board chairman, and an ex-Cabinet member.[1]

Work on the unprecedented inquiry began in the spring of 1958 and the report (there was to be only one) was made public on June 19, 1961. During that time more than 100 persons, many of them leading scholars, contributed their thoughts to the final result. More than 100 papers, many of them later published in eight volumes, were prepared by experts for use by the committee and its task forces. A small staff of economists working under Bertram Fox, director of research at the Harvard Graduate School of Business Administration and Eli Shapiro, then professor of banking at Massachusetts Institute of Technology, now at Harvard University, wrote or rewrote scores of documents and digests. The full commission held twelve sessions, none for less than two days at a time and several that went on for five consecutive days. Each of the six task forces, one each on such subjects as monetary policy, fiscal policy,

---

[1] See p. 243 for the full list.

A Look at Money and Credit   223

coordination, etc., met at least six times as a body. Six trade organizations—banks, insurance, mortgagers, etc.—prepared full length monographs and the United States Treasury and the Federal Reserve System answered a series of questions at book length, in lieu of hearings. The monographs and the question-and-answer documents were later published in book form. Countless conferences by staff and commission members were held with Federal Reserve, Treasury, and other government staffs and officials, and with leaders of private financial institutions, for the same purpose.

Because of the diversity of interests, backgrounds, opinions, and aspirations represented by the commissioners, and the theories and ideologies of their advisors, the meetings were intense, argumentative, educational, and in the long run productive. Debates between Stanley Ruttenberg, then chief economist for the CIO-AFL, and David Rockefeller, chairman of the Chase Manhattan Bank, or between that veteran New Dealer, Isador Lubin, who never for a moment forgot to keep in mind the social values and social goals of policy, and Charles Shuman, the commission's and agriculture's stubbornly eloquent arch-conservative; or between the politically aware and articulate Henry Fowler, later Secretary of the Treasury, and sharp-minded, acidulous Philip Klutznick; or between that great self-made expert on the Federal Reserve, Marriner Eccles, and the entire commission, produced lively meetings.

Even when the final report—which was far more *their* report than that of its staff or learned advisors—was written, the debates continued, as some 140-odd footnotes to the 85 recommendations testify. Stanley Ruttenberg, for example, contributed 82 comments (not all were outright dissents) and Charles Shuman contributed 45. Ruttenberg's stemmed for the most part from his disagreements with the commission's conclusions concerning monetary policy, while Shuman's contributed a consistent critique of its stand on fiscal policy, especially where it called for increased governmental intervention into the manipulation of the economy. These comments (and almost every commissioner had something to say in the footnotes) reveal the many ideological, political, and even tempermental differences that had to be overcome in reaching what Mr. Wilde believed was a consensus of national economic belief.

Whether it was such a consensus or not, the *Report* attracted national attention upon publication. Indeed, it continues to this day to attract attention. The Information Division of CED, which directed its publication and distribution, has revealed that, six years later, hardly a week passes but that some reference to some aspect of the *Report* appears in CED's accumulation of press clippings, either in an editorial, a news story, or in the text of a speech.

The fact that the *Report*, which in effect had been "commissioned" by President Eisenhower, was presented by Mr. Wilde and other members of CMC to President Kennedy at a White House ceremony, helped get it off to a good start. But it quickly brought brickbats as well as praise.

Representative Wright Patman of Texas called it a "two-million dollar boondoggle," but that was before President Kennedy adopted it in part as his own. Then, despite its chairman's original sniff, Mr. Patman's Joint Economic Committee held a week of hearings in August, an unprecedented congressional action regarding a privately produced statement of this nature. Later, as we shall see, President Kennedy, in an equally unprecedented development, used the *Report* as the basis of his own *Economic Report* in January 1962.

There he said: "The Commission's *Report* represents the results of thorough analysis and deliberation by a private group of leading citizens representative of business, labor, finance, agriculture, and the professions. The Commission's findings and recommendations deserve careful consideration by the Congress, the Executive, and the public—consideration that should result in legislative and executive actions to strengthen government policy under the Employment Act and to improve the financial system of the United States."

President Kennedy was assassinated before he could translate his adaptations of the *Report* into a rounded political program. That he intended to do so is conjecture, but based on good evidence.

The report—entitled *Money and Credit: Their Influence on Jobs, Prices, and Growth*—had one undeniable virtue: it avoided that semantic quagmire in which so many reports, white papers, and policy statements have disappeared. In places, however, it suffered from a plethora of minutiae, and in others it seemingly failed to present enough supporting documentation to back the positions it arrived at. Many of its academic critics—and it was reviewed at length in nearly all of the leading economic journals both here and abroad—felt that it dwelt too often with the obvious, forgetting that it was not supposed primarily to be a learned dissertation on economics or a provocateur of untried theories, but a study in the political economy that lay behind the present financial institutions of the United States. Outside the economics profession it was generally received on that basis. For this reason, the two major recommendations that attracted the most journalistic attention were indeed more political than economic, although both were presented as rational means of achieving the economic results called for in the 282-page document. These were the sections dealing with fiscal reform and with the institutional machinery of the Federal Reserve System.

These two proposals for major changes in organization were not, perhaps, the most economically meaningful of the report's eighty-odd recommendations (which ranged from elimination of insurance "basket clauses" to elimination of the federal debt ceiling!), but they touched, bravely and outspokenly, on subjects that were certain to arouse emotional response in the public sectors.

One called for giving the President unprecedented power to use the federal tax system as a countercyclical tool.

The other would have deprived the Federal Reserve System, through basic reorganization, of what the mythologists have long called its "independence."

The controversy which these two sections of the report revived —for neither was original with CMC—is still with us. In 1967, when fiscal policy and monetary policy both were bubbling, *The Washington Post* was using it in its campaign against extended presidential taxing power. At the same time, *The New York Times* was using it as a pillar of strength in its lonely campaign to give the President just that power. At the time of publication, most objective critics felt that these predominantly political areas were either the strongest or the most dangerous in the report. Many, however, pointed out that it was not their contents that made them so important as it was the eminently respectable backing given them by the commission itself.

Whatever the cause, they struck fire.

In the *report's* section on fiscal policy the commission strongly recommended the use of a variety of hitherto untried techniques that would disassociate *"temporary and reversible changes for stabilization purposes from permanent and structural changes."* This, of course, was in line with a long-held CED position. But the commission went farther than CED had ever wanted to go. In its opinion the best way to achieve this desired flexibility was to write out a formula, which it proceeded to do with a will. And so it asked Congress to grant to the President of the United States limited, conditional power to make temporary countercyclical adjustments in the first-bracket rate of the individual income tax.

This power, the commission said, should be available only after the President had issued a statement that, in his judgment (presumably after consultation with Treasury, Federal Reserve, and Council), "economic conditions were running significantly counter to the objectives of the Employment Act." This adjustment could be either up or down. In either case it would be five percentage points, or one-quarter of the 1961 rate of 20 per cent. It would be limited for six months, unless Congress should decide to extend its duration. Before taking effect, this conditional power would be subject to legislative veto by a concurrent resolution of both houses of Congress. The presidential request would lie before Congress for up to 60 days. During this time Congress would approve it by rejecting the concurrent resolution, or disapprove it by voting for the resolution. If no action were taken by Congress, the tax raise or tax cut would become effective at the end of the 60 days.

Monetary policy, as CED had long contended, *is* the Federal Reserve. For this reason the commission's controversial chapter on monetary policy is, to a great extent, an analysis and critique of the central banking system of the United States. This system probably has more sensitive defenders and outspoken opponents than any other adjunct of the federal policy-making process. It is little wonder that the *Report* came in for considerable chastisement for its severe but direct efforts moderately to change certain methods of operating this quasi-public institution. If carried out its suggestions would undoubtedly have a lasting effect on its institutional makeup and on national economic trends.

Although William McC. Martin, the long-revered chairman of the Federal Reserve Board, agreed with segments of the *Report*, even his words did not soften the reception it received at the hands of many who labored under the delusion that the Federal Reserve System had been designed as an organization set apart from all others concerned with money and credit in the United States. This school maintained that the strength of the System lay in its complete disassociation from any form of control over monetary policy —even suggestive control—by Congress or the executive branch. It was indeed a separate institution, answerable only to Congress and the public in turgid annual reports. This "independence"—an independence owned by no other central bank, even the Bank of England—was mostly reverenced by supporters of "tight money," those whose greatest fear was even an ounce of inflation. Although this was, of course, an impossible position to maintain in the face of economic reality, this school had nevertheless managed to make "independence of the Federal Reserve" a part of the litany of national policy, until it was even half-believed by those who knew better.

The commission was not against "independence," but it wanted the Federal Reserve System to be a coordinate part of the entire machinery of money and credit and wanted to make it more effective in carrying out economic policy. It wanted it to function with speed and determination and in that flexible manner which CED had espoused several years before. The commission did not believe that monetary policy should exist in a vacuum. It felt that fiscal policy had to bear the brunt of the economic load. By the very means it suggested, which nibbled at the mythical independence, it hoped to make monetary policy a more formidable weapon to be used in the fight for stable prices, high employment, and growth.

The aspect of the *Report* with the greatest shock effect in the monetary area was the proposal that the chairman and vice chairman of the Federal Reserve Board, who should be chosen from among the board's membership, should serve a four-year term *coterminous* with that of the President.

Although historians agree the coterminous rule was the intention of the original Federal Reserve Act, the vicissitudes of human behavior had long since thrown this schedule askew. Now that its revival was suggested it was looked upon as a "plot" to bring the System under the presidential—and therefore political—thumbscrew, rather than as an honest attempt to bring the central bank into the administrative echelons of government policy.

Other suggestions were suspect for the same reason. The commission would cut the size of the Board to five members with overlapping ten-year terms, one expiring each odd-numbered year. Members, who would be eligible for reappointment, should not be chosen for their geographical and occupational qualifications, as the Act then decreed, but for their brains and ability. They should be paid at the highest level for appointive government officers. This Board, rather than the present "open market committee," should handle the all-important open market operations, setting open market policy after consultation with the heads of the twelve Federal Reserve Banks. The Board also should determine the discount rate, the

System's second most important function, for all banks, where it should be the same rate.

In January 1962, President Kennedy used the *Report* to good purpose, devoting many pages of his *Economic Report* to its contents. From the CMC paper he drew up an agenda for a program of fiscal and monetary reform that he did not live to see carried out.

President Kennedy called upon Congress to help him in "erecting a defense-in-depth against future recession." The basic elements of this defense were "(1) Presidential standby authority for prompt, temporary income tax reductions, (2) Presidential standby authority for capital improvements expenditures, and (3) a permanent strengthening of the unemployment compensation system." As he said, all three measures paralleled important proposals of the CMC *Report*.

In addition to its proposal for standby tax authority the CMC *Report* had strongly recommended "more adequate planning for postponable projects," backed by "suitable expenditure programs . . . enacted . . . so as to permit greater executive flexibility and timing." The standby authority now asked by President Kennedy would merely be an executive device for turning on a potent recovery measure that had previously been planned by Congress. CMC had not gone quite as far as suggesting this power. The CED, of course, had also supported advance planning of public works but only for use when a serious depression threatened.

The standby authority to cut taxes to avoid recession which President Kennedy called for did, indeed, parallel CMC's except for its one-way feature. Its application was simpler. He would have the President first make "a finding that such action [temporary uniform reduction in all individual income tax rates of not more than five percentage points lower than the existing tax rates] is required to meet the objectives of the Employment Act of 1946." This would go into effect thirty days after submission, unless rejected by a joint resolution of Congress, and would remain in effect six months, subject to revision, renewal, or rejection by the same congressional process.

"The business cycle does not have the inevitability of the calendar," President Kennedy said, and for this compelling reason it was necessary "to equip the government to act more promptly, more flexibly, and more forcefully to stabilize the economy—to carry out more effectively its charge under the Employment Act."

President Kennedy never made clear why he felt that he should be given power only to *cut* taxes to avoid recession and not be given power to raise them (under similar congressional restraint) to combat inflation. He probably felt that while Congress would not object to a tax reduction, it would consider a tax raise an executive interference with the constitutional taxing powers of Congress. Of course, at that time, he had not had to face up to an inflationary situation. But at any rate he had done what no President had dared do before him.

The issue is far from dead. While Congress will probably long be reluctant to extend this upward or downward revisionary power to any President, many students believe that the possibility of such a system has already had its effect. In 1964, and in 1966–67 Congress moved faster than many people had ever expected it would in responding to the Administration's requests for fiscal action to meet the needs of a swiftly fluctuating economy. Nevertheless there are many observers of the economic scene who believe with *The New York Times* that the commission's two-way formula should be on the books for the discretionary use of the President whenever necessary.

It is interesting to note that in 1954, in *Defense Against Recession*, CED had fully discussed ways and means of speeding up the tax-reducing process as an anti-recession measure. "In principle," it said, "it might be possible to short-cut (the) process by legislation providing for a tax cut to go into effect automatically under certain conditions, or by giving the President authority to reduce certain taxes under specified conditions." In January 1962, in *Fiscal and Monetary Policy for High Employment*, it discussed the CMC proposal. Although CED again recognized the need for devising means for "putting the tax cut quickly into effect and for assuring its termination at some point" it was not convinced of the rectitude of the CMC proposal. "What is desired is not to tip the balance of power between the President and Congress but to obtain a prompt decision." It felt that this could be done by amending the rules of Congress so that a proposal for a temporary tax reduction, within limits of duration and character specified by previous law, should come up for a vote without amendment in each House within a reasonable period of time, say 60 days."

In his 1965 State of the Union message President Johnson reverted to the Kennedy proposal based on the CMC *Report*. He said, "Congress can reinforce . . . confidence in the 'continued flourishing of the American economy' by insuring that its procedures permit rapid action on temporary income tax cuts; and special funds for job-creating public works when recession threatens." Notice that he did not mention tax *increases*.

No move in either direction was undertaken by Congress and President Johnson did not again ask for any special power or procedure in his January 1966 economic messages, although even at that time there was some reason to believe that the time might not be too far distant when an "overheated" economy might require a tax increase. Mr. Johnson recognized this, of course, in 1967, when he asked for a 10 per cent surtax on the income tax. He refrained from any reference to the need for temporary tax-changing power. But during this period the subject was not abandoned, by any means. Economists and journalists continued to discuss the issue, with the former group almost universally favoring some version of the 1961 CMC up-and-down presidential prerogative as necessary to insure fiscal flexibility in an uncertain economy.

President Kennedy stretched the point a little when in his 1962 message he based his requests for permanent unemployment insurance reform on the CMC *Report*. Without making a specific recommendation, the CMC had put itself on the side of reform in this area, but only to the extent of calling for a strengthening of "the existing degree of built-in stabilization." This, of course, included unemployment insurance, which was a powerful ingredient. By inference it did support increased benefit payments and longer benefit periods on "a self-financing basis." In such statements as *Defense Against Inflation* (1958) CED had also urged similar liberalization.

In his proposals for unemployment insurance reform and for increased authority to undertake capital expenditures as anti-inflationary devices, President Kennedy had gone beyond the commission's recommendations in this field. In so doing he had offered something for both the "structuralists" and the "fiscalists," as the historian Arthur M. Schlesinger has neatly divided the two major divisions of economic thought. But the existence and value of both were recognized by CMC as having merit, although it stressed the latter.

The President next turned to the CMC's proposals to strengthen the financial system, and here he hewed even closer to the CMC line. The *Report*, he pointed out, raised important issues of public policy in three fields which Congress ought not to ignore in the immediate future. These related to (1) the objectives and machinery of government for economic stabilization and growth, (2) federal direct lending and credit guarantee programs, and (3) the structure and regulations of private financial institutions and markets. The first he had already taken care of, but he also intended to do something about the rest. The commission had raised the issues, but had not given *all* the answers. With the help of his Administration's key officers he would look for them, using the commission's work as his springboard.

Specifically the President mentioned the CMC's strong criticism of the ceiling on the public debt, the ceiling on the permissible interest rates on United States Treasury bonds, and the required gold reserve against Federal Reserve notes and deposits. He urged the Congress to examine carefully the commission's recommendations for abandonment of these restrictions which, he said, "unnecessarily complicate or obstruct other government policies."

There were two suggested reforms in the *Report*, he said optimistically, "on which there appears to be sufficiently general agreement to proceed at once." Both were of "direct concern to the President in the exercise of his responsibility to the Federal Reserve System." One was to raise the salaries of the Board to a level that would allow them to walk on even ground with their counterparts in the central banks of other nations. This matter has since been attended to, in part at least.

The other change was to revise the terms of office of the officers and members of the Board so that a new President will be able to nominate a chairman of his choice for a term of four years coterminous with his own. To do this he urged having the terms of members begin in odd-numbered years, starting in 1965, which would give "the President a free choice when he begins his term."

President Kennedy foresaw little difficulty in getting Congress quickly and quietly to adopt this reform. But it was just this proposal that brought conservative wrath. Although it would seem that no rational student of government or finance would object to it, the bill to this purpose which went to the Hill from the White House never got to the floor.

President Kennedy found other parts of the CMC *Report* worthy of "careful appraisal" by the executive branch as a basis for "future legislative recommendations." These had to do with unspecified recommendations concerning banks and other financial institutions, federal lending and loan guarantee programs, and corporate pension and other private retirement programs. He thereupon created three "interagency working groups," headed by Secretary of the Treasury Douglas Dillon, Economic Adviser Walter Heller, and Secretary of Labor Arthur Goldberg (later taken over by his successor Willard Wirtz). Their reports, unfortunately, were not quickly forthcoming nor did they attract much attention when they were at last delivered, although CMC's suggestion for stricter controls over private pension funds did lend weight to Administration proposals in this field. Congress was discussing private pension reforms along the CMC lines in the summer of 1967.

There was, of course, a great deal more in the *Report* than that singled out by President Kennedy. It called for many other small but highly important changes in the existing public and private financial institutions of the United States. But these did not add up to finding any compelling need to propose any basic "overhaul of our financial structure."

The *Report* ranged over a wide variety of important areas—monetary policy, fiscal policy, and public debt, private financial institutions, government credit programs, international monetary relations, and the organization and coordination of governmental institutions. There are far too many to be mentioned in detail here. Within the institutions involved many were considered daring, although non-institutional commentators were disinclined to go beyond *The* (London) *Economist's* remark that they were "logical and constructive."

Several recommendations hit boldly (and sometimes ambivalently) at banking custom and tradition, raising the hackles of those who would be affected were they ever imposed. CMC's proposals for relaxing state barriers against branch banking, for instance, were regarded as rank heresy by independent banking units. Its suggestions for liberalizing investment policy for savings banks and other thrift institutions aroused the ire of the investment trusts. Savings banks and savings and loan associations disliked its proposal to equalize taxation between savings institutions and the commercial banks.

Again, it was in the realm of monetary policy—the Federal Reserve System—that it was most critical (along lines not taken up by President Kennedy).

The commission would also definitely deprive the presidents of the twelve regional Federal Reserve Banks of the power they now have over open market operations and the discount rate. Changes in the discount rate, it said, should be uniform all over the country. It stressed the virtual disappearance of regional differences in the United States, a belief that was behind its desire to make the Federal Reserve a truly central bank.

The *Report* joined many critics of Federal Reserve practices in attacking the "bills only" policy the Board had followed throughout the 1950's, but which it had already abandoned for the policy of trading in government securities of varying maturities before the paper was made public.

In the important and highly controversial area of general controls vs. specific controls, the expected ideological differences of the commission members came to the fore. Although it recognized the fact that the Federal Reserve's existing powers tended to discriminate against some classes of borrowers, its majority rejected extending these powers over such matters as consumer credits. It apparently felt the Federal Reserve had tools of sufficient efficiency already to carry out its countercyclical assignments. In order to strengthen these powers the commission strongly urged that all commercial banks *be required to* be members of the Federal Reserve System.[2] But it would not go so far as to support giving the System controls over the rapidly growing non-bank financial institutions that many observers felt necessary for the maintenance of over-all economic stability.

The *Report* had its measure of ambivalence—"conservative" at one spot, "liberal" at an other. Its stand on the public debt, for example, was acceptable to the orthodox in its "conservative" demand for a stop in the shortening of the maturity of the debt. But it shocked the orthodox in its "liberal," almost New Deal, defense of the use of public works as a powerful anti-recession instrument. It stood with the "planners" in its proposal for the advance blueprinting of plans and the allocation of funds for public works over a five-year period. Its section on international economic policy failed to face up to the balance-of-payments question or to add any new solutions to the international monetary problems then arising.

In an interesting article on "Managing the Money Managers" in the August, 1967, issue of *Banking*, the journal of the American Bankers Association, Professor George J. Viksnins discusses the need for modification of the Federal Reserve System. "Criticism of the Fed among academicians has recently been growing," he writes, "and

---

[2] About 7,000 banks were outside the Federal Reserve System in 1961.

politicians are listening with interest." Representative Wright Patman had again introduced his familiar bill—in many respects similar to the CMC suggestions—to change the structure and functions of the System. As seems inevitable Professor Viksnins turned to the 1961 CMC *Report* and said, "The Commission's rather conservative recommendations should be the starting point for a reshaping of monetary management." For the benefit of those who would leave the Fed alone he quoted Walter Bagehot's 1873 comment in *Lombard Street*:

> There should be no delicacy as to altering the Constitution of the Bank of England. The existing constitution was framed in times that have passed away, and was intended to be used for purposes very different from the present. . . . "Putting new wine into old bottles" is safe only when you watch the condition of the bottle, and adopt its structure most carefully.

In his introduction to the *Report* chairman Frazar B. Wilde said that its conclusions "represent a consensus of American philosophy and economic judgment today." An investigation of the vast literature—learned and polemical—that the document has engendered would probably lead one to believe that there is no permanent consensus in the highly complicated realm of money and credit. The survey of public and private financial institutions, policies, and practices which CMC published in 1961 will have to be done again, perhaps in the near future.

In this event, the new economic problems that arise continually in our free society will call for the same kind of objective investigation as was set forth in the CMC *Report*. No organization is probably better equipped to carry this work forward than the Committee for Economic Development, whose first quarter of a century quest for ways to attain the goals of adequate economic growth, high employment, reasonable price stability, and better economic education at all levels of society, has been one of the brighter chapters in the political–economic history of the 20th Century in the United States.

Appendix

237

A CHRONOLOGICAL BIBLIOGRAPHY OF CED STATEMENTS ON NATIONAL POLICY

1943

Postwar Employment and the Settlement of Terminated War Contracts (*October*).

1944

Postwar Employment and the Liquidation of War Production (*July*).
A Postwar Federal Tax Plan for High Employment (*August*).

1945

Postwar Employment and the Removal of Wartime Controls (*April*).
International Trade, Foreign Investment and Domestic Employment, including Bretton Woods Proposals (*May*).
The Problem of Changeover Unemployment (*August*).
Toward More Production, More Jobs and More Freedom (*October*).
Agriculture In An Expanding Economy (*December*).

1946

The End of Price Control—How and When? (*April*).
Fiscal Policy to Fight Inflation (*September*).

1947

Collective Bargaining: How to Make It More Effective (*February*).

Meeting the Special Problems of Small Business (*June*).
Taxes and the Budget: A Program for Prosperity in a Free Economy (*November*).

1948

An American Program of European Economic Cooperation (*February*).
Monetary and Fiscal Policy for Greater Economic Stability (*December*).

1949

Tax and Expenditure Policy for 1949 (*May*).
The International Trade Organization and the Reconstruction of World Trade (*June*).
The Uses and Dangers of Direct Controls in Peacetime (*July*).
National Security and Our Individual Freedom (*December*).

1950

Tax and Expenditure Policy for 1950 (*January*).
How to Raise Real Wages (*June*).
Economic Policy for Rearmament (*August*).*
Paying for Defense (*November*).

1951

Conditions Necessary for Effective Price-Wage Controls (*February*).*

---

* Statements by the Program Committee

238   *Appendix*

An Emergency Tax Program for 1951 (March).
Economic Aspects of North Atlantic Security (May).
Price and Wage Controls (December).

1952

Tax and Expenditure Policy for 1952 (April).
Ending Price-Wage Controls (June).*
The Threat to Our National Security (September).

1953

Britain's Economic Problem and Its Meaning for America (March).
Flexible Monetary Policy: What It Is and How It Works (March).
Tax and Expenditure Policy for 1953 (April).

1954

Taxes, National Security and Economic Growth (January).
Defense Against Recession: Policy for Greater Economic Stability (March).
Managing the Federal Debt (September).
United States Tariff Policy (November).

1955

Control of Federal Government Expenditures (January).
Federal Tax Issues in 1955 (May).
Tax Policy in 1956 (December).*

1956

Modernizing the Nation's Highways (January).
Economic Policy for American Agriculture (January).
Economic Development Abroad and the Role of American Foreign Investment (February).
The Budget, the Economy and Tax Reduction in 1956 (June).

1957

Economic Development Assistance (April).

Tax Reduction and Tax Reform—When and How (May).
Toward A Realistic Farm Program (December).*

1958

Economic Growth in the United States—Its Past and Future (February).
Anti-Recession Policy for 1958 (March).*
Defense Against Inflation—Policies for Price Stability in a Growing Economy (July).
The Problem of National Security—Some Economic and Administrative Aspects (July).

1959

The National Economy (January).*
The Budget and the Economic Growth (April).
The European Common Market and Its Meaning to the United States (May).
Paying for Better Public Schools (December).

1960

National Objectives and the Balance of Payments Problem (February).
Guiding Metropolitan Growth (August).

1961

Growth and Taxes: Steps for 1961 (February).
Cooperation for Progress in Latin America (April).
The International Position of the Dollar (May).
Distressed Areas in a Growing Economy (June).

1962

Fiscal and Monetary Policy for High Employment (January).
Economic Literacy for Americans—A Program for Schools and for Citizens (February).
A New Trade Policy for the United States (April).

---

* Statements by the Program Committee

An Adaptive Program for Agriculture (*July*).

Reducing Tax Rates for Production and Growth (*December*).

1963

Japan in the Free World Economy (*April*).

1964

Union Powers and Union Functions: Toward a Better Balance (*March*).

Trade Negotiations for a Better Free World Economy (*May*).

Improving Executive Management in the Federal Government (*July*).

Educating Tomorrow's Managers—The Business Schools and the Business Community (*October*).

Economic Development of Central America (*November*).

1965

Presidential Succession and Inability (*January*).

Developing Metropolitan Transporta-tion Policies: A Guide for Local Leadership (*April*).

East-West Trade: A Common Policy for the West (*May*).

Raising Low Incomes Through Improved Education (*September*).

1966

Budgeting for National Objectives (*January*).

A Better Balance in Federal Taxes on Business (*April*).

Modernizing Local Government (*July*).

How Low Income Countries Can Advance Their Own Growth (*September*).

A Stabilizing Federal Budget for 1967 (*December*).*

The Dollar and the World Monetary System (*December*).

1967

A Fiscal Program for a Balanced Federalism (*June*).

Trade Policy Toward Low-Income Countries (*June*).

Modernizing State Government (*July*).

SUPPLEMENTARY PAPERS

1944

The Economics of a Free Society, by William Benton (*October*).

Personnel Problems of the Postwar Transition Period, by Charles A. Meyers (*December*).

1946

World Politics Faces Economics, by Harold D. Lasswell (*January*).

1954

Problems in Anti-Recession Policy, by CED Economists and Consultants (*September*).

1958

New Role of the Soviets in the World Economy, by Michael Sapir (*May*).

1959

The Changing Economic Function of the Central City, by Raymond Vernon (*January*).

Metropolis Against Itself, by Robert C. Wood (*March*).

Trends in Public Expenditures in the Next Decade, by Otto Eckstein (*April*).

Prices, Costs and Output for the Postwar Decade: 1947–1957, by Charles L. Schultze (*December*).

1960

Developing the "Little" Economies, by Donald R. Gilmore (*April*).

The Education of Businessmen, by Leonard S. Silk (*December*).

---

* Statements by the Program Committee

1961

Study Materials for Economic Education in the Schools, Reports of the Materials Evaluation Committees (*October*). Revised Oct. 1963.

1962

The Sources of Economic Growth in the United States and the Alternatives Before Us, by Edward F. Denison (*January*).

Farming, Farmers, and Markets for Farm Goods, by Karl A. Fox, Vernon W. Ruttan, Lawrence W. Witt (*November*).

The Community Economic Base Study, by Charles M. Tiebout (*December*).

1963

Comparative Tariffs and Trade—The United States and the European Common Market, by Frances K. Topping (*March*).

How A Region Grows—Area Development in the United States Economy, by Harvey S. Perloff, with Vera W. Dodds (*March*).

1964

Community Economic Development Efforts: Five Case Studies, by W. Paul Brann, V. C. Crisafulli, Donald R. Gilmore, Jacob J. Kaufman, Halsey R. Jones, Jr., J. W. Milliman, John H. Nixon, W. G. Pinnell (*December*).

1965

Crisis in World Communism—Marxism in Search of Efficiency, by Frank O'Brien (*January*).

1966

Men Near the Top: Filling Key Posts in the Federal Service, by John J. Corson and R. Shale Paul (*April*).

1967

Economic Development Issues: Latin America, by Roberto Alemann (Argentina), Mario Henrique Simonsen (Brazil), Sergio Undurraga Saavedra (Chile), Hernan Echavarria (Colombia), Gustavo Romero Kolbeck (Mexico), Romulo A. Ferrero (Peru) (*August*).

OTHER CED PUBLICATIONS

Problems of United States Economic Development

Vol. I: Papers by 49 free world leaders on the most important problems facing the United States in the next twenty years.

Vol. II: The 50 winning papers in CED's free-world-wide competition on "The Most Important Economic Problems to be Faced in the United States in the Next Twenty Years."

The "Little" Economies: Problems of United States Area Development

Papers delivered at the semi-annual meeting of the Board of Trustees of CED, New York, May 29, 1958, by Donald K. David, Jervis J. Babb, Raymond Vernon, Luther Gulick, Arthur B. Van Buskirk, William R. Davlin and H. Bruce Palmer.

Taxes and Trade: Twenty Years of CED Policy

Addresses to the Board of Trustees of CED, Washington, May 9, 1963, by Theodore V. Houser, J. Cameron Thomson, President John F. Kennedy, Philip D. Reed and others, May, 1963.

Better Management of the Public's Business

Three Papers on the Improvement of Management in Government, by Marion B. Folsom, Don K. Price and Sir Eric Roll, July, 1964.

Gold, the Dollar, and the World Monetary System
A CED Symposium on the International Position of the Dollar. Papers by Frazar B. Wilde, Jacob Viner, Emilio G. Collado, and Henry A. Fowler, June, 1965.

Managing A Full Employment Economy
A CED Symposium. Papers delivered at the Annual Meeting of the Trustees of CED, Los Angeles, May 1966, by Frazar B. Wilde, Walter W. Heller, John D. Harper, Pierre-Paul Schweitzer and others, June, 1966.

RESEARCH STUDIES

1944

Production, Jobs and Taxes, by Harold M. Groves (June).
The Liquidation of War Production, by A.D.H. Kaplan (July).

1945

Demobilization of Wartime Economic Controls, by J. M. Clark (January).
Providing for Unemployed Workers in the Transition, by Richard Lester (January).

1946

Agriculture in an Unstable Economy, by Theodore W. Schultz (January).
Jobs and Markets—How to Prevent Inflation and Depression in the Transition, by Members of CED Research Staff (March).
Financing Business During the Transition, by Charles C. Abbott (May).
Postwar Taxation and Economic Progress, by Harold M. Groves (May).
International Trade and Domestic Employment, by Calvin B. Hoover, (September).
Controlling World Trade: Cartels and

Commodity Agreements, by Edward S. Mason (August).

1948

Small Business: Its Place and Problems, by A.D.H. Kaplan (September).

1949

Monetary Management, by E.A. Goldenweiser (July).

1950

National Security and Individual Freedom, by Harold D. Lasswell (October).

1951

American Monetary Policy, by E.A. Goldenweiser (July).

1952

Stabilizing Construction: The Record and Potential, by Miles L. Colean and Robinson Newcomb (December).

1955

The Budgetary Process in the United States, by Arthur Smithies (March).

SPECIAL ISSUES OF THE SATURDAY REVIEW

The American Economy 1959 (January 17, 1959)
Maximum Challenge: Is the Economy of the Western World Splitting Apart? (January 16, 1960)
Inside the Soviet Economy: What Does

Its Growth Mean to the Free World? (January 21, 1961)
Collective Bargaining and the American Economy (January 11, 1962)
The Pacific and the World Economy (January 12, 1963)

National Agenda for 1964: Business Faces A Presidential Year (*January 11, 1964*)

The Challenge of Prosperity (*January 9, 1965*)

Making American Cities More Livable (*January 9, 1966*)

Changing Directions in American Education (*January 14, 1967*)

MEMBERS OF THE COMMISSION ON MONEY AND CREDIT—1958–1961

FRAZAR B. WILDE, *Chairman*
Chairman, Connecticut General Life Insurance Company

H. CHRISTIAN SONNE, *Vice Chairman*
New York, New York

ADOLF A. BERLE, JR.
New York, New York
(Withdrew to serve as Chairman of the U.S. State Department Latin American Task Force.)

JAMES B. BLACK
Chairman of the Board, Pacific Gas & Electric Company

JOSEPH M. DODGE
Chairman of the Board, The Detroit Bank and Trust Company (Resigned October 7, 1960.)

MARRINER S. ECCLES
Chairman of the Board, First Security Corporation

LAMAR FLEMING, JR.
Chairman of the Board, Anderson, Clayton & Co.

HENRY H. FOWLER
Fowler, Leva, Hawes & Symington (Resigned February 3, 1961, on his appointment as Under Secretary of the Treasury.)

GAYLORD A. FREEMAN, JR.
President, The First National Bank of Chicago (Appointed April 29, 1960.)

FRED T. GREENE
President, Federal Home Loan Bank

of Indianapolis (Died March 17, 1961.)

PHILIP M. KLUTZNICK
Park Forest, Illinois (Resigned February 8, 1961, on his appointment as United States Representative to the Economic and Social Council of the United Nations.)

FRED LAZARUS, JR.
Chairman of the Board, Federated Department Stores, Inc.

ISADOR LUBIN
Arthur T. Vanderbilt Professor of Public Affairs, Rutgers University

J. IRWIN MILLER
Chairman of the Board, Cummins Engine Company

ROBERT R. NATHAN
Robert R. Nathan Associates, Inc.

EMIL RIEVE
President Emeritus, Textile Workers of America, AFL-CIO (Appointed May 19, 1960.)

DAVID ROCKEFELLER
President, The Chase Manhattan Bank

BEARDSLEY RUML
New York, New York (Died April 18, 1960.)

STANLEY H. RUTTENBERG
Director, Department of Research, AFL-CIO

CHARLES SAWYER
Taft, Stettinius & Hollister

WILLIAM F. SCHNITZLER
Secretary-Treasurer, AFL-CIO (Resigned April 28, 1960.)

THE LIBRARY OF MONEY AND CREDIT

Money and Credit: Their Influence on Jobs, Prices and Growth. The Report
of the Commission on Money and Credit (Englewood Cliffs, N. J.: Prentice-
Hall, Inc., 1961).

Papers Prepared for the Use of the Commission on Money and Credit

Financial Institutions

The Commercial Banking Industry
The American Bankers Association

The Consumer Finance Industry
National Consumer Finance Association

Life Insurance Companies as Financial
Institutions
Life Insurance Association of America

Management Investment Companies
Investment Company Institute

Mortgage Companies: Their Place in
the Financial Structure
Miles L. Colean, for the Mortgage
Bankers Association of America

Mutual Savings Banking: Basic Characteristics and Role in the National
Economy
National Association of Mutual Savings Banks

Property and Casualty Insurance Companies: Their Role as Financial Intermediaries
American Mutual Insurance Alliance
Association of Casualty and Surety
Companies
National Board of Fire Underwriters

The Savings and Loan Business: Its
Purposes, Functions, and Economic Justification
Leon T. Kendall, for the United
States Savings and Loan League

The Federal Reserve and the Treasury:
Answers to Questions from the Commission on Money and Credit

Monetary and Fiscal Policy

Federal Credit Agencies
by George F. Break, Jack Guttentag,
Ernest Bloch, D. Gale Johnson, Dale
E. Hathaway, George S. Tolley,
Jack McGroskey.

Federal Credit Programs
by Stewart Johnson, Warren A. Law,
James W. McKie, D. Gale Johnson, James Gillies, Robert C. Turner
and Ross M. Robertson, J. Fred
Weston.

Fiscal and Debt Management Policies
by William Fellner, Richard A.
Musgrave, James Tobin, James R.
Schlesinger, Paul H. Cootner, Irving
Auerbach, Ralph K. Huitt, John
Lindeman.

Impacts of Monetary Policy
by Daniel B. Suits, Robert Eisner
and Robert H. Strotz, with a bibliography by George R. Post, Edwin
Kuh and John R. Meyer, Leo Greb-
ler and Sherman J. Maisel, Charlotte
DeMonte Phelps, Irwin Friend.

Inflation, Growth and Employment
by Joseph W. Conard, Jesse W.
Markham, Franklyn D. Holzman,
John W. Kendrick, Daniel Creamer,
Stanley Lebergott, Lawrence R.
Klein and Ronald G. Bodkin, Tibor
and Anne Scitovsky.

Monetary Management
by Frank M. Tamagna, Warren L.
Smith, Clark Warburton, Michael
D. Reagan, Charles P. Kindleberger,
Robert Z. Aliber.

Private Capital Markets
by Irwin Friend, Hyman P. Minsky,
Victor L. Andrews.

Private Financial Institutions
by Paul M. Horvitz, Deane Carson
and Paul H. Cootner, Thomas G.
Gies, Thomas Mayer and Edward
C. Ettin, Lawrence L. Werboff and
Marvin E. Rosen, Fred H. Klop-
stock, E. Gordon Keith.

Stabilization Policies
by E. Cary Brown, Robert M. Solow,
Albert Ando and John Kareken,
Milton Friedman and David Meisel-
man, Lawrence E. Thompson, Arthur M. Okun, Merton H. Miller,
Allan H. Meltzer, Oswald Brownlee
and Alfred Conrad.

Index

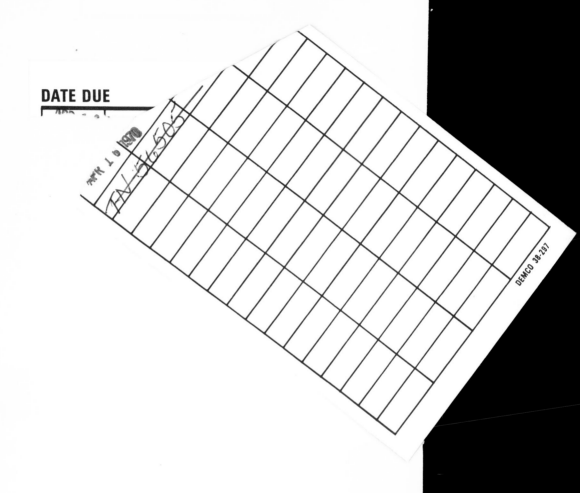

DATE DUE